HAWAI'I BY CRUISE

DOCUMENTATION
Passenger Name_____
Ship Name _____
Date of Voyage_____
Stateroom_____

Valley of the Temples, Oahu

HAWAII By Cruise Ship

THE COMPLETE GUIDE TO CRUISING THE HAWAIIAN ISLANDS

ANNE VIPOND

*YOUR PORTHOLE
COMPANION*

**OCEAN
CRUISE
GUIDES**

Vancouver, Canada   Pt. Roberts, USA

Published by: Ocean Cruise Guides Ltd.

Canada:
325 English Bluff Road
Delta, B.C. V4M 2M9

USA:
PO Box 2041
Pt. Roberts, WA 98281-2041

Editors: Mel-Lynda Andersen, Richard Rogers, William Kelly
Contributing Editors: Michael DeFreitas, Marguerite Short
Addt'l Photography: Michael DeFreitas, Phil Hersee, Alan Nakano, Wayne Messenger, Peter Stevens
Front cover artwork by Alan H. Nakano
Back cover photos: (top) Joe Solem, (bottom) Hawaii Tourism
Cartography: Reid Jopson, Cartesia, OCG
Design: Ocean Cruise Guides
Publisher: William Kelly
Phone: (604) 948-0594 Email: info@oceancruiseguides.com
Visit our website: www.oceancruiseguides.com
Printed in China

ISBN 13: 978-0-9688389-4-5
Library and Archives Canada Cataloguing in Publication

Vipond, Anne, 1957-
 Hawaii by cruise ship : the complete guide to cruising the Hawaiian Islands / Anne Vipond.

Includes index.
"Your porthole companion".
ISBN 0-9688389-4-4

    1. Cruise ships--Hawaii--Guidebooks. 2. Hawaii--Guidebooks.
I. Title.

DU622.V56 2006   919.6904'42   C2006-905320-0

Wailua Falls, Maui

CONTENTS

PART ONE

GENERAL INFORMATION

CONTENTS

PART TWO

THE VOYAGE & THE PORTS

Ever since Captain James Cook chanced upon the Hawaiian Islands in 1778 and introduced this Polynesian paradise to the outside world, visitors haven't stopped coming – first by ship, then by jet plane, and now by a combination of the two, thanks to Hawai'i's burgeoning cruise industry.

If ever there was an ideal cruise destination, Hawai'i is it. What better way to experience the languid pace and natural beauty of these lush volcanic islands than by slowly cruising among them, spending full days in port exploring each island or lazing on a beach, then traveling by night under a tropical sky.

While most of Polynesia's farflung islands lie south of the equator, the Hawaiian chain straddles the Tropic of Cancer and is one of the most isolated archipelagos in the world. It is also one of the most beautiful – a green oasis of plunging waterfalls, tropical flowers and palm-fringed beaches. Outdoor recreation ranges from surfing, snorkeling and other water sports to golfing on championship courses and cycling the slopes of volcanoes. An American state, Hawai'i is exotic yet familiar, offering all the conveniences of home.

But perhaps the most alluring aspect of Hawai'i is the people who live there, described as "the very incarnation of generosity, unselfishness, and hospitality" by Mark Twain in his *Letters from Hawai'i*, written in 1866. In it he recounts the arrival by open boat of some shipwreck survivors, greeted by two Hawaiians who swam out through the surf to climb aboard the small craft and pilot it safely to shore. As soon as this weary boatload was beached, a crowd of locals gathered round with heaps of bananas, melons and other foodstuffs.

Twain comments that they "would soon have killed the starving men with kindness" had someone not intervened and prompted the helpful Hawaiians to take these emaciated mariners in their arms "like so many children" and carry them to a nearby house where they were given medical care and attention.

To this day, the people of Hawai'i embody the aloha spirit of welcoming strangers, despite an annual inundation of visitors numbering some seven million per year. The traditional lei greeting is still widely practised, and Hawai'i remains, as characterized by Mark Twain, "the loveliest fleet of islands that lies anchored in any ocean."

PART I

General Information

Hawai'i Cruise Options

Lihu'e

KAUA'I

```
0        25
|---|---|
Miles
```

N

HAWAI'I CRUISING DISTANCES			
FROM HONOLULU IN NAUTICAL MILES:			
Nawiliwili		Big Island of Hawai'i	
(Lihu'e)	110 miles		
Kahului	103 miles	Hilo	220 miles
Lahaina	83 miles	Kona	165 miles

O'AHU

Honolulu

Located some 2,500 miles west-southwest of the U.S. mainland, Hawai'i is about five hours by air from Los Angeles and about four days by sea from Los Angeles or San Diego. Whether you arrive by jet plane or by cruise ship, an island-hopping cruise relieves you of the dilemma facing resort-based visitors to Hawai'i – namely, which island to visit? An inter-island cruise allows you to spend a day or two on each of the four major islands – O'ahu, Maui, Kaua'i and the Big Island. If your cruise begins or terminates in Honolulu, you can extend your time in Hawai'i by spending some pre- or post-cruise days at a land-based resort.

Which Cruise?

Only one cruise line – Norwegian Cruise Line – has ships dedicated to the Hawaiian Islands on round-trip cruises from Honolulu. This is because NCL America's U.S.-flagged ships are eligible to cruise solely in American waters and do not have to make a foreign port call to satisfy U.S. shipping regulations. NCL America's inter-island itineraries are seven, 10 and 11 days in duration. The seven-day itineraries include overnight stops at Kaua'i and Maui, and a day in Hilo and a day in Kona (the two Big Island ports of call). The 10-day itinerary includes an overnight in Honolulu, two full days in Kauai, three days in Maui (two in Kahului, one in Lahaina) and full days in Hilo and Kona. The 11-day version of this Hawai'i-only itinerary adds a day at sea. Another 11-day itinerary includes a visit to Fanning Island, with less time spent at Hawaiian ports and more days spent at sea.

Other cruise lines offer round-trip cruises from the mainland. The main base ports are San Diego and Los Angeles, and this type of cruise is about two weeks in duration. These cruises are appealing for their relaxing days spent at sea (four days each way) and the elimination of the trans-Pacific flight to Hawai'i.

Another option is a one-way cruise between the mainland and Hawai'i, which entails a flight at the beginning or end of the cruise. These itineraries are offered each spring and fall when many cruise ships are repositioning between the Caribbean and Alaska. A typical 11-day itinerary runs between Honolulu and one of several mainland ports between Ensenada and Vancouver. There are many variations to the Hawaiian itineraries described above. *For details on each cruise line's itineraries, please consult the Cruise Line Glossary at the back of this book.*

travel and is affiliated with Cruise Lines International Asssociation. CLIA is an independent marketing and training organization for the North American cruise industry and offers courses for travel agents, which earn them Cruise Counselor certification.

An informed and experienced cruise agent will be able to guide you through the maze of ship choices, cabin considerations and itineraries. You can book cruises online, but this isn't necessarily where you will find the best deals or advice (which can be crucial when selecting a ship and cabin). The cruise lines work closely with cruise agents, whose specialized services are valued in this niche market.

Hawai'i is a popular destination for families, so it's a natural fit to visit these islands on a cruise ship. There is much to do on shore with children, and plenty

MOLOKA'I

MAUI

Lahaina **Kahului**

LANA'I

KAHOOLAWE

Which Ship?

Once you have chosen an itinerary, the next step is choosing a ship. The overall onboard experience is comparable among most of the mainstream ships servicing Hawai'i, but each cruise line has an individual style that appeals to different travelers. The best way to choose a ship that suits your personal taste and lifestyle is to consult an experienced cruise agent who specializes in cruise

HAWAI'I

Hilo

Kailua-Kona

Newer cruise ships feature an abundance of balcony cabins.

of organized activities on board the ship to keep the kids entertained. If you're traveling with children, be sure to choose a ship with extensive youth facilities.

For information on stateroom choices, see 'Life Aboard' on page 41.

Air Flights

The cruise lines offer air rates that usually are at a discount of normal 'rack' fares and can arrange your air flights and ground transfers. If you want this convenience, the 'air/sea package' should be booked all at once. If you make your own flight arrangements, be sure to allow a large enough window of time to get from the airport to the cruise port if you are making same-day connections. Most ships begin checking in passengers at 1:00 p.m. on the day of sailing, and all passengers must be on board within 30 minutes of when the ship departs.

There are advantages and disadvantages to booking your air flights with the cruise line. If your flight is delayed, the cruise line will make arrangements to ensure you connect with your cruise. However, be sure to check the seating arrangements, as your seats may not be together. Also, the cruise line may not put you on a direct flight. It is usually worth paying the optional variation fee (about $50), which lets you pick your dates of travel, airline, routing and advance seat assignment.

When To Go?

The weather is ideal year-round in Hawai'i, thanks to its tropical heat being tempered by steady trade winds. Air temperatures at sea level rarely rise above 90 degrees Fahrenheit (32° C) during the day or drop below 65 degrees Fahrenheit (18° C) at night. The ocean temperature is between 71 and 81 degrees Fahrenheit (22-27° C) year-round. Temperatures at higher elevations can be much cooler, with Maui's Haleakala

Crater experiencing temperatures in the 40–65 degree Fahrenheit (4-18° C) range and the Big Island's Mauna Kea receiving snow on its upper slopes during the winter months.

In winter the islands receive more rainfall than in summer, especially at higher elevations and along the windward coastlines. The beaches also receive more surf in winter, when distant storms in the North Pacific send large breakers and strong currents onto the Hawaiian Islands' north and east shores.

Hawai'i cruises are available year-round out of Honolulu, where you can extend your vacation with a pre- or post-cruise stay. Busy times coincide, not surprisingly, with Christmas holidays and summer vacation. High-season rates for hotels are in

Weddings and Honeymoons

Hawai'i has long been a popular place to get married. The only requirements are that both parties be at least 18 years old when they appear before a local license agent to fill out an application and pay a $60 fee in cash. The issued marriage license is good for 30 days.

A couple planning a pre-cruise wedding in Hawai'i could tie the knot on O'ahu or Maui, then board a cruise ship for a seven-day, island-hopping honeymoon. Best Bridal Hawai'i (808-922-4130, www.bestbridal.com) offers an assortment of wedding packages in Hawai'i, and now operates the 85-seat Ocean Crystal Chapel at Hilton Hawaiian Village. Unveiled in March 2006, this is the first free-standing resort chapel in Waikiki.

Kaua'i is home to one of Hawai'i's most enduring wedding venues – the Coco Palms Resort's lagoon-filled grounds. This is where Tropical Dream Wedding (888-615-5655, www.tropicaldreamwedding.com) can recreate a 'Blue Hawaii' wedding similar to the ceremony portrayed in the 1961 movie starring Elvis Presley, in which the bride and groom are transported to a thatched-roof chapel in a flower-festooned, double-hulled canoe.

Another option is to marry aboard the ship. Most cruise lines offer wedding, honeymoon and anniversary packages. In addition to its onboard wedding packages, Norwegian Cruise Line can arrange an onshore wedding on O'ahu, Maui or Kaua'i.

For couples who want to renew their vows, the Sheraton Moana Surfrider in Waikiki hosts a complimentary ceremony every Saturday night in the hotel's Banyan Courtyard. Members of the general public as well as hotel guests are invited to attend.

Temperature Ranges	High	Low
January – April	81	66
May – August	86	72
Sept – Dec	85	70

effect from Christmas to Easter and throughout the summer. One-way repositioning cruises between the mainland and Hawai'i are available in spring and fall. Round-trip Hawai'i cruises from Los Angeles and San Diego are offered by a number of cruise lines throughout the winter.

(For more detail, see the Cruise Lines Glossary at the back of this book.)

Shore Excursions

Whether or not to take a ship-organized shore excursion depends on several factors. Generally speaking, it makes sense to book through the cruise line any activities involving transfers, equipment and experienced guides. This applies to boat tours and helicopter tours, whose operators rarely undercut the cruise lines' pricing.

When choosing between excursions in an ocean raft (rigid-hulled inflatable craft) or on board a catamaran (a twin-hulled sailing vessel), bear in mind that the catamaran will be a smoother and dryer rider than an ocean raft, but the latter allows your skipper more flexibility to explore coastal nooks and crannies.

Helicopter tours, although expensive, are an amazing experience. Because tour helicopters resemble airborne glass bubbles, all passengers have an excellent view as their chopper soars over breathtaking scenery. A person gains a big picture of how these volcanic islands rose from the sea millions of years ago when treated to a bird's-eye view of their rugged interiors and cliff-edged coastlines.

If you are simply seeking a splendid beach to do some swimming or snorkeling or take a surfing lesson, such activities

(Above left) Helicopter view of Hawai'i. (Left) Catamarans are often used for snorkel tours.

can easily be done on your own. A snorkel mask and fins can be rented for about $10, and other watersports equipment is also widely available. However, if you are a beginner at any of the watersports, lessons or guided excursions are recommended. For instance, kayaking is often more rewarding when booked with an outfitter, whose guides are familiar with local sea conditions and know the best spots for snorkeling or beach picnics.

A rental car is one way to get to the beach of your choice. Sometimes there is a local shuttle or, in the case of Oahu, a good bus system. And at several ports of call, good beaches are within easy walking distance of the cruise pier.

If you are extremely interested in a particular land-based attraction and want to explore this venue at your leisure, you should visit it independently rather than with a group.

When renting a car, it's best to reserve a vehicle ahead of time, especially during the popular summer months and mid-December through to April. This is especially true in Lahaina on West Maui, where the car rental agencies seem to have a limited number of vehicles and are reluctant to arrange

(Top to bottom) Guided excursions include novice and advanced scuba diving, and kayaking. All of the islands can be explored by rental car.

last-minute daily rentals to cruise visitors. (Other ports are more flexible on this.) Reserving a vehicle can be done on the Internet before leaving home, and most agencies supply a printout map of their airport location. Most also provide a free shuttle for their cruise-ship customers.

The islands are simple to navigate, with paved coastal highways winding past beautiful beaches and turn-off roads lead-

(Below) A roadside fruit stand. (Bottom) The seas can be rough on Oahu's north shore but not in sheltered Kuilima Cove.

ing inland to verdant valleys, hidden waterfalls and volcanic peaks. Rental agencies, however, will warn you not to leave valuables in your parked vehicle.

When driving around the islands, you may want to pause at a roadside produce stand. Locals set these up to sell the flowers, fruit and vegetables that they grow in their back yards. Treat yourself to a lychee, which looks like a dried-up chestnut until peeled to reveal a succulent fruit resembling a grape but tasting quite different.

If you are pursuing shoreside activities independently, keep in mind that you must be back at the ship no later than a half hour before it departs. Ships only wait for passengers who are on ship-organized shore excursions and they rarely remain in port past their designated departure time. If you miss your ship, you are responsible for getting to the next port of call on your own.

Beaches in Hawai'i

A beach is not just a beach in Hawai'i. Not only are there dozens to choose from, each beach is different. Some are perfect for swimming, others for surfing, and these conditions can change from season to season, from day to day, and from hour to hour. All beaches in the State of Hawai'i are public and people are guaranteed legal access. Some of the best can often be found at one of the county or state parks, where facilities usually include parking, picnic tables, washrooms and outdoor showers for rinsing off sand and saltwater. Many of the beach parks have lifeguards on duty year-round.

Talk to the lifeguard on duty to get the lowdown on sea conditions before going swimming.

The ocean is powerful and unpredictable, and visitors to Hawai'i are sometimes unaware of the dangers, with several dozen people drowning in Hawaiian waters each year. May through September are usually fine for swimming, but wind and wave conditions can be highly localized, changing from day to day, and some areas can experience a large south swell in summer. If you're unsure of the swimming conditions, ask the lifeguard on duty and

A quiet section of Waikiki Beach lies in front of Fort DeRussy.

always take note of any warning signs posted. If the red flags are up, do not enter the water.

A distant storm out in the open Pacific will send large swells onto beaches and create strong currents that can carry over-confident swimmers away from shore. If you get caught in a current, don't exhaust yourself by trying to swim against it. Instead, swim with the current, gradually crossing it until you are free of its grip.

Waves come in sets and the seas can look deceptively calm in between these sets when in fact there could be dangerous rip currents and cross currents.

One word of advice is to use swim fins when swimming in large surf. Do not swim alone; always be with a companion. Never turn your back on the ocean but face seaward so you can see incoming waves and respond appropriately. Be especially vigilant when supervising young children.

Watersports equipment and lessons are widely available at Hawai'i's beaches. **Surfing** lessons are often offered at beaches that receive a gentle surf and present perfect conditions for beginners. **Boogie (body) boarding**, a variation of surf boarding, uses a shorter, wider board. The rider remains lying on the board, unlike surfing in which the rider stands upright.

Bodysurfing requires no equipment (except flippers), just superb swimming skills and the athleticism of a dolphin. Dedicated bodysurfers enjoy their affinity with the ocean, with nothing between them and the wave they are riding. When learning to body surf, do so at an angle to the waves; if you're perpendicular, a wave can flip you upside down

Dr. Beach 🏖

When Stephen Leatherman, a professor who studies beaches at Florida International University, was asked by a travel magazine editor to name the top 10 American beaches, he rattled off a list of his favorites in no particular order. That was back in 1991 and since then, the release of Dr. Beach's annual list has become a major media event, covered by newspapers and travel magazines across North America.

Leatherman has devised a numerical rating for beaches, applying a range of scientific criteria, such as temperature, cleanliness and prevailing wind conditions. Hawaiian beaches dominate his annual list, one of their built-in advantages being a year-round water temperature that is ideal. Previous Hawaiian winners include Kapalua, Maui (1991), Hapuna, Big Island (1993), Lanikai, O'ahu (1996), Hulopoe, Lanai (1997), Kailua, O'ahu (1998), Wailea, Maui (1999), Mauna Kea, Big Island (2000), Poipu, Kaua'i (2001), Ka'anapali, Maui (2003) and D.T. Fleming, Maui (2006). When a beach wins top honors, it is excluded from future lists.

(Above) Stephen Leatherman.
(Below) D.T. Fleming Beach.

and cause serious injury.

Hawai'i offers excellent **snorkeling** with plenty of reefs close to the shoreline. If you are a beginner, practice in shallow water and learn how to clear water from the snorkel and put your mask back on while treading water. Take along a disposable, waterproof camera for capturing the underwater sights on film and always wear waterproof sunscreen. Do not touch the coral; it is against the law to damage or remove any stony coral from Hawaiian waters.

It is generally preferable to snorkel in the morning when water clarity is best and the fish are most active. The tradewinds usually strengthen as the day progresses and afternoon breezes will create currents that stir up the ocean floor and make the water cloudy. In such conditions, avoid snorkeling over shallow, sandy bottoms and instead snorkel right over the reef. In locations sheltered from the prevailing wind, afternoon light can enhance underwater viewing.

Kiteboarding (also called kitesurfing) is a hybrid of windsurfing, paragliding and wakeboarding. A person stands strapped onto a kiteboard (small surfboard) and is pulled across the water by a big kite. Some beaches are off-limits while others have kiteboarding zones. For information about lessons, call the Hawai'i Kiteboarding Association at 873-0015.

Golf Courses

When Robert Trent Jones, Sr. devised a way to build golf courses on old lava flows (by crushing the top layer of rock, then adding gravel and topsoil), he initiated Hawai'i's emergence as one of the world's most desirable golf destinations. That was in the early 1960s, and today Hawai'i is home to more than 70 golf courses and hosts numerous professional tournaments, including the PGA Grand Slam. The courses are stunning with their varied terrain of cool tropical valleys and lava sea cliffs. They are also challenging, with uneven lies and greens of aggressive Bermuda grass, which has a pronounced grain that effects the speed of a breaking putt. The steady trade winds are another factor, adding to the challenge of these championship courses.

The cruise lines offer golf programs to their passengers,

(Above left) Kiteboarding in Kahului Bay on Maui.

(Left) Turtle Bay Resort's Arnold Palmer Course.

but if you want to reserve a tee time independently, visit www.teetimeshawaii.com or call 1-888-675-GOLF. You can reach Stand-by Golf, a last-minute discount tee service, at 888-645-2665. Greens fees on championship courses will exceed $100 while fees at municipal courses tend to be about half that amount.

Hiking

Walking a wilderness trail deep into a verdant valley is a pleasant pastime. However, if you are not part of a guided group, there are a few precautions you should take. Hike with a partner, and take plenty of drinking water as well as sunscreen, insect repellent, a high-energy snack and a rain slicker. Narrow valleys should be avoided during or right after heavy rains, due to the risk of flash flooding and falling rocks. Because volcanic rock is crumbly, rock climbing is not advised in any weather conditions. For both safety and courtesy, keep to marked trails and respect posted signs. Use extra caution when hiking near clifftops.

Freshwater streams and ponds are sometimes tainted with the Leptospira bacteria, making their water unsuitable for drinking and questionable

(Above, right) Kalalau Foot Trail and Wailua Falls (right) on Kaua'i.

for swimming, especially if you have an open cut. This particular bacteria is expelled in the urine of infected animals and washed into freshwater pools by rainwater carrying soil downstream. Symptoms of a human infection include high fever, muscle aches and nausea, which appear about two weeks after exposure to the bacteria. Check with the locals (or your guide) before jumping in. If no one else is around and you can't resist going for a dip, avoid submerging your face in the water.

Ranch Activities

Although horses are not allowed on Hawai'i's beaches, trail riding is popular and widely available to visitors. There are working ranches on all the main island, and these stables often offer guided trail rides. Several of these large private ranches also offer other tourist activities, including ATV rides over rolling hills and zipline rides across rainforest canopies.

Cruise & Stay Options

Hawai'i, with its extensive visitor infrastructure, is an ideal place to extend your cruise vacation. One-way cruises from the mainland either originate or terminate in Honolulu, the megacenter of Hawai'i's tourism industry. There is much to see in Honolulu, a vibrant city flanked by Waikiki

Cycling and ATV excursions are offered on all the islands.

Beach and Diamond Head at one end, and Pearl Harbor at the other. Competition for the tourist dollar keeps prices here the lowest of any of the Hawaiian islands, with accommodations in Waikiki ranging from penthouse hotel suites overlooking the water to modest hotel rooms a few blocks from the beach.

Norwegian Cruise Lines (NCL) offers round-trip cruises from both Honolulu and Maui, the latter offering myriad accommodations ranging from luxury resorts to budget-priced condos. For detail on recommended hotels on both Oahu and Maui, please see the Where to Stay section in their respective chapters.

Hawai'i is not a cheap place to visit. The resorts here are not the all-inclusive type found at some tropical destinations and tourists do not remain within the confines of their chosen resort but venture to all corners of the island, visiting local attractions and exploring beaches and towns along the way.

Hawai'i is family friendly and the major resorts offer children's programs which, for an extra charge, provide supervised activities for youngsters (aged 5 to 12), including water sports and Hawaiian crafts.

In keeping with the new awareness of Hawai'i's rich culture, most major resorts offer cultural activities, often overseen by a full-time cultural advisor. Activities include lessons in hula dancing, lei making and ukulele playing, as well as cooking demonstrations.

For more information, visit www.gohawaii.com or call 1-800-GoHawaii. The Hawai'i Visitors and Convention Bureau can be reached at (808) 923-1811.

A sunset view from the Fairmont Kea Lani on Maui.

Documentation & Currency

A valid passport is the best proof of citizenship a traveler can carry and one that is required of American citizens embarking on some, but not all, Hawai'i cruises. American citizens flying to Hawai'i to embark on a round-trip NCL America cruise do not need a passport, but must carry proof of U.S. citizenship, such as a birth certificate, accompanied by an official photo identification, such as a current driver's license. American citizens taking a Hawai'i cruise that includes a foreign port call, such as Fanning Island, Ensenada or Vancouver, must carry a passport. Canadian citizens must carry a passport for all Hawai'i cruises. Permanent residents of the United States must carry a valid Alien Resident Card, a passport from their country of citizenship, and any relative visas. Verify with your travel agent the existing identification requirements. It is important that you have all required documents; if not, you could be denied boarding your ship, with no refund issued. Most cruise lines post the current passport and visa requirements on their websites.

In the interests of U.S. homeland security, pre-registration for a cruise is mandatory. This can be done online, or by faxing or mailing a form supplied by the cruise company. Before your departure, leave a detailed travel itinerary with a family member, friend or neighbor. Include the name of your ship, its phone number and the applicable ocean code, as well as your stateroom number – all of which will be provided with your cruise documentation. With this information, a person back home can place a satellite call to your ship in an emergency. Another precaution is to photocopy, on a single sheet of paper, the identification page of your passport, your driver's license and all credit cards. Keep one copy of this sheet with you, separate from your passport and wallet, and leave another one at home.

Travel insurance is recommended. A comprehensive policy will cover travel cancellation, delayed departure, medical expenses, personal accident and liability, lost baggage and money, and legal expenses. You may already have supplementary health insurance through a credit card, automobile club policy or employment health plan, but you should check these carefully. Carry details of your policy with you and documentation showing that you are covered by a plan.

The U.S. dollar is the official currency of Hawai'i, and there are ATM's throughout the Hawaiian Islands. Most cruise ships also have an ATM on board, but the fee might be higher than on shore (up to $5 per transaction). Visa, MasterCard and American Express credit cards are widely accepted throughout the islands. Carry a handful of small bills for tipping tour guides.

What to Pack

Resort casual is the norm everywhere in Hawai'i, even at luxury resorts, where a suit and tie is a rarity. Your best choice for daytime attire is cool cotton shirts and shorts, along with a wide-brimmed hat and sunglasses. Also wear comfortable walking shoes or sandals. And bring a bathing suit of course, both for beach visits and for lounging by the ship's pools. It's easy to 'go native' in Hawai'i, with shops selling a wide variety of aloha wear – brightly colored *pareos* (sarong-style wraps), muumuus and Hawaiian shirts.

If you plan to go hiking in the rainforest, bring cotton pants and a long-sleeved cotton shirt, as well as a sweat top and waterproof windbreaker. If you plan to visit the summit of a volcano, where temperatures are much

Cotton shirts and muumuus are ideal attire in Hawai'i.

cooler than at sea level, bring a sweater or fleece-lined jacket.

Your evening wear should include something suitable for the one or two formal nights held on board the ship (formal wear is optional on the NCL ships). Women wear gowns or cocktail

dresses on these occasions and men favor dark suits or tuxedos. For informal evenings, women wear dresses, skirts or slacks, and men wear a shirt and tie, or a sports jacket with an open-necked shirt.

Check with your travel agent regarding your ship's onboard facilities, such as whether there will be a hair dryer in your cabin, and whether the ship has coin-operated laundrettes with irons and ironing boards. Those that don't will provide a laundering service (the cost is approximately $15 for a bag of clothes, washed and pressed), and hand washing can be done in your cabin. Dry cleaning is another onboard service. Basic toiletries can be purchased aboard the ship.

Pack sunscreen for the beach and insect repellant for rainforest hikes. Restrictions may apply to what air passengers can carry aboard an airplane, and your agent will know what is allowed. Be sure to keep all documentation (tickets, passport, etc.), prescrip-tion medicines and eyeglasses with you. Keep prescribed medication in original, labeled containers and carry a doctor's prescription for any controlled drug. If you wear prescription eyeglasses or contact lenses, consider packing a spare pair.

Health Precautions

All large ships have a fully equipped medical center with a doctor and nurses. Passengers needing medical attention are billed at private rates, which are added to their shipboard account. This invoice can be submitted to your insurance company upon your return home.

Sea sickness is not a wide-spread or prolonged problem on modern ships, which use stabilizers to reduce any rolling motion when in open seas. However, if you're susceptible to motion sickness, there are a number of remedies. One is to wear special wrist bands, the balls of which rest on an acupressure point. Over-the-counter medications include Dramamine or Gravol pills, which should be taken ahead of time, before you start to feel nauseous. Another option is to chew Meclizine tablets (available at the ship's infirmary). Check first with your doctor before taking any medication. Natural remedies include taking ginger in capsule

When a ship is at sea, it is sometimes necessary to airlift a passenger requiring emergency surgery to the nearest hospital.

form or sipping on ginger ale and nibbling on dry crackers. Fresh air is another antidote.

When swimming or snorkeling off Hawai'i's beaches, be careful not to touch any jelly fish, either in the water or on the beach. If stung by a Portuguese man-of-war (which looks like blue balloon with trailing tentacles), use a stick or gloves to remove any remaining matter, then rinse with salt or fresh water. If stung by a box jelly (which looks like a clear plastic bag with tentacles), apply vinegar to relieve the pain and seek medical help.

Vacation Photos

Photographs are often your most cherished vacation souvenirs, whether they are prints, slides or digital images. When using an

(Below) Shipboard photo galleries sell film, batteries and other accessories as well as souvenir prints of passengers taken by the ship's photographers.

automatic camera, 200-ASA print film is your best choice for all-around lighting conditions, and this speed of film is less likely to be damaged by the powerful X-ray machines now used at airports. Exposed but undeveloped film should not be put in checked luggage but placed in a carry-on bag where it can withstand about five X-rays at walk-through security checkpoints before becoming damaged. Another option is to place your rolls of film in a see-through plastic bag and ask for a hand inspection, or have your film developed on board the ship before returning home.

If you're using a digital camera, be sure to have a total of at least 128 mb of flash card memory storage and shoot at a fine setting for print quality reproduction. A laptop computer will of course provide lots of storage, and most on-board photo departments can develop digital images into prints. Print film can be bought on most ships or in the ports of call, but slide film is sometimes harder to find. Put fresh batteries in your camera before leaving home, or pack an extra battery pack if you're using a digital camera. Battery packs can be recharged in your cabin. Flash cards can be purchased in most ports in Hawai'i.

A disposable waterproof camera is ideal for taking to the beach and for shooting underwater images while snorkeling. Be aware that water absorbs light, with red and orange colors reaching only a short distance below the surface, which is why a blue tint dominates underwater photos unless special lighting is used.

Phoning & E-mailing 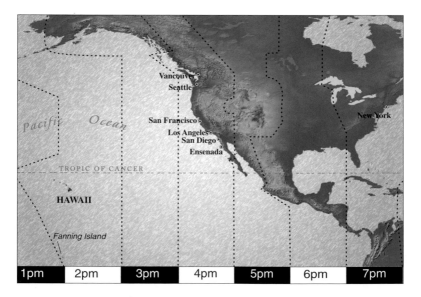 Home

You can phone home from the ship, either through the ship's radio office or by placing a direct satellite telephone call, which is expensive (about $10 per minute). Non-urgent calls can be placed from a land-based phone at the ports of call. Cell phones can be used in Hawai'i, where the ships are usually close enough to land to receive a signal.

Hawai'i Standard Time is +2 hours Pacific Standard Time and +5 hours Eastern Standard Time. However, Hawai'i does not observe daylight savings time, so be sure to add one hour to the

Be sure to check the time zone before you call from Hawai'i.

Vancouver
Seattle
San Francisco
Los Angeles
San Diego
Ensenada
New York

Pacific Ocean

TROPIC OF CANCER

HAWAII

Fanning Island

| 1pm | 2pm | 3pm | 4pm | 5pm | 6pm | 7pm |

(Above) An onboard Internet cafe. (Right) Handweaving a hat out of palm fronds.

time difference when this is in effect on the mainland (April through October).

Another way to contact family and friends back home is the Internet. Most ships have an Internet cafe on board and offer flat-rate use (about $10 for 15 minutes, sometimes less). Passengers log into the internet through their shipboard card, issued on boarding, and within seconds are online. At the end of the session, the ship's system shows how much time the passenger logged on the Internet and the total cost. No matter where you are, at sea or in port, you can send an e-mail instantly. On some ships, passengers can use their own laptop computers to plug into the ship's connection, which is about a 56k speed or better.

Shopping

The Hawaiian peoples' tradition of creating everything they needed from the local flora and fauna has produced the unique clothing and decorative arts that are readily associated with Hawai'i. Each Polynesian nation developed its own artistic traditions, and the Hawaiians excelled at feather-

work and wood carving. They also pursued weaving and tapa art, which features geometric patterns on bark cloth.

Traditional items sold today in the islands include hula drums and an array of wood carvings, ranging in size from miniature tikis to large statues. Skillfully woven goods include bowls, mats and sun hats. Other items to look for are handmade ukuleles and aloha wear (see page 27). Art from other Polynesian nations is also featured at galleries in Hawai'i, including masks from Fiji and tapa art from Tonga.

Locally crafted jewelery often reflects Hawaiian themes, such as the sea turtle (*honu*), which symbolizes good luck in Hawaiian culture. Fine jewelry is handcrafted of gold and set with a variety of gemstones, including cultured black Tahitian pearls. Hawaiian black coral, which divers discovered in 1958 in the deep waters off Molokai Channel, is considered the most lustrous coral in the world and is featured in the collections of Maui Divers Jewelry, which has outlets on all the major islands. The company's Jewelry Design Center, toured annually by 350,000 visitors, is located in Honolulu on King Street.

(Top to bottom) Wood carvings; hand-woven bowls; tapa art depicting the honu (sea turtle).

Scrimshaw, first practised by American whalers who engraved pictures into whale bone and whale ivory, still thrives in Hawai'i. Contemporary artists work with fossil ivory that is 2,000 or more years old, and their hand-engraved scrimshaw is featured on such items as jack knives and money clips. Lahaina Scrimshaw, located in Whalers Village at Ka'anapali on Maui, is a good place to purchase scrimshaw.

nounced KAH-ney), whose paintings depict the historic events and ancient legends of Hawai'i. Born in 1928 and raised on the Big Island of Hawai'i, Kane holds a masters degree from the Art Institute of Chicago and has won numerous awards. His books, beautifully illustrated, include *Voyagers* (1991) and *Ancient Hawai'i* (1998). A selection of his paintings appear in the History section of this book. (www.herbkaneart.com).

Hawaiian painting reflects a range of styles, including vintage art posters and postcards. One of Hawai'i's best known artists is **Herb Kawainui Kane** (pro-

(Above) Fijian mask. (Right) Hawaiian music CD. (Below) Shops on board the ships sell Hawaiian merchandise.

Sailing ships had long plied the waters of Hawai'i when Mark Twain arrived by steamship from San Francisco in 1866. He commented that the voyage had taken just over 10 days, whereas the fast clippers took three weeks. Twain next embarked on an inter-island cruise to Maui and the Big Island, which was something Hawaiian royalty had been doing for centuries. King Kamehameha II in particular liked sailing from island to island accompanied by his chiefs and attendants. In 1820, the same year he moved his official residence from Kailua-Kona on the Big Island to Honolulu, he purchased an 83-foot yacht replete with wood-paneled staterooms. He renamed the yacht *Haaheo o Hawai'i (Pride of Hawai'i)* and continued his custom of wandering from island to island.

The first detailed charts of the Hawaiian Islands were produced by Captain Vancouver of Britain's Royal Navy, who surveyed these waters in the early 1790s. He and other ships' captains quickly became aware of consider-able currents along the islands' coastlines, and they often found their square-rigged sailing ships being pushed out to sea when standing off an island. This was especially pronounced in the wake of a storm. Once, while attemping to sail in a counter-clockwise direction around the top end of Kaua'i, Captain Vancouver was thwarted by a contrary current that sets south along the island's east coast.

Modern cruise ships are not at the mercy of wind and current, but local pilotage can still be challenging, with extensive reefs ringing the entrances to harbors. Honolulu, Hilo and Kahului harbors all require close vigilance by a ship's captain due to reefs bordering their entrance channels. Lahaina Harbor is also encumbered with reefs, which caused numerous sinkings in the days of sailing ships. One of the most notorious shores in Lahaina Roads is Ship Wreck Beach on the north coast of Lanai Island, where a few old wrecks still lie.

Cruise ships are rarely affected by wind but very strong northeast winds (over 35 knots) can make

A Celebrity ship lies to anchor off Lahaina on Maui.

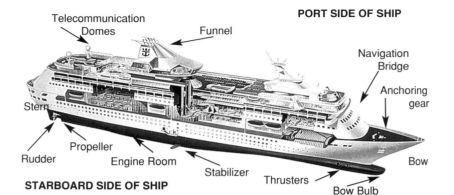

PORT SIDE OF SHIP

Telecommunication Domes

Funnel

Navigation Bridge

Anchoring gear

Stern

Propeller

Rudder

Engine Room

Stabilizer

Thrusters

Bow

Bow Bulb

STARBOARD SIDE OF SHIP

(Above) Diagram of a cruise ship. (Right) Lanai Island's infamous Ship Wreck Beach.

docking at Kahului on Maui's north side impossible, forcing the captain to anchor his ship off Lahaina on the island's other side. This anchorage provides shelter from northeast winds but a strong Kona wind (from the southwest) will blast through Auau Channel and create rough water for the ship's tenders.

Cruise lines reserve the right to change the itinerary of any of their ships, which rarely happens and is usually due to weather conditions.

How Ships Move

Ships are pushed through the water by the turning of propellers, two of which are mounted at the stern. A propeller is like a screw threading its way through the sea, pushing water away from its pitched blades. Props are 15 to 20 feet in diameter on large cruise ships and normally turn at 100 to 150 revolutions per minute. It

takes a lot of horsepower – about 60,000 on a large ship – to make these propellers push a ship along. The bridge crew can tap into any amount of engine power by moving small levers that adjust the propeller blades to determine the speed of the ship. Most modern ships use diesel engines to deliver large amounts of electricity to motors that smoothly turn the propeller shafts.

Ship vibration is minimal using these sophisticated systems to deliver power. Some ships use electric motors mounted on pods hung from the stern of the ship, like huge outboard engines. These pods can swivel 360 degrees.

Ships normally cruise at a sedate speed of 10 to 16 knots, as the distances between islands are not great. One exception is the 320-mile trip between Nawiliwili on Kaua'i and Hilo on the Big Island. Distances at sea are measured in nautical miles (1 nautical mile = 1.15 statute miles = 1.85 kilometers).

The majority of cruise ships currently sailing Hawaiian waters were built in the last decade – a testament to the booming cruise industry. These new ships have been dubbed 'floating resorts' for their extensive onboard facilities, from swimming pools and health spas to show lounges and movie theaters. Cabins, formerly equipped with portholes, now are fitted with picture windows or sliding glass doors that open onto private verandas. Modern cruise ships are quite different from those of the Golden Age of ocean

liners, which were designed for the rigors of winter storms in the North Atlantic. Ships built today are generally taller, shallower, lighter and powered by smaller, more compact engines. Although their steel hulls are thinner and welded together in numerous sections, modern ships are as strong as the older ocean liners because of advances in construction technology and metallurgy.

A ship's size is determined by measurements that result in a figure called tonnage. There are approximately 100 cubic feet to a measured ton. Cruise ships used to be considered large if they exceeded 30,000 tons. Most new ships being built today are over 80,000 tons and carry about 2,000 passengers.

At the stern of every ship, below its name, is the ship's country of registry, which is not necessarily where the cruise company's head office is located. Certain countries grant registry to

NCL's Pride of Hawai'i sails from Honolulu.

ships for a flat fee, with few restrictions or onerous charges, and ships often fly these 'flags of convenience' for tax reasons. Foreign-flagged ships cannot cruise solely in Hawaiian waters; they must make at least one foreign port call in the course of a cruise. NCL America's ships are U.S.-flagged, which is why they can cruise exclusively in Hawaiian waters.

The Engine Room

Located many decks below passenger cabins is the engine room, a labyrinth of tunnels, catwalks and bulkheads connecting and supporting the machinery that generates the vast amount of power needed to operate a ship. A large, proficient crew keeps everything running smoothly, but this is a far cry from the hundreds once needed to operate coal-burning steam engines used before the advent of diesel fuel.

Recent technical advancements (in the last 40 to 50 years) have helped reduce fuel consumption and improve control of the ship.

These include the bow bulb, stabilizers and thrusters. The bow bulb is just below the waterline and displaces the same amount of water that would be pushed out of the way by the ship's bow. This virtually eliminates a bow wave, resulting in fuel savings as less energy is needed to push the ship forward. Stabilizers are small, wing-like appendages that protrude amidships below the waterline and act to dampen the ship's roll in beam seas. Thrusters are port-like openings with small propellers at the bow and sometimes also at the stern, which push the front or rear of the ship as it is approaching or leaving a dock. Thrusters have virtually eliminated the need for tugs in most situations when docking.

The Bridge

The bridge (located at the bow or front of the ship) is an elevated, enclosed platform bridging (or crossing) the width of the ship

The bridge on modern ships has space-age features.

with an unobstructed view ahead and to either side. It is from the ship's bridge that the highest-ranking officer, the captain, oversees the operation of the ship. The bridge is manned 24 hours a day by two officers working four hours on, eight hours off, in a three-watch system. They all report to the captain, and their various duties include recording all course changes, keeping lookout and making sure the junior officer keeps a fresh pot of coffee going. The captain does not usually have a set watch but will be on the bridge when the ship is

entering or leaving port, and transiting a channel. Other conditions that would bring the captain to the bridge would be poor weather or when there are numerous vessels in the area, such as commercial fishboats.

An array of instrumentation provides the ship's officers with pertinent information. Radar is used most intensely in foggy conditions or at night. Radar's electronic signals can survey the ocean for many miles, and anything solid – such as land or other boats – appears on its screen. Radar is also used for plotting the course of other ships and for alerting the crew of a potential collision situation. Depth sounders track the bottom of the seabed to ensure the ship's course agrees with the depth of water shown on the official chart.

The helm on modern ships is a surprisingly small wheel. An automatic telemotor transmission connects the wheel to the steering mechanism at the stern of the ship. Ships also use an 'autopilot' which works through an electronic compass to steer a set course. The autopilot is used when the ship is in open water.

Other instruments monitor engine speed, power, angle of list, speed through water, speed over ground and time arrival estimations. When entering a harbor,

(Top) NCL captain of Pride of Aloha on bridge deck. (Left) Tendering takes place at Lahaina and Kai'ua-Kona.

large ships must have a pilot on board to provide navigational advice to the ship's officers. When a ship is in open waters, a pilot is not required.

Tendering

At some ports, the ship will anchor off a distance from the town and passengers are tendered ashore with the ship's launches. People on organized shore excursions will be taken ashore first, so if you have booked a shore trip you will assemble with your group in one of the ship's public areas. Otherwise, wait an hour or so and the line-ups will be shorter. On Hawai'i cruises, ships use tenders at Lahaina on Maui and Kailua-Kona on the Big Island.

Ship Safety

Cruise ships are one of the safest modes of travel, and the cruise lines treat passenger safety as a top priority. The International Maritime Organization maintains high standards for safety at sea, including regular fire and lifeboat drills, as well as frequent ship inspections for cleanliness and seaworthiness.

Cruise ships must adhere to a law requiring that a lifeboat drill take place within 24 hours of embarkation, and many ships schedule this drill just before leaving port. You will be asked to don one of the life jackets kept in your cabin and proceed to your lifeboat station (directions will be displayed somewhere in your cabin, and the ship's staff will be on hand to guide you through the safety drill).

Hotel Staff

The Front Desk (or Purser's Office) is the pleasure center of the ship. And, in view of the fact that a cruise is meant to be an

The front desk handles all passenger queries and accounts.

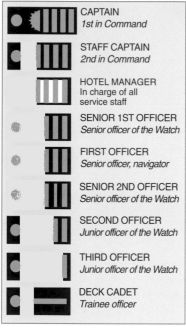

	CAPTAIN 1st in Command
	STAFF CAPTAIN 2nd in Command
	HOTEL MANAGER In charge of all service staff
	SENIOR 1ST OFFICER Senior officer of the Watch
	FIRST OFFICER Senior officer, navigator
	SENIOR 2ND OFFICER Senior officer of the Watch
	SECOND OFFICER Junior officer of the Watch
	THIRD OFFICER Junior officer of the Watch
	DECK CADET Trainee officer

The ship's hotel manager oversees all of the service staff.

extremely enjoyable experience, it is fitting that the Hotel Manager's rank is second only to that of the Captain. In terms of staff, the Hotel Manager (or Passenger Services Director) has by far the largest. It is his responsibility to make sure beds are made, meals are served, wines are poured, entertainment is provided and tour buses arrive on time – all while keeping a smile on his face. Hotel managers generally have many years' experience on ships working in various departments before rising to this position, and usually have graduated from a university or college program in management and train in the hotel or food industries, where they learn the logistics of feeding hundreds of people at a sitting.

A Hotel Manager's management staff includes a Purser, Food Service Manager, Beverage Manager, Chief Housekeeper, Cruise Director and Shore Excursion Manager. All ship's staff wear a uniform and even if a hotel officer doesn't recognize a staff member, he will know at a glance that person's duties by

(Top) Balcony cabin on Pride of Hawai'i. (Right) Most new ships have extensive sports facilities.

their uniform's color and the distinguishing bars on its sleeves. The hotel staff on cruise ships come from countries around the world, with the exception of NCL America's ships servicing Hawai'i, which are staffed by American citizens.

Checking In

Upon arrival the your cruise ship pier, you will be directed to a check-in counter and asked to offer up a credit card to be swiped for any onboard expenses. In exchange, you will receive a personalized plastic card with a magnetic strip. This card acts both as your onboard credit card and the door key to your stateroom. It is also your security pass for getting off and on the ship at each port of call. Carry this card with you at all times.

Life Aboard

Cruise ship cabins – also called staterooms – vary in size, from standard inside cabins to outside suites complete with a verandah. Whatever the size of your accommodation, it will be clean and comfortable. Telephone and television are standard

(Above and bottom left) Specialty restaurants are an alternative to the ship's main dining room. (Left) An inviting lounge on Pride of Aloha.

features in cabins, and storage space includes closets and drawers ample enough to hold your clothes and miscellaneous items. Valuables can be left in your stateroom safe or in a safety deposit box at the front office, also called the purser's office.

If your budget permits, an outside cabin – especially one with a verandah – is preferable for enjoying the coastal scenery and orienting yourself at a new port. When selecting a cabin, keep in mind its location in relation to decks above and below. Being above or below the disco is fine if that is where you plan to be in the wee hours, but if you are below the dining room, you'll likely

hear the scraping of chairs as a wake-up call. For those prone to seasickness, cabins located on lower decks near the middle of the ship will have less motion than a top outside cabin near the bow or stern. If you have preferences for cabin location, be sure to discuss these with your cruise agent when booking. Cruise lines often reward passengers who book early with free upgrades to a more expensive stateroom.

Both casual and formal dining are offered on the large ships, with breakfast and lunch served in the buffet-style lido restaurant or at an open seating in the main dining room. Dinner is served at two sittings in the dining room and, when booking your cruise,

(Above right) Pride of Aloha's Hawaiian cultural center.
(Right) Passengers are treated to Hawaiian music at dinner.

you will be asked to indicate your preference for first or second sitting at dinner. Norwegian Cruise Line features Freestyle Dining on its ships, allowing passengers the flexibility to choose from one of several restaurants each evening.

Most ships now offer alternative dining – small specialty restaurants that require a reservation and for which there is usually a surcharge (about $20 per person). Room service is also available, free of charge, for all meals and in-between snacks.

Things to Do

There are so many things to do on a modern cruise ship, you would have to spend a few months onboard to participate in every activity and enjoy all of the ship's

(Top to bottom) An early jogger on the sun deck; the pool area on Pride of Hawai'i; a putting green on Serenade of the Seas.

facilities. A daily newsletter, slipped under your door, will keep you informed of all the ship's happenings. If exercise is a priority, you can swim in the pool, work out in the gym, jog around the promenade deck, join the aerobics and dance classes or join in the pingpong and volleyball tournaments. Perhaps you just want to soak in the jacuzzi, relax in the sauna or treat yourself to a massage and facial at the spa.

Stop by the library if you're looking for a good book, a board game or an informal hand of bridge with your fellow passengers. Check your newsletter to see which films are scheduled for the movie theater or just settle into a deck chair, breathing the fresh sea air. Your days on the ship can be as busy or as relaxed as you want. You can stay up late every night, enjoying the varied entertainment in the ship's lounges, or you can retire early and rise at dawn to watch the ship pull into port. When the ship is in port, you can remain onboard if you wish or you can head ashore, returning to the ship as many times as you like before it leaves for the next port. Ships are punctual about departing, so be sure to get back to the ship at least a half hour before it is scheduled to leave.

Children and teenagers are welcome on most cruise ships, which offer an ideal environment for a family vacation. Youth facilities on the large ships usually include a playroom for children and a disco-type club for teenagers. Supervised activities are offered

(Above) A poolside bar. (Below) Children's facilities often include water slides, splash pools and a play room.

on a daily basis, and security measures include parents checking their children in and out of the playroom. Kids have a great time participating in activities ranging from ball games to arts and crafts, all overseen by staff with degrees in education, recreation or a related field. Each cruise line has a minimum age for participation (usually two or three years old), and some also offer private babysitting. Youth facilities and programs vary from line to line, and from ship to ship.

Extra Expenses

There are few additional expenses once you board a cruise ship. Your stateroom and all meals (including 24-hour room service) are paid for, as are any stage shows, lectures, movies, lounge acts, exercise classes and other activities held in the ship's public areas. If you make use of the personal services offered on board – such as dry cleaning or a spa treatment – these are not covered in the basic price of a cruise. Neither are any drinks you might order in a lounge. You will also be charged for any wine or alcoholic beverages you order with your meals. Some cruise lines offer beverage programs for teens and children, in which their parents pre-pay for a booklet of soft-drink tickets or for unlimited soda fountain fill-ups.

(Above left) The atrium is the focal point of a ship's interior.
(Left) The promenade deck.

Tipping is extra, with each cruise line providing its own guidelines on how much each crewmember should be tipped – provided you are happy with the service. On some cruise lines tipping is a personal choice while on others it is expected. A general amount for gratuities US $3.50 per day per passenger for both your cabin steward and dining room steward, half that amount for your assistant waiter, and 10 to 15 percent of your total wine bill for the wine steward (unless this is automatically added to your receipt). Tips are usually given the last night at sea, preferably in American cash. Some cruise lines offer a service that automatically bills a daily amount for gratuities to your shipboard account. Most ships are cashless societies in which passengers sign for incidental expenses, which are itemized on a final statement that is slipped under your cabin door during the last night of your cruise and settled at the front office by credit card or cash.

(Right) A quiet moment at the ship's rail. (Below) A young passenger sizes up the ship's bridge, which spans an upper deck.

Volcanoes

The Hawaiian islands are a string of shield volcanoes that rise from the ocean floor. They are part of the Hawaiian Island-Emperor Seamount chain, which extends for 3,500 miles (5630 km) and began forming some 70 million years ago. The Hawaiian islands are the newest additions to this chain. Kaua'i is five to six million years old, O'ahu is three to four million years old, and Maui is one to two million years old. The Big Island, which is about half a million years old, is still creating new shoreline along its southeast side.

The islands initially formed one by one above a 'hot spot' located deep within the earth's mantle. Each one began as a seamount when magma from this extra-hot zone pushed its way to the surface where it erupted on the sea floor. After countless eruptions over several hundred thousand years, the seamount emerged above sea level and became an island, continuing to grow upward and outward with each new layer of erupted lava.

The earth's crust is divided into sections of rock referred to as 'plates.' Unlike volcanoes that form along the edge of continental plates, the Hawaiian islands sit in the middle of the Pacific plate. This plate is moving in a north-west direction at a rate of about four inches (10 cm) per year, its leading edge descending beneath the North American plate along a deepsea subduction zone called the Aleutian Trench. The Pacific plate acts as a conveyor belt, carrying each new Hawaiian island away from the hot spot, where a new seamount then forms and eventually emerges as an island. A seamount called Lo'ihi is already rising from the ocean floor southeast of the Big Island and will likely become an island in about 60,000 years.

The Pacific plate, like other ocean plates, consists of basalt and produces shield volcanoes, which are gently sloped and massive in size. Their rounded shape is due to basaltic lava remaining

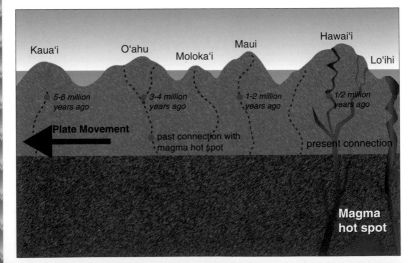

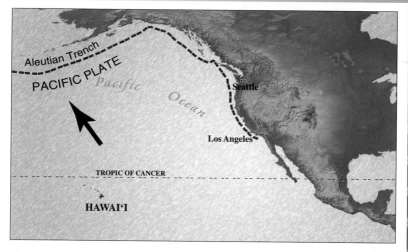

fluid as it flows from the volcano's vent, unlike the more gaseous lava of cone-shaped continental volcanoes, which erupt with explosive force, blowing bits of hardened lava rock (called cinders) straight into the air. Hawai'i's shield volcanoes also contain cinder cones within their calderas (large craters), which were formed by steam explosions that are triggered by magma and

Steam rises from Hawai'i's active Kilauea Caldera.

That Sinking Feeling

When a Hawaiian island is growing, it is simultaneously sinking. This is due to the fact that the Earth's crust lies atop a partially molten layer of rock. As the weight of the growing island increases, it depresses the lithosphere directly beneath it. When the island achieves a floating balance (called isostatic equilibrium, which is similar to a boat floating in water), it stops sinking.

groundwater mixing when the floor of an active crater sinks below the water table. When magma erupts from within a volcano, there is little support for the floor of its summit crater, which collapses and forms a deep, large crater called a caldera.

As rising magma fills the reservoir beneath a shield volcano's summit, the pent-up pressure is

(Below) 'The Discovery of Hawai'i' by Herb Kane.
(Bottom) Lava streams from Pu'u O'o vent.

eventually released by an eruption (often heralded by a preceding earthquake). Lava streams from the volcano's summit or along a rift zone, sometimes appearing as surface flow but more often concealed within lava tubes that form when the outer layer of lava cools and hardens into a crust, while the lava inside continues flowing.

Upon reaching the ocean, the hot lava enters the water as submarine flows and forms unstable land called a 'bench.' When one of these lava benches collapses, the lava flowing within a tube beneath it is suddenly exposed to the water, heating it into steam and triggering an explosion called a steam blast. If waves splash onto molten lava, they explode into tephra jets – clouds of steam, boiling hot water and tephra (fragments of volcanic glass). Bench collapses are a common occurrence along the southern flank of Kilauea on

THE LOWDOWN ON LAVA

The two principal forms of lava found at Kilauea are *pahoehoe* (smooth, ropy lava) and *a'a* (gravelly, jagged lava). Molten *pahoehoe* is less viscous (sticky) than *a'a* due to its high dissolved gas content and extreme temperature (in excess of 2000° F/1100° C). As hot *pahoehoe* lava flows down a mountainside, it loses gases and cools, becoming slow-moving *a'a* lava that is stirred up and tumbled as it moves across rough ground and hardens into rugged rock. Both types of lava are challenging to walk across after they have hardened. Shelly *pahoehoe* in particular presents an extremely glassy, brittle and thin crust, beneath which are numerous cavities into which a person can easily fall or get cut.

Lava bombs are rounded rock fragments that are partly molten when ejected from a volcano. A round bomb is one that hardens before hitting the ground; a pancake bomb is still fluid. Pele's tears are solidified droplets of lava that fall from a lava fountain, and Pele's hair consists of glassy threads of lava that harden in the air. Droplets that are fluid molten lava when they fall around the base of a lava fountain are called spatter. Pillow lava forms underwater when *pahoehoe* lava enters the sea. (Ash is volcanic dust and tuff is ash that has consolidated into rock.)

Lava tubes are open-ended caves that form within lava flows, when the outer layers of fast-flowing *pahoehoe* cool into a hardened crust while the molten lava continues flowing inside like a river. When the flow of lava stops and the empty lava tube cools, the lava dripping from the ceiling can cool and harden into icicles of rock called stalactites. Holes in the roof of a lava tube are called skylights. (See photos on pages 272 and 273.) Lava trees are hollow pillars of lava left standing where a tree was encased during a lava flow.

(Top to bottom) Molten lava oozes to the surface of Kilauea; hardened pahoehoe; a lava fountain erupts from Kilauea.

the Big Island, where the volcano slopes off into the ocean and is weakly supported, in contrast to its northwest side, which abuts Mauna Loa. Mauna Loa and Kilauea present an opportunity for scientists to observe and study active volcanoes. Kilauea has been in constant eruption since 1983, and is the world's best understood volcano as well as one of the most efficient. Magma rising from the mantle 25 to 35 miles (40-60 km) beneath Kilauea's summit spends little time in the volcano's magma chamber before it is channeled to the surface via Pu'u O'o Vent on Kilauea's southeast rift zone.

Erosion

In Hawai'i, the islands that rose from the sea will eventually return to the sea, on a journey lasting millions of years. When a seamount growing on the ocean floor emerges above sea level to become an island, its barren peaks continue to rise until high enough to catch the rain clouds. As volcanic eruptions subside, the island's wet, windward side gradually becomes covered with lichen, which breaks down rock and allows plants to grow in the nutrient-rich volcanic soil. Plant life arrives from seeds carried by wind and water or in bird droppings. Insects and other small animals hitch a ride on drifting logs and other debris. Over time a variety of vegetation takes root and flourishes in the warm, moist climate.

The steady trade winds and tropical rains that bring life to the

Kaua'i's Na Pali Coast reflects several million years of erosion.

Black Sand Beaches

Hana Bay, Maui

Littoral (coastal) cones form along the shorelines of active volcanoes when seawater penetrates the rubble-strewn top of an *a'a* lava flow to reach the liquid core and trigger a strong steam explosion. Wave action quickly removes most of the cone and, if the shoreline configuration is favorable, a beach of black volcanic sand will form. Rare green-sand beaches, such as the one near South Point on the southwestern flank of Mauna Loa, consist of olivine and pyroxene sands, which have been filtered by local currents from ground-mass lava to form separate beaches.

island also erode its landforms. The erosive forces of wind and water easily break down basalt rock, and the mountain streams flowing seaward carve deep valleys separated by high ridges, which are gradually worn into sheer cliffs called *pali*. During heavy rains, mudslides and landslides hasten the erosion. Over millions of years, the once-mountainous island is reduced to an islet that is flat, barren and dry.

Meanwhile, the coral reef that grew on the sea-level slopes of the young volcanic island continues to grow upwards, remaining just beneath the water's surface, while the island itself slowly contracts. Initially a lagoon forms between the shrinking island and the encircling reef. Eventually the island disappears beneath the water, leaving behind a coral atoll. It too will ultimately disappear when the Pacific plate moves it into colder waters and the reef dies. What remains of the old volcano resting on the sea

Molokini Island, off Maui, is an eroded volcanic cone.

Residents flee a tsunami as it rolls into Hilo Bay on Hawai'i.

bottom ultimately will return to the Earth's crust as the Pacific plate carries it to a subduction zone (the Aleutian Trench), where it descends beneath the North American plate.

Earthquakes & Tsunamis

The movement of magma within Hawai'i's active volcanoes creates a complex push-pull balancing act that results in frequent tremors and earthquakes. When a volcano is growing, which is the case with Kilauea on the Big Island, its seaward flanks are unstable as they slope steeply to the sea floor. An earthquake can trigger a submarine landslide, which can in turn generate a tsunami. Such was the case on the Big Island's south coast in 1868 when the Great Kau quake caused violent tremors, a devastating mudflow and a tsunami that washed away 180 houses, drowned 46 people and destroyed Keauhou town near Halape.

In 1975 an earthquake registering 7.2 on the Richter scale again struck the Big Island's south coast. It happened in the middle of the night, causing the shoreline to subside 11 feet (3.5 m) into the sea. A tsunami washed ashore, destroying the shelter at Halape Campground where some boy scouts were dragged out to sea and miraculously survived. One survivor recalls fighting his way back to the water's surface where the branches and bushes were so thick he could walk over them back to shore. The scout leader and one other camper drowned.

Not all tsunamis in Hawai'i are generated locally. Distant earthquakes generated two major tsunamis to hit Hawai'i in the last century. In 1946, an earthquake in the Aleutian Trench sent a killer wave racing across the North Pacific to Hawai'i, and in 1960 an earthquake in southern Chile triggered a tsunami that reached Hawai'i. These ocean-crossing waves are not dangerous when in deep water, where they are only a few feet high and undetected by ships at sea. They are, however, several hundred miles in length and can build into a series of waves of catastrophic proportion upon approaching a shelving coastline.

Anywhere from 10 to 40 minutes can pass between crests and the highest wave may occur several hours after the first wave. The sudden withdrawal of water from a shoreline could be the trough of an approaching tsunami, so people who venture onto these newly exposed beaches risk becoming engulfed by a wave's huge crest. A tsunami warning system is in place for the Pacific Ocean. Countries with gauge systems include the United States, Canada, Japan, Chile, New Zealand and the Philippines. Should any of the stations record a drastic change in water elevation, direct telephone contact is made with the warning center in Honolulu. A 24-hour Tsunami

A winter wave rolls ashore at Waimea Bay on O'ahu.

Warning System has been in operation in Hawai'i since 1946, and a steady one-minute siren warns the public if a tsunami is approaching Hawaiian waters.

A tsunami – meaning 'harbor wave' in Japanese – is often referred to as a tidal wave. However, tsunamis are not caused by tidal action (although a high tide can increase their onshore damage) but by sea floor earthquakes or underwater landslides.

Waves & Tidal Action

The maximum tidal range in the Hawaiian islands is only 1.5 feet (.45 m) due to their close proximity to the North Pacific's amphidromic point, which is a 'pivot point' from which the tide propagates northward in a counterclockwise direction toward the coast of North America. Much

more variable is the surf that rolls ashore. Many factors determine the size and shape of these waves, including the speed and direction of the wind and the orientation and bathymetry of each bay.

Winter generally brings high surf and dangerous currents to many of Hawai'i's beaches, generated by distant storms in the North Pacific. For serious surfers, however, winter waves are the best for surfing, unless an onshore wind is pushing the top of the waves down and making them break too fast. In big seas, an offshore wind will make the waves stand up to their full height and provide the ultimate surfing wave.

Weather buoys positioned around the main Hawaiian Islands provide data on sea conditions (height and direction of waves), allowing meteorologists to predict localized surf conditions.

Rain clouds collect over Maui.

Weather

Most visitors to Hawai'i expect the weather to be ideal, and for the most part this is the case. Cloudbursts in winter are frequent but are usually short-lived. There's almost always a sunny beach somewhere, even if the island's mountainous interior is shrouded with clouds. However, heavy rains can cause flash flooding in mountainous areas when the water levels of valley streams rise rapidly, spilling onto their banks and turning into raging torrents. Hurricanes are also a menace, but are infrequent. Rarely does a hurricane make landfall at the Hawaiian islands. Most pass south of Hawai'i, although Kaua'i was hit hard by Hurricane Iwa in November 1982 and by Hurricane Iniki in September 1992.

On the Big Island, where the active volcano Kilauea emits about 2,000 tons of sulfur dioxide

each day from Puʻu Oʻo vent, a visible haze called 'vog' (volcanic smog) often forms. It is caused when sulfur dioxide and other volcanic gases interact chemically with oxygen, moisture, dust and sunlight. The trade winds dissipate these harmful gases but they are hazardous if a person is directly downwind of concentrated fumes emitting from ground cracks along lava tubes. Pregnant women, small children and adults with breathing and heart conditions should avoid such situations.

Rainbows

In his *Letters from Hawaii*, Mark Twain states, "Why did not Captain Cook have taste enough to call his great discovery the Rainbow Islands?"

Rainbows, which form when the sun shines through water droplets, are a common phenomena in Hawaiʻi. They occur most frequently in the late afternoon when the sun shines following a downpour. This is due to the air being filled with sheets of water droplets that refract and reflect the sun's rays. Rainbows cannot appear if the sun is high in the sky; conversely, a complete 180° arc will form when the sun is at the horizon. Less common is the lunary rainbow, which occurs soon after dark if a full moon is shining. Sailors called these 'rain dogs' and Mark Twain described them as "drifting about the heavens in these latitudes, like stained cathedral windows."

Ancient cultures around the world perceived the rainbow as a mystical occurrence, and the Hawaiians believed a rainbow signified the presence of royalty.

A rainbow appears over Moʻoheau County Park in Hilo, where showers occur about 270 days per year.

The lush islands of Polynesia are the stuff of legend. They hold a seductive sway over the hearts and souls of anyone who has visited – or dreamed of visiting – their shores. Once under their spell, anything is possible. They have lured sailors to commit mutiny, inspired artists to create great works, and prompted mainland city dwellers to abandon lucrative careers in favor of barefoot days at the beach.

Polynesia, meaning *many islands*, is one of the three main ethnological divisions of Oceania, the other two being Melanesia and Micronesia. Together these three oceanic regions encompass some 25,000 islands that are scattered across the central and south Pacific Ocean. Polynesia's principal island groups include Hawai'i, Samoa, Tonga, French Polynesia and Fiji, the latter lying along the border between Polynesia and Melanesia. Polynesia also includes New Zealand, the home of Maori tribes.

The Hawaiian islands, which form the apex of the Polynesian triangle, are the only major island group of Polynesia that lies north of the equator. Within the Hawaiian chain are approximately 100 islands and islets strung across the central Pacific for more than a thousand miles, from the Big Island of Hawai'i to the tiny Kure Atoll. The eight major islands in the chain are Hawai'i (known as the Big Island), Maui,

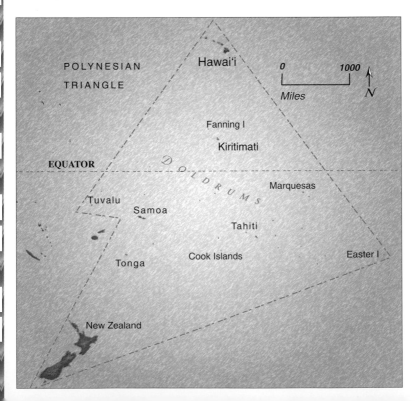

Kahoʻolawe, Lanaʻi, Molokaʻi, Oʻahu, Kauaʻi and Niʻihau. The rest of the island chain – called the Northwestern (or Leeward) Islands – consists mostly of coral atolls, which are protected as a fish and wildlife conservation area. One exception is Midway Island, which is a military base administered by the U.S. Department of the Interior.

Midway Island, which actually comprises two small islands enclosed by a circular atoll six miles in diameter, was uninhabited when discovered in 1859 by an American sea captain. Many of these remote islands and atolls were discovered the hard way – when ships grounded on their treacherous reefs. Shipwrecks were common in these uncharted waters, a fact that accentuates the impressive seamanship of the early Polynesians who first put to sea in search of new lands.

Early Seafarers

The Pacific Ocean is the world's largest and deepest ocean. It covers one-third of the earth's surface and spans 11,000 miles (18000 km) at its greatest width, from the Isthmus of Panama to the Malay Peninsula. The Pacific Ocean's immense size was not fully comprehended until the Portuguese navigator Ferdinand Magellan led a Spanish seafaring expedition across its uncharted expanse in 1520 – a crossing that took more than three months, during which the ships' crews suffered miserably from scurvy and starvation. Yet, great as his epic

Traditonal Polynesian craft remain as a motif in Hawaiʻi.

sea journey was, Magellan was not the first to traverse the open waters of the South Pacific. As early as 1100 BC, intrepid mariners were sailing across this vast sea.

Where these ancient mariners came from and the sea routes they followed are still open to speculation. Shortly after European explorers began discovering these remote Pacific islands, two theories emerged. One proposed that Polynesian peoples had originated in Asia and island-hopped their way across the Pacific. However, sea captains of that era viewed as implausible an eastward migration from Asia, due to the contrary winds and currents. They speculated that the only way to reach the islands of Polynesia was by sailing westward from the Americas.

Neither theory explained, however, the presence in Polynesia of both Asian and American influences. The sweet potato and dog breeds of South America were found on many an island alongside the chicken, pig and outrigger canoe, all of which originated in Asia. There were also physical and cultural similarities between the aboriginals of coastal British Columbia and Washington State, and those of Polynesia, such as their swift ocean-going canoes carved from large logs. The people living on the geographically remote islands of Polynesia spoke similar languages, with variations of the name Hawai'i used in New Zealand (Havaiki), the Cook Islands (Avaiki) and Samoa (Savaii). These cultural similarities all pointed to the existence of a great ancient seafaring culture.

Regardless of the mounting evidence, the accepted scientific theory of a direct Asian migration to Polynesia endured until the mid-20th century. Then, in 1947, the Norwegian explorer and anthropologist Thor Heyerdahl challenged mainstream academia. With the help of five crewmen, Heyerdahl built *Kon-Tiki* – a replica of the ancient rafts used by the Incas. They launched this primitive raft from Peru and sailed in a westerly direction across the South Pacific Ocean.

Bobbing like a cork on the Pacific swells, *Kon-Tiki* drifted with the prevailing ocean currents and southeasterly trade winds for 4,300 miles and 101 days before making landfall on the island of Raroia in the Tuamotos. This epic voyage proved that ancient seafarers were capable of sailing long distances in primitive craft. It also proved that the initial migration to Polynesia could have originated from South America, followed by a second major migration from Asia, which entailed sailing a circuitous route across the North Pacific to North America, then swinging south and west to Polynesia.

The migrating Polynesians traveled in huge canoes that they carved from logs, 60 to 80 feet

A double-hulled ocean canoe.

long, two of which were lashed together with massive crossbeams for extended voyages. They built a platform between the two hulls to hold a cabin, and an A-frame mast was mounted for rigging a claw-like sail made of plaited leaves. Vines and woven coconut fiber were used for making ropes and lines.

Skilled navigators, the Polynesians steered by the sun, moon and stars, and rode the prevailing winds and currents to their next landfall. Signs of land ahead included a change of water color and wave motion, as well as the presence of seaweed and turtles, which indicated a reef in the vicinity. They also observed and followed seabirds flying to their island homes; it has even been suggested that the annual migrations of the Pacific plover and the long-tailed curlew could have led Polynesians north to Hawai'i.

Tonga likely was the first Polynesian island to be colonized by migrating mariners, in about 1150 BC. Over time, one by one, the other islands were discovered and colonized. including the Hawaiian Islands which were settled sometime between 500 and 750 AD. The first boat load may have landed near Ka Lae (South Point) on the Big Island. Wherever this seminal landing took place, the men and women who first set foot on the pristine shores of Hawai'i were beginning a new life for themselves and their descendants. Their great seafaring quest had ended.

Village Life, Hawaiian Style

The men and women who travelled great distances to reach the Hawaiian islands did not arrive empty handed. They brought with them plants and animals for cultivation, and wasted no time establishing villages around which their everyday lives were centered. These villages were situated in groves of coconut palms overlooking a beach or lagoon where residents could fish the local waters and cultivate taro fields in the nearby valleys. Their houses, called *hales* (haw-lays), were huts thatched with clumps of *pili* grass on the exterior and *lauhala* (pandanus leaves) on the interior walls. Mats of woven

A replica boat house at Pu'uhonua o Honaunau.

lauhala covered the floor upon which people would sit and sleep.

Sleeping, cooking and dining were pursued in separate *hales*, and men and women were forbidden to eat together. Other *hales* with specific roles were the drum house (for storing hula implements), the weaving house (where women created baskets, mats and other items from dried pandanus leaves), and the boat house, where canoes were built, repaired and sheltered close to the water. Nearby was the fishing house, where nets and fishing gear were stored and mended. Fish hooks were made of bone or shell, poles were made from bamboo, and nets were woven with cordage made from vines or coconut husk fibers.

Artist-historian Herb Kane depicts early Hawai'i in 'Ka'anapali in Ancient Times'.

The *hale ali'i* (chief's or king's residence) occupied a prominent rise and consisted of three hales enclosed by a stone wall. The king's was the largest house, about thirty feet long, its open interior floored with layers of cloth and bordered with pillow-like folds of the same. The king's bed, also made of layers of fine soft cloth, was raised several feet off the ground at one end of his apartment. His favorite queen occupied a smaller *hale*, and neither were allowed to enter each other's house. The smallest hut of the three, the royal bed chamber, stood between the two others.

Feathered standards, called *kahili*, were displayed inside and outside a chief's *hale* to indicate his royal status, and his attendants would carry these when he moved about. The blowing of a conch shell announced the approach of a royal procession, and common people would bow or prostrate themselves to a passing chief.

(Above) 'Council of Chiefs' by Herb Kane. Note the feather cape worn only by high-ranking chiefs. (Right) A taro field. (Below, right) Pounding the poi.

Ruling chiefs inherited their royal rank but were often called upon to defend their territory from rival chiefs. Thus, royal sons were trained from a young age to become skilled warriors, and mock battles were staged to sharpen their skills with spears and other weapons. This elite military training took place apart from men of the common class who would form armies when their chiefs called them to battle but who otherwise spent their days farming or fishing.

Taro – a tuberous root plant – was widely cultivated and was a mainstay of the Hawaiian diet. To irrigate their crops of taro, the Hawaiians built dams and canals to redirect stream water and carry it onto their fields. Causeways provided access to the fields, which were divided by low stone walls. Different stages of inundation required field laborers working in the deepest portions to be waist deep in mud as they planted, weeded and gathered taro plants. These fields were an ideal habitat for ducks, which the Hawaiians hunted for food. Sugar cane was planted along the borders and partitions of the taro fields, and sweet potatoes were grown on dry ground. The cloth plant *kapa* was also cultivated.

The local fishermen caught *aku* (bonito) from small canoes that were paddled quickly by three or four people while one angler fished with a rod from the stern. Salt was used for preserving fish, and pans were positioned in shallow saltwater reservoirs separated from the ocean by walls of mud and stones. Royal fishponds, fed by freshwater streams, were also situated near the ocean and were enclosed by a rock wall with sluice gates.

While Hawaiian villagers lived in isolation, European explorers were expanding their horizons. Starting in 1565, Spain's Manila galleons sailed annually back and forth across the Pacific, between Acapulco and the Philippines, but their routes – determined by the prevailing winds and ocean currents – bypassed the Hawaiian Islands, which remained undiscovered by the outside world.

Yet, according to Hawaiian legends, there were a few visitors. These people arrived either as shipwreck survivors or as castaways. They may have been Spanish or Asian, but exactly who they were and how they got there remains shrouded in the mists of antiquity. Those who did wash up on the shores of Hawai'i remained there and adopted the Polynesian way of life, their fate a mystery to the outside world.

Meanwhile, rumors circulated in naval circles that a Spanish explorer had discovered a group of Pacific islands, identified as Los Majos islands on early Spanish charts and shown to lie at the same latitude as the Hawaiian islands

Captain James Cook of Britain's Royal Navy.

but about 10 degrees of longitude east of the Big Island of Hawai'i. These rumors were never substantiated by Spain, which had boldly claimed the Pacific Ocean to be its own 'Spanish Lake.' However, the rise of Great Britain and other rival sea powers meant that Spain's monopoly of the Pacific could not endure forever. The isolated islands of Polynesia were destined for discovery.

The Modern World Discovers Hawai'i

"How shall we account for this nation spreading itself so far over this vast ocean?"
– Captain James Cook

The 18th century was a great era of naval exploration. While merchant ships were pursuing the riches of trade, the sea powers of Europe were sending naval expeditions on voyages of discovery. Great explorers included France's LaPerouse, Spain's Alejandro Malaspina and Vitus Bering under the employ of the Russian Tsar. But the man whose name is synonomous with Pacific exploration is Britain's James Cook.

A genius among navigators and a brilliant leader, Cook charted more of the Pacific Ocean in the course of a decade than had all other explorers in the previous 250 years. When his ships appeared on the horizon off the Hawaiian islands on January 19, 1778, a new era had arrived for the people of Hawai'i. Cook wondered if the islands he was approaching were inhabited, but this question was soon answered

Herb Kane's 'Visitors From Another World' shows the ancient Hawaiians witnessing what they believed to be the return of their god Lono.

by the sight of canoes setting off from shore toward the ships. Cook promptly noted the similarities between the people paddling these canoes and those he had met in Tahiti.

As excited as Cook and his crew were at finding an uncharted Polynesian island, their surprise was nothing compared to the Hawaiians' reaction. Cook arrived during *makahiti* (the winter season and time of celebration) and he struck a startling resemblance to Lono, the Hawaiian god of the harvest. Even before Cook stepped ashore, the sight of his square-rigged ships' white sails was so similar to the Hawaiians' symbol of Lono, namely a banner of tapa held aloft by a long staff, the island inhabitants believed that their great god had returned as promised by legend.

They launched their canoes and paddled out to greet Cook's two ships, *Resolution* and *Discovery*, as they anchored at Waimea Bay on the southwest coast of Kaua'i. The Hawaiiains offered roasting pigs and taro in trade for iron nails, which they used for making weapons and were familiar with from their salvaging of driftwood that would wash ashore from distant shipwrecks.

Fortunately, several of Cook's officers, including George Vancouver, were able to communicate with the Hawaiians using a sort of pidgin-Tahitian dialect. The Hawaiian chiefs who came aboard the ships were astonished at the array of unfamiliar objects – everything from telescopes and other nautical instruments to logbooks and table flatware. One chief spotted an anchor and tried to pick it up, not realizing how heavy it was.

'Moment of Contact' by Herb Kane shows Cook's first meeting with the people of Hawai'i.

The Naming of Owhyhee

JOHN *Earl of* SANDWICH,

When explorers such as James Cook and George Vancouver began charting the Hawaiian islands, they named the various coves and bays they examined after the villages or districts bordering that particular body of water. However, when Cook sought a name for the entire island chain, he chose to call them the Sandwich Islands in honor of John Montagu, the 4th Earl of Sandwich, who was then First Lord of the Admiralty. A dissolute aristocrat, Montagu was criticized for Britain's naval defeats during the American Revolution, but is today remembered for popularizing the sandwich – which was his preferred method of dining so he wouldn't have to leave the gambling table. The British name of Sandwich Islands did not endure and the islands are now known by their original name of Hawai'i.

in the *Fortyninth* — Year of His Majesty's Reign.

Sandwich

Chichester

By Command

Printed by H. Teape, Tower-hill, for His Majesty's Stationary-Office.

Upon heading ashore with three armed boats to find fresh water, Cook was treated to an amazing scene. The Hawaiians waiting there immediately fell flat on their faces at the sight of the incarnation of their god Lono and would not rise until beseeched to do so. They offered foodstuffs and performed a ceremony with prayers, after which Cook handed out the presents he had brought from the ships. The next day, the Hawaiians eagerly helped the British sailors fill their water casks, rolling them to and from a nearby freshwater pool.

Cook's initial visit was brief before heading to North America in search of a northwest passage. When he returned to the Hawaiian islands in late November, it was once again the *makahiki* season and by then the news of his earlier visit had spread to all of the islands. With awe and anticipation, the residents of the Big Island watched Cook's ships sailing around their island. Cook was seeking a sheltered anchorage, but unfavorable winds had prevented his ships from venturing too close to shore until they came upon Kealakekua Bay on the west side of the island. Here they dropped anchor, not realizing they had chosen the site of a *heiau* (temple) dedicated to Lono.

Throngs of joyful people greeted Cook and his men. They came by the hundreds in canoes and on surf boards. Many swam out to the ships while thousands more lined the shores, eagerly awaiting a closer look at the incarnation of Lono, their beloved god who had returned to them at last. Unaware of the aura of godliness bestowed upon him, Cook was escorted past the prostrated masses by high-ranking priests who led him to the *heiau* for a ceremonial

Herb Kane's 'Death of Cook' depicts one of history's most tragic events.

feast. Later, formal visits were paid to Cook's ships by King Kalani'opu'u and his chiefs, followed by a ceremony on shore at which the elderly king removed his feathered cloak and helmut and placed these on the shoulders and head of Cook. Then, as a strong pledge of friendship, the Hawaiian king exchanged names with the British naval commander. Two weeks later, Cook would be dead at the hands of the Hawaiians.

When Cook departed the Hawaiian Islands on February 4, 1779, his departure was a great relief to his Hawaiian hosts who had felt compelled to lavish Cook and his men with vast quantities of food for their long voyage. By the time the ships set sail, doubts as to Cook's godliness had already surfaced, due in part to the death of one of his crewmen whose body had been buried on shore. Just days after leaving Kealakekua Bay, the foremast of the *Resolution* – whose rigging had been an ongoing problem – was damaged in gale-force winds. Reluctantly, and tragically, Cook brought his two ships back to Kealakekua Bay.

There was no jubilant welcome this time, as the British sailors unstepped the *Resolution*'s mast and rowed it ashore for repair on the beach. Tensions began to manifest in petty thievery and minor scuffles. Then, the increasingly sullen Hawaiians became outright alarmed when they saw Cook and his armed men come ashore one morning to retrieve a ship's boat that had been stolen in the night. Cook marched straight to the home of King Kalani'opu'u and persuaded him to return to the ship with him. When they reached the beach, however, the Hawaiian king had second thoughts about going with Cook. A melee broke out and Cook was struck down from behind with a club, then stabbed in the back before being clubbed to death.

The body of Cook and four marines who were killed in the fracas had to be left behind as the rest of the party escaped to the waiting boats. It took a week to recover Cook's body, which had been treated like that of a Hawaiian chief – the flesh stripped from the bones, which were saved and worshipped. Meanwhile, Cook's officers had to restrain their enraged crewmen

An obelisk stands near the spot where Captain Cook was murdered in Kealakekua Bay.

from wreaking a bloody revenge, but they did allow them to vent their grief and anger by burning the village at Kealakekua Bay to the ground. Upon the begrudging return of Cook's bones, the two British ships weighed anchor and took their final leave.

One of the officers who had been instrumental in negotiating the return of Cook's remains was a 21-year-old midshipman named George Vancouver. Twelve years later, Vancouver returned to the Sandwich Islands as the commander of a British naval expedition. Proficient in the Polynesian dialects, Vancouver developed a keen interest in the affairs of the Hawaiians and tried to reconcile the islands' warring chiefs. In the process he formed a remarkable friendship with the most important figure in Hawaiian history – Kamehameha the Great.

The newborn Kamehameha was hidden in the Waipi'o Valley.

Kamehameha, The Warrior King

A high-born royal, Kamehameha possessed all the qualities of a great leader: brave, strong and ruthless as a conqueror; wise, compassionate and respected as a ruler. He was born in about about 1758, during a lightening storm one November night in Kohala, on the Big Island of Hawai'i. Given the name Paiea, the royal infant was immediately taken from his mother and hidden away in the remote Waipi'o valley because of a death threat issued by King Alapai, an elderly uncle, who suspected that the child's father was not in fact the chief of Kohala but a rival chief from Maui. Five years later, the young boy was returned to his parents' custody. His once-hostile uncle, now weak and frail, was ready to accept the child. He gave his nephew the new name of Kamehameha, meaning The Lonely One.

When his father died, the 14-year-old Kamehameha was adopted by another uncle, King Kalani'opu'u, who sent the boy to the district of Kau, on the slopes of Mauna Loa. There, like most male children of royal blood, Kamehameha received special tutoring in navigation, astronomy and religious rites, all taught through oral recitation and memorization, for there was no written language. He was also trained to become a warrior, mastering such battle skills as throwing and dodging spears. Kamehameha grew into a tall, muscular young man whose fearless countenance and powerful aura belied his good-natured disposition.

When Kalani'opu'u died in 1782, his kingship passed to his son, but custody of the war god Ku passed to his nephew Kamehameha, who was soon battling his cousin for control of the island. Kamehameha also launched a successful attack on the island of Maui, then returned to Hawai'i for a final confrontation with the last remaining rival chief on the Big Island. By 1791, Kamehameha had become the undisputed ruler of the island of Hawai'i and his royal stature was unquestionably that of a great warrior king.

Back in England, the publication of Cook's journals had sparked great interest in the sea otter trade. This was a highly lucrative enterprise, for these thick fur pelts fetched a phenomenal price in China. The Hawaiian islands, due to their

Kamehameha the Great is commemorated throughout Hawai'i.

strategic location, became a principal stop-over port for British and American fur-trading ships traveling between the Pacific Northwest and China. These merchant ships would take on water and provisions in Hawai'i, and their commanders soon discovered that the Hawaiian chiefs coveted firearms – muskets, pistols, gunpowder, cannons and balls – to use in their protracted civil wars. Rival district chiefs, often members of the same extended family, would frequently battle one another, or they would join forces to battle the ruler of a neighboring island.

When Captain George Vancouver arrived off the southern tip of the Big Island on March 1, 1792, he was commanding two ships of Britain's Royal Navy. His instructions were to explore and thoroughly chart the northwest coast of North America in search of a northwest passage, but the Hawaiian islands were a convenient place to spend the winters in between summers spent surveying northern waters.

Hawai'i held many attractions. With a pleasant climate, clean villages and appetizing food, these islands were an ideal place for rest and recreation. In fact, the arrival of merchant ships was a harbinger of Hawai'i's future tourism industry, and already there was a market for souvenirs. In exchange for native handicrafts, the British sailors happily traded iron nails, knives and scissors, the latter item coveted by Hawaiian women for cutting their hair. However, unlike during Captain Cook's visit to the islands, when one sixpenny nail was worth several small pigs, the Hawaiians now wanted firearms.

Captain Vancouver refused to enter the arms trade, explaining to the Hawaiian chiefs that his cannons and firearms belonged to England's King George. But he did offer goats, sheep and geese in trade, as well as pieces of red cloth, which the Hawaiian rulers especially valued for their regalia. They also respected Vancouver as an emissary of England's mighty King George, whom they perceived as powerful and wealthy enough to fund a navy of well-armed ships manned with disciplined crew.

The natives no longer prostrated themselves on the ground at the sight of white men. The reverence the Hawaiians once displayed had disappeared in the ensuing years since Cook's visit, for the behavior of many a merchant sea captain and his crew had been anything but godlike. Several incidents of treachery and violence had erupted between the Hawaiians and ship captains, who were quick to punish or kill anyone they caught stealing. Vancouver, on the other hand, was the consumate diplomat, whose interactions with the local chiefs were conducted with respectful decorum and a strict adherence to protocol. He was also extremely cautious, always

HMS Discovery under the command of George Vancouver.

gaining
the friendship
of a local chief
before sending an
armed watering
party ashore.

The Hawaiian rulers
were equally apprehen-
sive about their visitors. In
one instance, an elderly
Kauian chief was reluctant to
go aboard Captain Vancouver's
ship for a visit but agreed to the
plan once it was determined that
one of Vancouver's midshipmen
would remain on shore until the
safe return of the chief. The
young man chosen for this role,
Thomas Manby, was a willing
hostage and afterwards he wrote
in his logbook that his time
ashore was spent in "ecstatic
enjoyment" entertaining the old
chief's wives who "without reluc-
tance yielded to the encircling
arms of youth."

After briefly stopping at the
Hawaiian islands in March 1792,
Vancouver's ships returned the
next winter and it was then that
King Kamehameha greeted the
British sea captain. The two men
instantly recognized each other as
a person of importance, and a
friendship quickly formed based
on a mutual deference to the
other's authority.

Captain Vancouver's chart.

When Vancouver's two ships
arrived at Kealakekua Bay, they
were greeted by thousands of
Hawaiians, who encircled the
ships with their canoes and
helped tow them into the bay. By
noon the two ships lay at anchor
and an official reception took
place with great fanfare. While
Captain Vancouver and his officers waited on the ships' decks to
receive King Kamehameha, his
flotilla of 11 large canoes set off
from shore in a V-shaped formation. Kamehameha, resplendent
in a yellow-feathered cape and
helmut, stood in the lead canoe,
which was paddled by three
dozen men. Under his orders, all
of the men in the canoes kept an
exact and regular time with their
paddles as they paraded round the

'A Ceremony at Pu'ukohola Heiau' by Herb Kane depicts the temple Kamehameha built to please the war god Ku.

two ships, then drew up in a line under the *Discovery*'s stern while Kamehameha's canoe pulled up alongside the starboard side of the ship and came to a swift stop beside the gangway. The king promptly climbed up the gangway where Captain Vancouver awaited with an outstretched hand, which Kamehameha took in his. The two men declared their friendship toward one another, then saluted by touching noses. Gifts were exchanged, and chiefs and royal wives were invited aboard.

Vancouver took a sincere interest in the welfare of the Hawaiians, adopting the role of peace negotiator. During his time spent among the islands, he sought to end the inter-island fighting. Although Vancouver was unable to negotiate a peace agreement between Kamehameha and Kahekili (ruler of Maui and O'ahu), he did persuade Kamehameha and his district chiefs to cede the Sandwich Islands to Great Britain. Vancouver foresaw an increase in the importance of these islands as commerce grew in the North Pacific, and Kamehameha saw benefits in having a powerful ally such as Great Britain to help his people defend themselves from exploitation by armed foreigners visiting the islands. However, Kamehameha wasn't totally convinced of the benefits of entering an alliance with Britain until Vancouver's shipwrights constructed for him a 36-foot schooner called *Britannia* and outfitted it with equipment. Kamehameha already had acquired cannons with which to arm the *Britannia*, and he now owned a vessel unequaled by the other chiefs in the islands.

When it was time for Vancouver and Kamehameha to say their final farewells, Kamehameha presented Vancouver with a magnificent feather cloak as a gift for the English king, with strict orders that no one else be allowed to wear it. The affinity held by Hawaiian royalty for the faraway kingdom of Great Britain would endure for decades. One royal prince insisted he be addressed as King George by his people, while another adopted the name William Pitt. And the Union Jack, which Vancouver had presented

The stripes of Hawai'i's flag represent the eight major islands.

to Kamehameha, would eventually be incorporated in Hawai'i's state flag.

About a year after Vancouver's departure, the ruler of Maui and O'ahu died and control of his kingdom passed to his son Kalanikupule and his brother

Lady Washington

The 18th-century American brig *Lady Washington* was a well-known ship of the fur trade era. Her captain, John Kendrick, had been busy supplying the Hawaiians with firearms in exchange for local goods when he met an ironic end while anchored in Honolulu Harbor. As was the custom, another merchant ship at anchor was saluting the *Lady Washington* when one of its cannon shots accidentally killed Kendrick. A replica of the ship (shown here) was a stand-in for the *Interceptor* in the movie *Pirates of the Caribbean,* starring Johnny Depp.

Kamehameha's troops force their enemies off Pali Lookout in 'Nu'uanu Battle' by Herb Kane.

Kaeo. Friction between the two men soon resulted in a pitched battle on the shores of Pearl Harbor at which Kaeo was defeated and killed. It was now Kamehameha's time to strike. Setting off from the island of Hawai'i, he led his flotilla of 16,000 men across Alenuihaha Channel to attack Maui. The island soon fell to Kamehameha's army, which next captured Moloka'i on its way to O'ahu where he and his well-trained and well-armed forces landed at Waikiki in April, 1795. The island's defenders retreated up the Nu'uanu Valley where they made their last, futile stand atop a cliff-edged lookout. This decisive battle was Kamehameha's most important victory, making him the ruler of all the Hawaiian islands except Kaua'i.

A year later Kamehameha had to return to the Big Island to quash a rebellion started by a rival chief and re-establish his supremacy. A ruthless warrior, Kamehemeha was also a wise leader who consulted with his loyal chiefs and encouraged peaceful activities among his subjects, all while planning his final conquest, of Kaua'i. In the end, a peace agreement was reached between Kamehameha and the ruler of Kaua'i in which the latter would continue to rule over his island while agreeing to acknowledge Kamehameha as his sovereign. Thus, in 1810, Kamehameha became the supreme ruler of the Hawaiian islands, ushering in an era of peace and prosperity.

The Kingdom of Hawai'i

As the years went by and the loyal chiefs who had helped

Kamehameha conquer all of Hawai'i were replaced by sons upon their deaths, the Hawaiian king's authority became absolute. This was used in a constructive manner, for Kamehameha was a benevolent ruler who brought law and order to his kingdom by preserving the *kapu* system of ancient customs and religious beliefs. This was the Hawaiians' only code of law and it governed every area of life with prohibitions and restrictions that were ordered by the ruling chiefs.

When Kamehameha died in 1819, his kingdom was plunged into mourning. Never again would the Hawaiians see a ruler of his stature. Kamehameha's descendants carried on the family's royal dynasty until the death of Kamehemeha V in 1872, but the intervening years were ones of change and instability. The profitable sandalwood trade (which became active under Kamehameha the Great) eventually stripped the islands of these trees. The whaling ships brought wealth – and vice – to the islands. Infectious diseases to which the Hawaiians had no immunity decimated the population, which

(Top to bottom) Kamehameha I in his later years; half a million feathers collected from over 60,000 mamoa birds were used to make Kamehameha's feather cloak on display in the Bishop Museum; Kamehameha's last royal compound in Kailua-Kona.

Queen Ka'ahumanu encouraged the new king, Kamehameha II, to abolish the ancient kapus.

plunged from about 300,000 at the time of Captain Cook's visit to about 54,000 by 1876.

The ongoing visits from American and European ships brought political intrigue and diplomatic sparring to Hawai'i's domestic scene, which foreigners increasingly controlled by purchasing tracts of land and establishing sugar plantations and other business interests.

But it was the arrival of missionaries from New England that fundamentally changed Hawaiian society. Idealistic, educated and well intentioned, the missionaries soon exerted great influence over the monarchy. The young, self-indulgent Kamehameha II, who succeeded his father Kamehameha the Great to the throne, had already succumbed to foreign influences and recently rejected the *kapu* system when New

England missionaries first landed on the shores of his island kingdom and requested permission to preach the gospel. Their arrival was timely, for this new religion would fill the spiritual vacuum created by Kamehameha II's orders to destroy the *heiaus* and burn the idols.

The missionaries introduced literacy and Christian values, and won the approval of Kamehameha II's regent, Queen Ka'ahumanu. The favorite wife of Kamehameha I, she followed in her late husband's footsteps, and emerged as a powerful leader and advisor to the king. Tall and portly (considered a mark of prestige among royalty), she was related by blood to most of the kingdom's leading chiefs, and her edicts were seldom questioned. She became a devout Christian and spent her later years living in a Boston-style house in Honolulu. Yet, as death drew near, she chose to return to a former residence – a small grass hut in the Manoa Valley – where she met her maker.

The missionaries disapproved of many aspects of Hawaiian life , including the propensity some members of the royal court had for drinking, gambling and other vices. A moral tug-of-war emerged between members of the royalty and the missionaries, both sides seeking to influence the common people. When the missionaries lost one of their most powerful advocates with the death of Queen Ka'ahumanu, they were mortified by the self-indulgent behavior of the young, handsome Kamehameha III, second son of Kamehameha the Great, who now sought to gain full control of the Hawaiian nation. He was forced, however, by a council of chiefs to share his power with a new regent, his half sister and a staunch Christian, to whom he left the responsibilities of governing while he indulged in the pursuit of pleasure. The young king urged his people to reject Christian teachings and rally round their own cultural symbols of surfing, hula and other pastimes. But when his favorite sister died suddenly at the age of 20, Kamehameha III called a halt to his indulgences and adopted Christian ways.

By the end of his reign in 1854, Hawai'i had become a constitutional monarchy. Influenced by western ideals, the kingdom had adopted a constitution guaranteeing religious freedom, representative government and an independent judiciary. The old feudal land system had been replaced with a land commission that

Kamehameha II ordered the destruction of the idols.

granted native tenants the opportunity to claim ownership on the plots of land they currently occupied and cultivated.

This division of land was called the Great Mahele. Yet, for generations the Hawaiians had lived as feudal tenants who followed directives and submitted to authorities without question, so many did not immediately grasp the concept of liberty and owning land. Foreigners living on the islands were quick to buy the land that many of the natives were more than willing to sell. As foreign land owners gained power, financially and politically, the native Hawaiians became a people under siege. The missionaries tried to protect the Hawaiians from exploitation by foreigners through education and conversion to Christianity, but because the missionaries considered much of Hawaiian culture to be pagan and depraved, the Hawaiians lost their sense of identity and self respect.

For many Hawaiians, their king was the most tangible symbol of a lost culture. When Kamehameha IV ascended the throne in 1855, he and his wife, Queen Emma, tried to reassert the monarch's power and resist foreign influence, as did his brother and successor Kamehameha V, who abolished the constitution. When Kamehameha V died in 1872 without an heir, the Kamehameha dynasty came to an end. His successor, King Lunalilo, was chosen by a vote in the legislature but his reign lasted for just one year.

Upon Lunalilo's death in 1874, David Kalakaua ascended the throne. King Kalakaua, the 'Merrie Monarch,' loved military pomp and royal pageantry. He

The hula was revived during the reign of King Kalakaua.

revived the hula and island music, introduced opera, and ordered a new Iolani Palace to be built. On the ninth anniversary of his inauguration, Kalakaua held a lavish, two-week-long coronation celebration that included a state dinner and ball at the palace. His crown, designed in the traditional European style, was embellished with gold taro leaves. An avid sailor, Kalakaua liked to host extravagant parties at his royal boathouse near Honolulu Harbor. He held annual regattas, and his fleet of koa wood racing canoes were manned by his own team of highly trained paddlers.

By now, Honolulu had become the commercial center of the islands and the pacific headquarters for many a merchant shipping line. As steamship travel increased, so did the number of visitors to Hawai'i. One of these travelers was Mark Twain, a young reporter with the Sacramento *Union* who visited in 1866. A few years later Prince Alfred, the second son of Queen

Victoria, was the first foreign prince to visit the islands. Honolulu's first hotel, the Hawaiian Hotel, opened in 1872, and Robert Louis Stevenson came for a visit in 1889, spending six months at Waikiki Beach where he was regularly entertained at King Kalakau's beach house.

The expanding sugar industry, which depended on a reciprocity treaty with the United States to guarantee its markets, meant a growing demand for labourers. Immigrants came from other Pacific islands, as well as from China and Japan. Portuguese workers from the Madeira Islands introduced the ukelele to island music, and the Hawaiian islands, once isolated from the rest of the world, now contained one of its most cosmopolitan populations.

In 1887, Hawai'i granted the United States the exclusive right to establish a naval base at Pearl Harbor. In exchange, Hawai'i's sugar exports were guaranteed a favored position in American markets. This triggered a marked increase of American investment – and political influence – in Hawai'i.

When Queen Lili'uokalani ascended the Hawaiian throne in 1891, Hawai'i's sugar barons, many of whom were American, quickly grew impatient with the queen's imperious attitude and resistance to constitutional reform, for she believed in the divine right of an absolute monarch. Like other monarchs throughout history who have refused to adapt

(Above) King Kalakaua and Robert Louis Stevenson at Waikiki in 1889.
(Below) Sugar mill ruins.

to a changing political climate, Queen Lili'uokalani was overthrown in 1893 and a provisional government, led by the U.S. Minister to Hawai'i, was established. When President Cleveland learned of this development, he refused to annex Hawai'i because the majority of Hawaiians had not supported this bloodless revolution. He sent a special commisioner to Hawai'i to investigate and report on the circumstances of the queen's overthrow and the general attitude of the people

toward their new provisional government.

The resulting presidential report was critical of the political coup and supportive of the deposed queen. When the Cleveland administration's new minister to Hawai'i arrived with instructions from Washington, he presented Lili'uokalani with the conditions for her reinstatement as queen, but she refused to grant amnesty for the revolutionists, declaring that they would be executed. Her unbending attitude troubled the American minister, who consequently doubted the politcal stability of a restored monarchy. It was however, the determination of the new provisional government to retain power that prompted Cleveland to refer the matter to Congress for debate. Congress eventually censured the actions of the provisional government, but no further action was taken.

Back in Hawai'i, the new government decided to form a republic. The person chosen to be president was 50-year-old Sanford Ballard Dole. Born in Honolulu of American missionary parents, Dole had returned to Hawai'i after receiving an education in the United States. Prominent in Hawaiian public life, he did not approve of the revolution but, once it had transpired, he became an articulate defender of its goals. On the fourth of July, 1894, the respected statesman Dole stood

(Above left) Royal Coat of Arms.
(Left) Queen Lili'uokalani.

on the steps of Iolani Palace and proclaimed the formation of the Republic of Hawai'i.

The deposed queen attempted a counter-revolution but her plot was revealed and a cache of weapons was found buried in the garden of her private residence. Lili'uokalani was arrested and held at the palace where she was pressured into signing an abdication document. Found guilty at her trial for complicity with her Royalist supporters' act of treason, she was fined and released, and departed a year later for the United States where she wrote her memoirs. These were published in 1898, the year that the Spanish-American war highlighted the strategic importance of the Hawaiian Islands as a military base. In August of that year, Hawai'i was finally annexed.

At the official ceremony, attended by hundreds of troops from two American warships docked in Honolulu Harbor, President Dole offically rendered Hawai'i's sovereignty to the United States. In the presence of dozens of dignitaries crowded onto the terrace of Iolani Palace, the Hawaiian national anthem *Hawai'i Ponoi* was heard one last time by the citizens of an independent nation and their flag lowered. The band then played *The Star Spangled Banner*, and the American flag was raised. The people of Hawai'i were now American citizens, and the United States had become the rising imperial power in the Pacific.

Japan's surprise attack on Pearl Harbor in December 1941 plunged the United States into World War II, and Hawai'i became the chief Pacific base for U.S. forces. (See page 188 for extensive detail on Pearl Harbor.)

After the war, tourists began

Japan launched a surprise attack on Pearl Harbor in 1941.

arriving in mass numbers with the introduction of jet travel. In 1955, the annual visitor count to Hawai'i was 110,000. Today, the annual visitor count is seven million and the extensive infrastructure of island airports, highways and hotel resorts has transformed the landscape. A recent trend among visitors is to invest in time-share condominiums and stay for extended periods of time. The sheer number of people visiting and living – full-time and part-time – on the islands has created environmental and social stresses. Erosion and flooding are a concern in some areas where development has altered the natural terrain, while in other places the demand for fresh water is impacting local watersheds and the streams they supply. A movement among some indigenous

Hawaiians to reassert their independence as a sovereign nation is another issue the government must deal with. Yet, despite its imperfections and challenges, Hawai'i is still the closest that most of us will come to finding paradise on earth.

A Few Facts on Hawai'i

Located in the central Pacific, about 2,100 miles (3,380 km) from San Francisco, Hawai'i's total land area is 6,450 square miles (16,706 sq. km). The six major inhabited islands are Kaua'i, O'ahu, Maui, Lana'i, Moloka'i and Hawai'i, the latter being the largest in size and commonly referred to as the Big Island. The most populous island is O'ahu, where Honolulu – the state capital and Hawai'i's major city – is located.

Early tourists arrived first by steamship, then by airplane.

Hawai'i's Official Symbols

Flower: yellow hibiscus
Tree: *kukui* (candlenut tree)
Bird: *nene* (Hawaiian goose)
Marine Mammal: humpback whale
Fish: humuhumu'nukunuku'apua'a
(reef triggerfish)

The 50th state of the Union, Hawai'i was admitted on August 21, 1959. Its population is 1.26 million, with no ethnic majority. Approximately one-third of the population is Caucasian; about 22% is Japanese; 15% is Filipino; and a small percentage is Chinese. Residents of native Hawaiian ancestry comprise 20 to 25% of the population.

Major sources of economic wealth are tourism and military defence spending. Food processing is major industry, and the main agricultural products are sugarcane, pineapple, macadamia nuts and livestock.

(Below) Modern-day Waikiki Beach. (Bottom) Pride of Hawai'i departs Honolulu.

"Our reception and entertainment here by these unlettered people . . . is seldom equalled by the most civilized nations of Europe."

– Captain George Vancouver, February, 1794

There's no denying the immediate appeal of Hawaiian culture. The melodic sound of a slack-key guitar, the swaying grass skirts, the sweetly scented floral lei – all aptly symbolize the aloha spirit and the gentle side of the

Hawaiian people. Although for a time it seemed that Hawaiian culture had been reduced to these popular clichés for the benefit of tourists, in recent decades native Hawaiians have rediscovered their Polynesian heritage on their own terms.

This reawakening of Hawaiian culture, like any renaissance, did not begin with a single event but is a movement that has gradually gained momentum. One accomplishment that played a major role in the rebirth of Polynesian pride took place in 1976, when a navigator from the Caroline Islands named Pius Mau Piailug sailed his 62-foot double-hulled canoe on a voyage from Tahiti to Hawai'i. In the tradition of Polynesia's ancient mariners, he and his crew successfully piloted their primitive vessel across 2,600 miles of open ocean without the aid of charts or modern

(Left) A ukulele lesson.
(Below) A replica boat house in Hana, Maui.

navigational instruments.

Piailug's impressive feat of seamanship inspired other Polynesians to rediscover their oceangoing heritage and learn the ancient skills of canoe building, sail handling and celestial navigation. While reconnecting with the ocean, the Hawaiian people also began revisiting their ancestors' appreciation of the land. Hawai'i's official motto is "The life of the land is preserved in righteousness," and for centuries the Hawaiians had nurtured their fields of taro – a plant whose roots are boiled and pounded into a paste called poi, the Hawaiian staff of life.

The Hawaiian people's intrinsic connection with the land and the sea has spawned Hawai'i's appeal as a healthy, healing destination. People seeking a retreat where they can relax and rejuvenate their minds and bodies come to the islands to partake in spa treatments based on ancient Hawaiian techniques such as *lomilomi* massage (which uses long, rhythmic strokes) and *lomilomi pohaku*, which is stone massage using steamed lava stones to rub avocado and olive oil into the skin. Adding to Hawai'i's healthy appeal is a regional cuisine based on local seafood, vegetables and tropical fruits.

The natural beauty of these lush islands draws tourists by the millions each year, but the pristine beauty of yesteryear is harder to find these days. The sheer popularity of Hawai'i threatens its idyllic setting, and some native Hawaiians resent tourists determined to experience the 'real' Hawai'i as they venture along remote trails that cross private property to reach hidden waterfalls and swim in pristine pools of fresh water.

Fortunately there is enough of Hawaii for everyone. All beaches are public and a visitor to these islands will find easy access to plenty of lagoons, trails and waterfalls, many situated within state or county parks, where you are more than welcome and where your presence does not unduly impose on the locals. Tour operators also provide access to private ranchlands where they guide visitors on foot, horseback or all-terrain vehicle into secluded valleys.

The Hawaiian Language

Hawaiian is one of the Malayo-Polynesian languages and is closely related to the other major Polynesian dialects. It was strictly an oral language until the arrival

Hawaiian Vowel Sounds

a – like *ah* in father
e – like *ai* in bait
i – like *ee* in see
o – like *oa* in boat
u – like *oo* in too
For example, Kamehameha is pronounced *Kah-may-ah-may-hah.*

Some useful Hawaiian words:
mahalo (*mah-ha-low*) – thank you
kane (*kah-nay*) – man
wahine (*wah-he-nay*) – woman
keiki (*kay-key*) – child
kupuna (*kuh-poonah*) – ancestors
ali'i (*ah-lee-ee*) – royalty
mana – spiritual power
kumu – teacher
heiau – sacred site or temple
kahuna – priest / expert
pu'uhonua – place of refuge
makai – toward the ocean
mauka – toward the mountain
moana - ocean
pali – cliffs
wai – water
hana or hono – bay
lanai – porch

of New England missionaries in the 1820s. After six years of consulting with native speakers, and with American and British scholars, the missionaries (who themselves were well educated) developed a written language using just 12 letters of the Roman alphabet.

The Hawaiian language has five vowels but only seven consonants, plus a glottal stop (indicated with an inverted apostrophe) which is similar to the pause in 'oh-oh.' Each of the five vowels (a, e, i, o, u) has a regular (unstressed) and lengthened

(stressed) sound, the latter indicated with a *kahako*, which is macron above the vowel to indicate it should be sounded longer but not differently than an unstressed vowel.

The consonants used in Hawaiian are h, k, l, m, n, p and w. Originally several of these consonants had an interchangeable counterpart, i.e. b-p, t-k, l-r, v-w. To avoid confusion, the missionaries deleted b, t, r and v from the Hawaiian alphabet. However, these deleted consonants have not completely disappeared from common usage. For example, *kapa* (a type of bark cloth) is often spelled *tapa.*

The letters chosen by the early missionaries match the significant sounds of Hawaiian, and it's said that if you hear a Hawaiian word, you can spell it. Errors in Hawaiian pronunciation do occur today because of the diminished number of native speakers, resulting in people failing to include the glottal stop or the lengthened vowel sound in the applicable words. We are now seeing words and placenames, such as Hawai'i, printed with the glottal stop to aid pronunciation.

English and Hawaiian are the official state languages of Hawai'i; the latter is spoken by relatively few residents but remains an important symbol of ethnic identity. Also, the Hawaiian language is enjoying a resurgence and is now taught statewide within the Department of Education through a Hawaiian immersion school program.

Ancient Customs

Just as the ancient Greeks worshipped a pantheon of immortal gods and legendary heroes, so too did the pre-historic inhabitants of Hawai'i. A stone-age people when discovered by Captain Cook in 1778, the Hawaiians had lived in isolation for hundreds of years and firmly believed in the almighty power of their gods. Myths that explained natural phenomena were passed orally from generation to generation, and Hawaiians of royal blood could recite their genealogy back to the gods, just as the early pharaohs of Ancient Egypt had done.

The important war god Ku.

The great gods of the Hawaiian pantheon include Kane, the creator. Acccording to a Hawaiian proverb, 'The great earth is animated and adorned by Kane.' Ku was the god of war, to whom human sacrifices would be made at *heiaus* (temples) to ensure victory in battle. Pele, a powerful goddess who personified volcanic eruptions, was feared for her fiery temper and jealous rages. She was also revered as a great force of destruction and of creation.

Lono was the god of peace and of the land, rain, thunder and winds. Each November a priest watching the sky for omens would wait for the rising of the constellation Makali'i (Pledades) in the east, and the setting of the new moon and sun in the west, before declaring the start of the Makahiki. This festival was dedicated to the god Lono and was a time of peace, when warfare would give way to sporting and religious events. During the four months of Makahiki, the ali'i (royalty) would travel in a procession along the alaloa (long road) encircling their island, stopping at villages along the way.

The sun was revered, for its energy was the source of all life, and its daily journey from dawn to darkness was honored from sacred points along the rims of volcanic craters.

Ancient Hawai'i's caste system consisted of *ali'i* (royalty), *kahuna* (priests and specialists) and commoners. Daily life was controlled by religious laws called *kapus* (taboos or restrictions). These controls which were regularly issued by the *ali'i* who were descended from the gods and thus wielded divine powers. Some kapu were seasonal, such as those that controlled the taking of specific species of fish. Some were permanent, such as men and

Pu'uhonua o Honaunau (Place of Refuge) on the Big Island.

women being forbidden to dine together. Others were enacted upon the death of a high-ranking chief or royal personage.

The *kapus* were administered by priests, who performed ceremonies at the *heiaus* (places of worship) and held authority at the *pu'uhonuas* (places of refuge), where someone who had broken a *kapu* could flee to safety and be absolved for their crime. Punishment for violating a *kapu* was severe – often death by clubbing – for the Hawaiians dared not risk angering one of their gods who might unleash a tidal wave or a volcanic eruption in a display of wrath unless appeased.

There was little mingling of royalty and commoners. Royal mothers would give birth at sacred stone sites in the presence of ruling chiefs to assure a high-ranking status for their child. A royal birth was announced by the pounding of bellstones and the beating of a *pahu heiau* (temple drum). Only priests and chiefs were allowed to beat these sacred drums, for they were considered a medium of direct communication with the gods. The sound of their beat carried an important message, be it the announcement of a royal birth or death, the beginning or end of a *kapu*, or a prayer and sacrifice to the gods. Another type of drum called *pahu hula* (dance drum) accompanied the chants of ancient hula.

When royal chiefs attended prayer ceremonies conducted by the priests, restraints on their behavior included their total seclusion from women, no dining on food not consecrated, no contact with sea water, and no touching of any articles handled by anyone who had not attended the ceremonies at the *heiau*. The ceremony, which lasted for two full nights and the intermediate day, would begin with the chanting of an invocation to the setting sun. The night was passed in prayer and at dawn, amid a profound silence, the high priest would repeat a prayer in a low voice, during which he would sacrifice a pig, tied by the legs, with such a quick blow that the silence was unbroken.

When a royal person lay on his or her deathbed, villagers living in the vicinity would gather by the hundreds, their collective cries and wails creating a loud, mournful din. Upon the person's expiration, the intensity of the mourning would increase to a feverish pitch and culminate in a human sacrifice. These sacrifices were often voluntary and while some commoners would flee for fear of being chosen, others willingly offered themselves. This practise was halted by King Kamehameha I.

Royal corpses were stripped of their flesh and their bones interred in sepulchral holes dug into the sides of steep hills. The remains of King Kamehameha were secretly interred and to this day it is not known where his remains are located. Upon the death of Kamehameha I in 1819, his son and successor Liholiho abolished the ancient religious traditions. Most of the *heiaus* were abandoned and the wooden idols were destroyed.

Life by the Sea

The Hawaiian word moana means 'open sea' – a place as important to Hawaiian culture as the land. The early Hawaiians traveled a great deal on the water, going from bay to bay in outrigger canoes or from island to island in double-hulled war canoes. The native koa tree provided the massive logs needed for constructing canoes; builders also used logs that washed ashore from North America's northern coastal forests, having drifted across the Pacific to the Hawaiian islands. Some were too decayed and worm-eaten to be of use upon

High school students hone their outrigger skills at Kailua-Kona.

arrival, but those that survived the sea journey were promptly carved into canoes.

The hull of a double canoe was about 65 feet (20 m) long, carved from a single log and joined together with eight beams. A double canoe could carry 50 paddlers (25 on each side) and up to 40 men could ride on the platform mounted on the crossbeams.

The Hawaiians were strong swimmers and skilled divers, whose dexterity in the water far exceeded the crews of sailing ships that began visiting the islands in the 1700s. If the sailors needed to inspect their ship's keel, they would call upon their Hawaiian hosts to dive beneath the hull and measure any damage to the keel with a piece of line held between two divers.

Hawai'i introduced surfing to the rest of the world.

Surfing, The Sport of Kings

When European sailors began visiting the Hawaiian islands, they were greeted by the sight of villagers setting off from shore in large numbers, not only in canoes but on swimming boards. Surfing was a favorite pastime for the Hawaiians, and the women were as adept as the men at this sport. The best surf spots were the exclusive domain of royalty, who also owned the best hardwood surf boards.

The long cumbersome wooden boards used by the early Hawaiians have been replaced with lightweight synthetic boards that are much more maneuverable, but the basics of surfing remain the same. Lying stomach down, a surfer paddles out from shore to the area where waves begin to form. Turning toward shore, the surfer paddles for the

beach ahead of an oncoming wave until it catches the board. This is when the surfer stands up and slides down the wave front like a skier on a hill, except that the slope is continually moving up (like a treadmill) which is why the surfer doesn't descend into the sea but keeps riding the wave. In the case of a large wave, its curling crest will form a 'tube' inside of which the surfer rides.

Hawai'i's most famous surfer was Duke Kahanamoku. Born on August 24, 1890, Duke was raised next to the ocean at Waikiki. An original 'beach boy' he spent his boyhood days swimming, surfing and running barefooted across the sand. When he wasn't in school, he was in the surf. He grew into a strong, athletic young man whose exceptional swimming skills included the powerful 'Kahanamoku kick' which propelled him through the water with such force that waves spread out behind him. When an amateur swim meet was held in Honolulu Harbor in 1911, Duke shattered the world record for the 100-yard freestyle. At first the Amateur Athletic Union was skeptical of Duke's time, with officials arguing he must have been aided by current in the harbor. But when Duke began breaking records at swim meets on the mainland, people took notice.

Duke made sports history at the 1912 Olympics in Stockholm, Sweden, winning almost every event in the water. He was called to the Royal Victory Stand where Sweden's King Gustaf personally

Duke Kahanamoku was an athlete of exceptional abilities.

presented Duke with his record-breaking gold medal in the 100-yard freestyle. Duke went on to compete in three more Olympic games. Meanwhile he became an ambassador for Hawai'i, introducing other regions of the world to the sport of surfing. He also appeared in Hollywood films, playing bit parts such as that of a

Polynesian chief opposite John Wayne in *The Wake of the Red Witch*.

In 1917, during a giant south swell off Waikiki, Duke made his famous Mile Ride on a 16-foot-long board. As 30-foot waves rolled toward shore, Duke paddled through the breakers, again and again turning turtle (wrapping his arms and legs around his board and hanging on from underneath) as the thundering waves washed over him. At last he reached the outlying waters where he sat resting on his board, watching the walls of water rolling toward shore, lifting and dropping his board as he waited for the right one – which Duke would ride for over a mile in an incredible display of skill, strength and courage.

Lu'au

The sound of the *pu* (conch shell) signals the start of a lu'au. Guests are greeted with leis draped over their shoulders, and are seated at long, low tables. Traditional foods served at a lu'au include sweet potatoes, marinated *lomilomi* (mashed salmon with chopped tomatoes and onions) and *poi* – which is made by pounding the taro root into a purplish paste and serving it in various forms, including *poe taro* (a kind of pudding). At modern lu'aus these traditional foods are often supplemented with popular mainland dishes such as potato salad and teriyaki steak. The centerpiece of any authentic lu'au is the

(Left) Poi is a traditional lu'au dish. (Below) Guests watch as the baked pig is unearthed.

unearthing of the pig, which is slowly baked in an *imu* (a pit in the ground). Following the sumptuous feast, the guests sit back and enjoy the entertainment which consists of Hawaiian music, chants and hula dancing. Other Polynesian cultures are frequently represented with Fijian dancing, Tahitian drums and the Samoan fire-knife dance, which is often the finale.

Hula

The ancient goddess Pele was the inspiration for the hula, which retells creation myths and legendary events of the Hawaiian people. The ancient style of hula

(Top and above right)
Traditional dances from other
Polynesian nations are often
performed at luaus. (Right)
Hula tells a story.

is called *kahiko* and is danced to drum beats and chanting. The modern style is called *auana* and is danced to guitar and ukulele. Hula is taught by a *kumu* (teacher) at *halau hula* (hula schools). Most *kumu* hold the equivalent of a masters degree in dance.

Music

The music of ancient Hawai'i was based on chanting and drum beats. When foreigners began visiting and settling on the islands, various influences modified Hawaiian music, such as choral

singing and European-style harmony introduced by the New England missionaries.

The ukulele was introduced by Portuguese workers who came from the Madeira Islands and this instrument quickly became part of the Hawaiian sound.

The guitar was brought to Hawai'i by the crews of trading ships and by Mexican cowboys who came to work the cattle ranches. By slackening the strings of their guitars to produce major chords, the Hawaiians invented slack-key tuning and introduced a unique sound to their music.

This full sound was further modified by steel guitar – an instrument invented by Joseph Kekuku who, as a child, would play the guitar by laying it across his knees and sliding a table knife up and down the strings. When Kekuku was in high school, his shop teacher helped him build a solid cylinder steel bar for sliding

(Left) Slack-key guitar. (Below) Hawaiian musicians, c. 1915.

along the strings. A converter nut was used to raise the strings above the fretboard, and the guitar's gut strings were replaced with metal piano wire.

The sweet and soulful sound of the slack-key guitar became a sound synonymous with the romantic, tropical paradise Hawai'i represented to America. However, by the 1970s, some native Hawaiians had come to regard *hapa-haole* (part-foreign, part-Hawaiian) music as colonialist and touristy. Others argue that there is always cross-over between musical styles and that *hapa-haole* music, which became hugely popular after a Hawaiian troupe performed at the Pan-Pacific Exposition in San Francisco in 1915, is a unique musical style reflective of the pre-rock era.

Aloha Wear

The colorful and casual clothing distinctive to Hawaii originated in the 1800s when the missionary women introduced long dresses to the ladies of Hawaii. The New England high-waisted pattern was modified to create a loose gown, known as a *holoku*, sewn with material acquired from sandalwood traders. Worn underneath was a muumuu, which was a short, simple slip. Until then, the Hawaiians had worn garments made of tapa, which was mulberry bark pounded to a soft texture and decorated with painted patterns.

Meanwhile, the Hawaiian men began wearing loose-fitting shirts (called frocks), which they acquired through trade from the crew of sailing ships. These untucked shirts took on a new look in the 1930s when a Honolulu tailor named Ellery Chun made his first Aloha-brand shirt with patterned silk. This new style of shirt quickly became popular, especially after a new high-quality rayon was introduced in the 1940s and the patterns of these 'silkies' became increasingly creative and colorful. Even businessmen began wearing them when the 'reversed' shirt was introduced in the early 1960s.

(Above right) Tapa cloth. (Below) Aloha shirt.

These were created when the brightly dyed fabric of an aloha shirt was turned inside out to reveal a more subtle design, and a button-down collar was added. A tasteful reversed shirt tucked into slacks is accepted office attire in Hawai'i (where lawyers heading to court can be identified by their suits and ties). Today a vintage 'silkie' from the 1940s is a collector's item. Classic motifs feature

coconut palms, tropical flowers and hula dancers. Aloha wear for women includes shirts, muumuus and *pareos* (sarong-style skirts).

Leis

The lei is Hawai'i's symbol of aloha, made from a variety of tropical flowers, including the exotic plumeria. O'ahu is known for leis made of orange *ilima,* which were once worn by kings and are today favored by male Hawaiians. The Big Island is known for leis made of red *lehua* and Maui for leis made of pink *lokelani.* The small island of Ni'ihau, lying southwest of Kaua'i, is known for its leis made not of flowers but of tiny shells. May 1st is Lei Day in Hawai'i, when everyone is encouraged to wear a lei, and when schools throughout the state hold May Day celebrations. A lei is worn loosely draped over the shoulders, not tight around the neck.

The Aloha Spirit

The word aloha, which means hello, good-bye or love, has come to represent the warmth and generosity with which Hawaiians greet one another and visitors to their islands. Some say aloha means the breath of life, for *ha* means breath and the Hawaiians' traditional greeting of rubbing noses was the sharing of *ha.* When foreigners began settling in

(Above left) Plumeria is strung into the traditional lei (left).

Hawai'i, they were called *haole*, which means 'those without breath' in reference to their shaking of hands instead of rubbing noses as a form of greeting.

One of the earliest recorded anecdotes illustrating the Hawaiians' ability to display kindness and compassion to complete strangers, even enemies, is recounted in the journals of Captain Vancouver. He describes the seizing of a small American schooner in 1791 by a large group of Hawaiians intent on revenge. One of the sailors who survived the attack, lying prostrate and badly beaten in a double canoe, looked up at his captor and uttered the words *maikai, maikai* (meaning good, good). The Hawaiian he had addressed instantly took pity on his captive and replied "aloha" before greeting him by touching noses, then tending to the injured man's wounds.

Another incident recorded by one of Vancouver's officers describes how he and his men nearly drowned when their open boat got caught in a sudden storm that was pushing them out to sea off the west coast of Maui. After bailing with their hats for five hours, a change in the wind allowed them to raise the sail and head for shore where a chief received them with kindness and hospitality – drying their wet clothes and serving a sumptuous feast.

The aloha spirit is still an integral part of Hawaiian culture, and most modern-day visitors soon realize it is not a slick slogan fabricated by the tourism industry but a genuine trait of the Hawaiian people. Whether receiving a traditional lei greeting or enjoying the relaxed and friendly attitude that everyone adopts (or should adopt) while in Hawai'i, a visitor can readily see that the aloha spirit is sincere and enduring.

(Below) Hawaiian crew on NCL America share their aloha.
(Bottom) Boat Day in Lahaina.

FLORA & FAUNA

The Hawaiian Islands are comparable to the Galapagos Islands for their abundance of unique species that have evolved in isolation for thousands of years. Originally only a few types of plants, insects and birds colonized the remote islands of Hawai'i. Insects were blown to the islands on the wind, and seeds were carried by birds or by logs drifting in ocean currents. Once these species arrived in Hawai'i, they flourished in a trop-ical paradise of warm weather and plentiful rainfall. With no natural predators, birds living here gradually lost their ability to fly and mutated into dozens of related species. One finch-like bird evolved into more than 50 different types of **honeycreeper**.

When Polynesian settlers arrived in this garden-like par-adise, they introduced new plant species, such as breadfruit, bananas, sugarcane and taro. They also brought small pigs,

who preyed on the islands' flightless birds, leading to the extinction of at least 35 species. Change was relatively slow during colonization by the Polynesians, but the pace speeded up following Captain Cook's historic visit in 1778. Soon afterwards, outsiders were introducing other species of animals, including cattle, goats, sheep and large European pigs.

Rats arrived as stowaways on ships, and mosquitoes first appeared in the 1820s, most likely arriving in a whaler's water casks, and were soon spreading avian malaria throughout the native bird populations, which had no resistance to the disease.

Over time, the natural habitat for Hawai'i's native species began to disappear as forests were denuded for their valuable wood and lowlands were converted into sugar and pineapple plantations. The mongoose was introduced to rid the cane fields of maurauding rats, but preyed instead on ground-nesting birds such as the **nene**, a cousin of the Canada goose. Reforestation in the early 1900s was done with alien species, such as eucalyptus and pine. The pace of development increased during the 20th century, with wetlands drained to make way for the construction of hotels and residential neighborhoods. Hawai'i's surviving species of native plants are now found mostly in uplands too steep for development, and it is in these remote valleys that biologists hack through dense vegetation to uproot alien plants or dangle from ropes along cliff faces to hand-pollinate native plants.

Much of this hard-to-access land lies within national preserves, where human impact can be controlled and park wardens are able to deal with threats to the native flora and fauna, the most prevalent one being the widespread and destructive presence of feral pigs. Some 100,000 feral pigs roam the islands and are hunted by park wardens, who also use fencing to protect habitat from grazing animals, including feral pigs and goats.

Plant Life

One refuge for Hawai'i's native plants is the National Tropical Botanical Garden, headquartered in Kalaheo on Kaua'i, which owns and administers four gar-

(Facing page) Hawaiian honeycreeper. (Right) Maui Tropical Plantation.

dens in Hawai'i. Three of these are situated on Kaua'i (the McBryde, Allerton and Limahuli gardens) and one is on Maui (the Kahuna Garden).

Many of the **flowers** that visitors associate with Hawai'i are not native species but were introduced during the colonial era and are now widely cultivated. The anthurium or 'Hawaiian Heart' is native to South America and was introduced into the Hawaiian Islands in 1889 by a government minister who grew them on his O'ahu estate. Other flowers grown commercially in Hawai'i include orchids, the bird of paradise (native to South Africa) and plumeria (or frangipani). which is also known as the lei flower.

Several species of hibiscus are native to Hawaii, including the yellow *ma'o hau hele*, which is the state flower; however, many of the hibiscus grown ornamentally throughout the islands are actually the Chinese hibiscus or one of its numerous hybrids. Hawai'i's cut-flower industry began in back yards in the 1940s when American servicemen wanted to send flowers to their sweethearts back home. It is now the state's fourth-largest industry, with flower farms producing high-quality tropical flowers for shipment to florists and individuals throughout the United States and other parts of the world.

Silversword is one of few

(Top to bottom) Red and white anthuriums; an orchid; petals of plumeria; the bird of paradise.

(Above) Hibiscus flowers.
(Right) Silversword plant.
(Bottom) Coco palm.

plants to grow in the harsh conditions of Haleakala volcano's upper slopes. Its shallow root system catches moisture in the porous, loose cinders while its long tap roots keep it anchored in high winds. It takes up to 30 years for the plant to sprout a three- to nine-foot stalk, its leaves covered with silvery hairs that conserve moisture and protect the plant from the intense sun.

Palm trees flourish in Hawaii, their flowing crowns of frond leaves swaying in the breeze and providing welcome shade. The coco palm, which grows 60 to 100 feet (18 - 30 m) tall, readily establishes itself on shorelines because its seeds, enclosed in a large buoyant pod, can float. Its fruit is the coconut – a hard woody shell encased in a brown fibrous husk, and a single coco palm can bear more than 200 nuts annually. A coconut has three round scars at one end; its embryo lies against the largest, which is easily punctured to drain the nutritious juice inside. Copra, from which oil is extracted to make soaps, cooking oil and sun-

PLANT LABELS

Over 90% of Hawai'i's flora and fauna is found nowhere else on earth. The following labels describe Hawai'i's plant and animal species: **endemic** – arrived naturally from elsewhere and evolved into something uniquely Hawaiian; **indigenous** – occur naturally in Hawai'i but are found in other parts of the world; **alien** – introduced by humans.

(Top to bottom) Red ginger; Irwin Memorial Park; a windbreak of wiliwili trees.

tan lotion, is produced when a ripened coconut is broken open and dried.

The *kukui*, or **candlenut tree**, is the State Tree of Hawai'i. Introduced by Polynesians, this tree grows to heights of 50 feet (15 m) on the slopes of mountains and valleys. Its leaves are pointed and pale green, and its small white flowers grow in clusters. The fruit contains one or two nuts, the oil of which was used for lighting torches, or the kernel of the nut itself could be lit like a candle (*kalakukui*). The burned soot of these round dark nuts was used for tatoos and for making designs on tapa cloth.

The **koa tree** is the Hawaiian mahogany, its wood taking on a red luster through which wavy lines show when the wood is polished. Used for crafting furniture and ukuleles, koa timber was formerly carved into war canoes, surf boards and calabashes. Growing taller than 50 feet (15 m), its thick trunk is tall and straight, its high crown of far-spreading branches consisting of broad-leaf stems.

The **rain tree**, also called monkeypod, grows to heights of 80 feet (24 m) with a branch spread reaching 100 feet (30 m), making this flat-topped tree ideal for providing shade to crops such as coffee. The leaves of the rain tree fold together during darkness and cloudy weather. Its edible pods are fed to livestock. The wood, which is durable and rich in color, is used for furniture and other items. Places to view this tree include the gardens of Irwin Memorial Park, opposite the Aloha Tower Marketplace at Honolulu's cruise port.

Because just about any kind of plant can grow in Hawai'i, many of the tropical fruits and flowers we associate with the islands are in fact alien species. **Pineapple** plants were first introduced to Hawai'i in the early 1800s and were initially more prickly and spongier than today's 'smooth cayenne' variety, which bears a large, juicy, golden fruit. This cultivated plant is a member of the Bromeliaceae family and grows in warm climates such as Hawai'i, which supplies a major portion of the world's canned pineapple, although increasing competition from Asia and Central America has resulted in the closure of several corporate plantations on the Hawaiian Islands. The red volcanic soil here is ideal for growing pineapples and black plastic mulch helps control weeds and conserve moisture and heat (which stimulate root growth). All plants are manually planted and harvested, and are grown year round, each crop taking 14 to 18 months to mature.

The **coffee tree**, a small ever-

(Top) Pineapple plant. (Above) The small red fruits of a coffee tree contain two beans each.

Outdoor Circle

In 1912, seven Oah'u women founded the Outdoor Circle with an original mission to plant trees and flowers in the Honolulu area. This simple goal led to public battles over such issues as ridding Hawai'i of billboards (Hawai'i is one of four U.S. states that bans billboards) and protecting historic trees. Intent on preserving Hawaii's scenic beauty for generations to come, this grass-roots organization is now 2,500 members strong and has been instrumental in preserving green, open spaces on all of the islands.

green, yields clusters of fragrant white flowers that mature into small red fruits containing two coffee beans each. Introduced to Hawaii in the 19th century, the coffee tree thrives at higher altitudes in fertile, well-drained soil of volcanic origin. The Big Island's Kona region is famous for its high-quality coffee.

The **Banyan tree** is native to India and its seeds usually germinate from bird droppings left on the branch of a host tree. The young banyan plant sends out aerial rootlets that take root upon reaching the ground, where secondary trunks then form to support the giant horizontal limbs. The branches of these trunks send out more roots and the host tree is eventually crowded out by the banyan's grovelike undergrowth. Places to see a banyan in Hawai'i include the Moana Surfrider on Waikiki Beach, the harborside park at Lahaina on Maui, and Banyan Drive in Hilo on the Big Island. An exceptional Indian Banyan, planted in 1863, can be seen on Magic Island in Ala Moana Beach Park. It's said that Princess Kaiulani sat in its shade while chatting with Robert Louis Stevenson.

(Top) A giant banyan tree.
(Above) A bamboo forest.
(Below) Eucalyptus trees.

Animal Life

Seabirds commonly sighted off Hawai'i's main islands include the wedge-tailed shearwater, Pacific golden plover, ruddy turnstone and long-tailed curlew. The Northwestern Hawaiian Islands are protected as a remote and uninhabited wildlife sanctuary

that supports huge colonies of seabirds. Biologists estimate that fourteen million seabirds breed and nest on these islands, including sooty terns and most of the world's black-footed albatrosses.

Forest birds frequently seen in Hawaii include the Hawaiian owl and the scarlet honeycreeper. However, other native birds – threatened by various predators and a shrinking habitat – are facing extinction. To prevent such a fate, the wildlife scientists at Keahou Bird Conservation Center are captively rearing endangered native birds, such as the Hawaiian hawk. Located near the town of Volcano on the Big Island, the center is locally staffed and managed, and its propagation programs are operated under the auspices of the San Diego Zoo.

Hawai'i's tropical foliage is home to the **gecko** – a small, harmless lizard that feeds at night on insects. Its brilliant red, green and yellow skin colors help to camouflage the gecko, by blending with the tropical vegetation. Take a close look at the plants growing on the grounds of resorts and public buildings, and you may spot a tiny gecko crawling on one of the leaves.

The only mammals to land on their own at the Hawaiian Islands were the hoary bat and the **monk seal** (all others were brought by canoe or sailing ship). The monk seal's population was seriously depleted by hunting in the past, with fewer than 30 now frequenting the waters and beaches of Hawai'i's main islands. It's esti-

The nene (top) and monk seal (above) are protected species.

mated that a total of 1,300 Hawaiian monk seals remain, and the majority of these find refuge on the Northwestern Hawaiian Islands. You can see monk seal at Waikiki Aquarium. If you see one sunning itself on the beach, do not approach closer than 100 feet. Seals spend much of their time in the water, but haul out once a year to breed, give birth and nurse their young.

Humpback Whales

The marine mammal that makes the biggest splash in Hawaiian waters is the humpback whale. Although large in size (up to 45 feet and weighing up to 40 tons), the humpback is an acrobatic whale that performs breaches, flipper slaps and deep dives. The whale's surface activity and close-to-shore feeding made it an easy target for commercial whalers in the 19th century. By the time humpbacks in the Pacific were placed under international protection in 1966, their numbers had dwindled to a few thousand from an estimated high of 125,000.

The Hawaiian Islands Humpback Whale National Marine Sanctuary was designated in 1992 and formally approved in 1997, following years of public information meetings and hearings. Since then the number of

A female adult and her calf in the waters off west Maui.

humpback whales frequenting the sanctuary keeps increasing at a rate of about 7% annually, and it's now estimated that 4,000 to 5,000 humpbacks are wintering in Hawaiian waters (approximately two-thirds of the North Pacific population).

Coastal Alaska is the Pacific humpback's summer feeding grounds, where this toothless whale feeds on schooling fish, plankton and other small organisms. Upon closing its mouth, the whale raises its tongue to force the scooped water out the sides, where the bristles of its baleen plates trap the food. The pleats on the sides of a humpback's mouth can create a pouch large enough to hold six adult humans.

Each fall, the humpback migrates to warmer waters to

spend the winter mating and giving birth to calves conceived during the previous year's breeding season. December and January are the birthing months, following a 12-month gestation period. Cows give birth to a single calf weighing about 3,000 pounds and measuring 10 to 15 feet in length. Calves are born without a blubber layer and nurse on their mother's milk, which contains 50 percent butter fat and enables the calf to gain 100 pounds a day.

Humpbacks travel in threesomes – a female, her calf and a male escort. The male earns his position as escort. He serenades the female by performing a song (a repeated pattern of sound) at depths of 60 feet or more. If this doesn't win her, the male will confront her current escort by smacking him with his fluked tail,

which packs 8,000 pounds of muscle and, studded with barnacles, is a humpback's most powerful weapon. The new mothers are uninterested in the antics of the males, for they are too busy nursing their babies and teaching them how to survive.

You can see humpback whales off Hawai'i as early as September and a few may linger till late May, but the prime whalewatching season is from mid-December to mid-April, with late February and early March considered the peak period with the greatest number of adults and calves in local waters, and the mothers and their calves coming the nearest they will to shore. The waters off Maui's west coast contain Hawai'i's highest concentration of wintering humpbacks (see Whalewatching section in the Maui chapter).

Na Pali Coast
Shipwreck Beach
Poipu Beach
Turtle Bay
Kaua'i

O'ahu
Honolulu
Makapuu Pt.
Hanauma Bay

Kaanapali
Lahaina
McGregor Pt
Kihei
Maui
Wailea
Makena Beach

Hawai'i
Hapuna Beach
Anaehoomalu Bay
Kona

Whalewatching Locations
KAUA'I:
Na Pali Coast, Poipu Beach, Shipwreck Beach
O'AHU:
Hanauma Bay, Makapuu Pt Lighthouse,
Turtle Bay Resort
MAUI:
McGregor Point Lookout, Makena Beach Park,
Wailea, Kihei, Kaanapali
HAWAI'I, BIG ISLAND:
Anaehoomalu Bay, Hapuna Beach Park, Honolii

*Spinner dolphins are friendly
and are often sighted from boats.*

Several species of dolphin can be sighted in the waters off Hawaii, but the most common is the **spinner dolphin**. Growing to seven feet in length, this marine mammal is gregarious and is often seen riding the bow waves of vessels. The name derives from the spinner's ability to leap clear of the water's surface and twirl like a top. These dolphins travel in large herds, which provides protection from predators such as tiger sharks. They hunt by night out at sea, using their sonar, then come into nearshore waters by day to rest in clear waters where they don't have to expend energy. Their main resting waters are the Wai'anae coastline of O'ahu and the Kealakekua coastline of the Big Island.

Until tuna fishermen in the eastern tropical Pacific modified their nets to reduce dolphin deaths, they inadvertently caught and killed hundreds of thousands of spinner dolphins. Hawaiians often refer to the Spinner dolphin as a porpoise so as not to confuse it with the dolphin fish, called mahi mahi, which is a popular catch for its white, flaky flesh and delicate flavor.

Hawai'i's **coral reefs**, which provide habitat for the 700 species of fish living in local waters, are themselves formed by living organisms – soft, saclike animals called polyps. Smaller than a pea, each polyp secretes an exoskeleton of limestone. A colony forms when polyps bud new polyps, which remain connected. These tiny polyps, each living inside its own limestone cavity, feed mainly at night on floating plankton, which they trap with their extended tentacles. Microscopic algae grow within the polyp tissues and are collectively responsible for the coral colony's vivid colors. These symbiotic algae, called zooxanthellae, need sunlight and clear water to take up carbon dioxide and photosynthesize, thus providing an internal supply of oxygen and organic nutrients to the polyp.

When coral colonies die, their surfaces are recolonized by new corals or other types of invertebrates, such as sponges or soft corals. Layers of skeletal materials gradually accumulate over time to form a coral reef. Although corals live in temperate as well as tropical waters, coral reefs are found only in tropical waters, within 30° of the equator, where the water temperature remains above 70° Fahrenheit (21° C) year round.

Coral reefs that extend from shore are called fringing reefs while those separated from shore by a wide lagoon are called barrier reefs. Rising like fortress walls from the sea floor, barrier reefs provide habitat for tropical fish and large predators, which feed here on the smaller fish. Fringe reefs, often within a few yards of the water's surface, serve as nurseries for hundreds of small tropical fish. Coral reefs also deflect incoming waves, their porous character allowing them to absorb and dissipate a pounding sea. In bays protected by strategically placed reefs, the steady shifting of particulate debris from the coral colony onto shore results in a beach of fine sand.

Most reef-forming corals belong to the stony or hard group of corals. There are many different types of hard corals; some are branch-like (such as antler and finger corals) and others are rounded (such as lobe and cauliflower corals). Sharing the marine environent are brilliantly

colored sponges, which attach themselves to coral reefs, often in colonies. They vary in shape and size, and show little movement.

Other members of the coral reef community include the **moray eel**, which hides in crevices by day and feeds at night. This snake-like fish is harmless unless provoked. The **trumpetfish** belongs to the same family as the seahorse and it breeds by forcing the female's

(Top right) Trumpetfish. (Right) Moray eel. (Below) Coral reef.

Tropical fish viewed at the Maui Ocean Center's reef exhibit include yellow tang and butterflyfish.

eggs into a pouch on the male's underside, where they are fertilized and nourished until expelled as miniature versions of the adult.

The shimmering tropical fish found along coral reefs come in an assortment of shapes, sizes, colors and markings, which often change as the juvenile fish mature. Angelfish are among the most beautiful of the small fish that inhabit shallow reefs, their flattened, disc-like shapes allowing them to slip through nooks and crannies as they feed on sponges and the ectoparasites of other fishes. Butterflyfish are similar to angelfish with yellow being their dominant color; they travel in pairs, feeding on coral polyps, sea anemones and algae. Parrotfish begin life as drably colored females, then turn into males with gaudy green and blue scales. They have molar-like teeth with which they grind algae off the corals, producing sand in the process.

About 25% of fish viewed along Hawaii's reefs are unique to these waters, such as the Hawaiian Cleaner Wrasse and the Milletseed Butterflyfish. In Hawai'i it is illegal to feed fish, for this practice encourages dependence and can upset their digestive systems.

Sharks are heavy fishes with skeletons made of cartilage. A shark must keep moving in order to breathe by taking water in through its mouth and passing it over the gills which form a line of slits down both sides of the fish. Worldwide, there are over 2,500 species of shark, ranging in size from two feet to 50 feet. Ancient Hawaiians believed sharks were *aumakua* (ancestral deities). According to Hawaiian legend, a huge shark led the first Polynesians to Hawai'i's shores.

Not all sharks are predatory and few are interested in humans. Those considered harmless include the Gray Reef Shark. To detect their prey, sharks have electromagnetic sensors on their snouts, which is why professional shark feeders wearing stainless-steel mesh suits and gloves can hypnotize a reef shark with a gentle stroke of the hand. Not so placid is the Tiger Shark, which is predatory and dangerous to humans.

In Hawaiian waters, shark sightings are rare and are usually made by surfers or boardsailors cruising outside a reef. On average, there are three or four shark attacks each year in Hawaii, but fatalities are much less frequent. In 2004, a surfer was attacked by a shark about 500 feet (150 m) off Kahana Beach in Maui. The 57-year-old man was bitten on the leg while paddling for waves at about 7:00 a.m. With the aid of fellow surfers he made it to the beach where he died from blood loss. This was the first shark fatality in Hawaii since 1992.

The first recorded shark attack on Kaua'i's north shore took place off Makua Beach in October, 2003, in an area called Tunnels, where sand-filled alleys run through the shallow part of the reef here. It was on the outer edges of this reef, about a quarter mile from shore, that 13-year-old Bethany Hamilton was attacked by a tiger shark. She was floating on her surfboard, looking out to sea and waiting for a good wave to roll in. Her left arm was dangling in the water, her shiny wristwatch glistening in the clear water, when a large gray object closed in on her left side. The shark severed her arm almost to the shoulder, and was gone.

Thanks to Bethany's calm reaction and the quick response of those around her, she survived the attack. An adult surfer used his rash guard as a tourniquet to staunch the flow of blood, then towed her back to shore – about a 15-minute paddle. On shore, a group of people rushed to assist, replacing the rash guard with a surf leash. Bethany was sped to the hospital in Lihu'e where doctors cleaned and closed her wound. Since the attack, Bethany has been interviewed on national television and featured in magazine articles. Her book *Soul Surfer* recounts the attack, the

A harmless reef shark.

aftermath and her triumphant return to surfing.

Several precautions can be taken by surfers and swimmers to minimize any potential encounters with sharks, such as avoiding waters made murky by runoff after a heavy rainfall or areas where fishermen have cleaned fish or tossed bait into the water. Don't go swimming or surfing at dawn or dusk, when sharks appear to be most active, or after dark. Refrain from wearing shiny jewelry, said to attract sharks because the reflected light resembles the sheen of fish scales. And leave the water right away if you get cut on a reef, for sharks have an acute sense of smell and are attracted to blood.

Rays are flat-bodied fish that are related to sharks. Shaped like kites with winglike pectoral fins that propel them through the water, rays also have long whip-like tails. There are three basic groups of rays: mantas, eagles and stingrays. Mantas (the largest) and eagles are active rays, whereas stingrays are bottom dwellers, lying like rugs on the sea floor as they dredge up shellfish and other small animals. The stingray's eyes and spiracles (breathing orifices) are on top of the head, its mouth and gill slits on the underside. It has rows of spines along its tail, which contain a poison that can inflict pain and be fatal to humans. Stingrays defend themselves against sharks by lashing with their tails, but they rarely attack humans unless provoked or stepped on. (If you are swimming or snorkeling in an area frequented by stingrays, avoid stepping on one by shuffling your feet across the sand.) Rays living in Hawaiian waters include the Brown Stingray and the Spotted Eagle Ray.

Turtles are the world's oldest surviving reptiles, in existence since the time of the earliest dinosaurs. There are 270 known species of turtles, some living on land, others in fresh water. Those living in the ocean are called marine (or sea) turtles. Equipped with streamlined shells and toeless, oar-like legs, sea turtles can dive to depths of 125 feet and can swim at speeds of 20 miles per hour. They will travel hundreds, even thousands, of ocean miles to reach their nesting sites.

Hawai'i's green sea turtles migrate 800 miles to their nesting beaches on the unpopulat-

Manta rays inhabit Hawaiian waters.

ed sand shoals of the Northwestern Islands. There, the females come ashore several times in a season to lay clutches of eggs the size of ping-pong balls. Each clutch consists of about 100 eggs, which are incubated in the warm sand, and take seven to 12 weeks to hatch, depending on the temperature of the sand. The hatchlings are two inches long when they dig out of their nest and rush to the sea, reappearing in coastal waters when they are the size of a dinner plate. About one in a thousand hatchlings reaches the age of sexual maturity at around 25 years. A mature female will nest every two to four years and live up to 80 years.

Called *honu* in Hawaiian, the green sea turtle is featured in mythology and is considered a source of good luck. Its shell, which reaches lengths of three to four feet, is colored dark brown to olive. Weighing 200 to 300 pounds, the green turtle can be seen eating seaweed along shorelines. Named for the greenish color of its body fat, this turtle was once a source of food for sailors. Three native species of turtle – green, hawksbill and leatherback – are found in Hawaiian waters, but the green turtle is the most common. The loggerhead and olive ridley are rare visitors. All sea turtles are protected by law, and commercial trade in endangered sea turtles is banned.

Green sea turtles can be seen at the Maui Ocean Center (right) and when snorkeling or diving along Hawai'i's reefs (below).

Makapu'u Point, O'ahu

PART II

The Voyage & the Ports

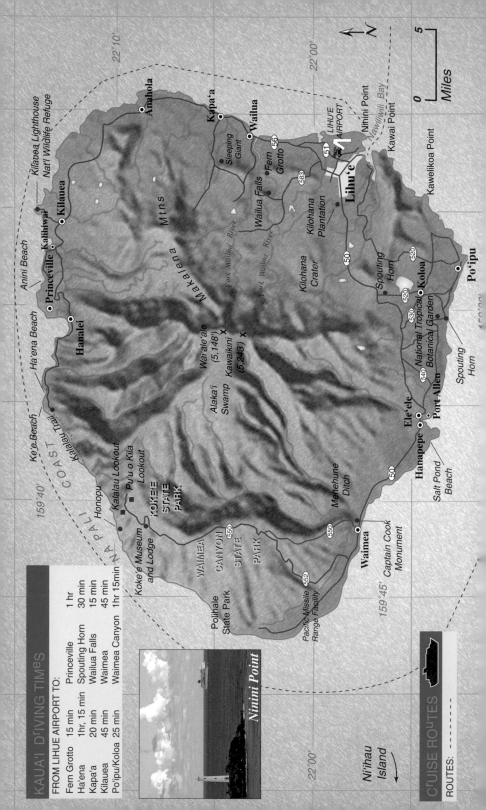

KAUA'I DRIVING TIMES

FROM LIHUE AIRPORT TO:

Fern Grotto	15 min	Princeville	1 hr
Ha'ena	1hr, 15 min	Spouting Horn	30 min
Kapa'a	20 min	Wailua Falls	15 min
Kilauea	45 min	Waimea	45 min
Po'ipu/Koloa	25 min	Waimea Canyon	1 hr 15min

Ni'ihau Island

Ninini Point

CRUISE ROUTES

ROUTES: - - - - - - - -

N

0   5

Miles

Kīlauea Lighthouse
Nat'l Wildlife Refuge

Anini Beach

Amahola

Kilauea

Kalihiwai

Princeville

Ha'ena Beach

Hanalei

Ke'e Beach

Kalalau Trail

NA PALI COAST

Honopu

Kalalau Lookout

Pu'u o Kila Lookout

KOKE'E STATE PARK

Koke'e Museum and Lodge

WAIMEA CANYON STATE PARK

Polihale State Park

Pacific Missile Range Facility

Makaleha Mtns

Wai'ale'ale (5,148') x

Kawaikini (5,243') x

Alaka'i Swamp

Menehune Ditch

Waimea

Captain Cook Monument

Salt Pond Beach

Hanapepe

Ele'ele

Port Allen

Spouting Horn

National Tropical Botanical Garden

Koloa

Spouting Horn

Po'ipu

Kawelikoa Point

Kawai Point

Ninini Point

Nawiliwili Bay

LIHUE AIRPORT

Lihu'e

Kilohana Plantation

Kilohana Crater

Kapa'a

Sleeping Giant

Wailua

Fern Grotto

Wailua Falls

North Fork Wailua River

South Fork Wailua River

56

51

583

50

520

520

530

540

550

550

552

22°10'

22°00'

22°00'

159°40'

159°45'

Na Pali Coast

be busy during rush hours. The north shore's two-lane road is dotted with one-lane bridges, requiring approaching drivers to yield to one another.

Shore Time Suggestions

For first-time visitors, Kaua'i has three 'must see' sights: the Na Pali Coast, Waimea Canyon and the North Shore. The most efficient – and spectacular – way to see all of these regions is by helicopter tour, which has become Kaua'i's signature attraction, thanks to the island's mountainous interior and vast tracts of tropical wilderness. However, driving tours and boat excursions will give you a closer look at these places of natural beauty, even if time constraints mean you may not be able to visit all three of them while your ship is in port.

If you are on Kaua'i for a full day and half of the next (which is often the case with Norwegian Cruise Line), consider renting a car for the first day (which you must reserve in advance) and driving up the Coconut Coast to the North Shore's beautiful beaches, such as Ha'ena or Ke'e, the latter providing access to the roadless Na Pali Coast via the Kalalau Trail. On day two, you can spend a leisurely morning at nearby Kalapaki Beach or take one of a variety of ship-organized shore excursions that will have you back to the ship in time for its mid-day departure and afternoon cruise past the Na Pali Coast. (Several NCL itineraries include a cruise around Kaua'i upon

Ha'ena Beach

SHIP-TO-SHORE EXCURSIONS

The outdoors is the major attraction on Kaua'i, whether you choose a scuba or snorkel excursion, a botanical garden tour or a coastal drive. Kaua'i's largely rural landscape makes it ideal for 'jungle trek' shore excursions involving the following activities: riding ziplines over rainforest canopies; hiking to hidden waterfalls; swimming in freshwater pools; kayaking past fern-covered river banks; and floating by inner tube along irrigation canals that criss-cross the lush countryside. These backcountry adventures often take place on private ranches. Although you can book some of these excursions upon arrival, for guaranteed reservations it is best to book them in advance through the cruise line, which will provide transportation to and from the venue. The following is a sampling of Kaua'i shore excursions available through the cruise lines. Times are approximate. For general information on shore excursions, please refer to the Cruise Options section in Part I. **More detail on the attractions listed below can be found within this chapter.**

• Waimea Canyon Tour (5 hrs)
• Scenic Hanalei (3.5 hrs)
• Helicopter Flightseeing (2 hrs in total with a 50-minute flight)
• Na Pali Coast by Raft or Catamaran (6 to 7 hrs)
• Wailua River / Fern Grotto (3.5 hrs)
• 4-W Backroads Adventure (4 hrs)
• Mountain Safari and Zipline Ride (8 hrs)
• Championship Golf (5 to 6.5 hrs)
• Botanical Garden Tour (4 hrs)
• Waterfall Hikes (4 to 6 hrs)
• ATV Ranch Adventure (4.5 hrs)
• Horseback Ride (3.5 hrs)
• Bicycling Tours (3.5 to 4.5 hrs)
• Po'ipu Beach Surfing (3 hrs)
• Beach Entry Snorkeling (4 hrs)
• SCUBA Beginner/Cert'd (6 hrs)
• Mudbug Safari (5 hrs)

Note: This is a general list of ship-organized shore excursions and will vary with each cruise line. For more detail, consult your shore excursions booklet (supplied by the cruise line) or log onto your cruise line's website.

departing Nawiliwili Harbor, treating passengers to a ship's rail view of the Na Pali Coast.)

If your ship will not be cruising past the Na Pali Coast (i.e. if your ship spends one full day in port and departs late in the afternoon) and you want to see this famous section of coast, your options are to: (1) rent a car and drive to the North Shore where you can hike part of the Kalalau Trail; (2) take a Na Pali Coast boat excursion from Port Allen; (3) take an island helicopter tour, the latter having the advantage of taking in

Kayakers on the Wailua River.

KAUA'I

both the Na Pali Coast and Waimea Canyon. You can book Na Pali Coast boat excursions and island helicopter tours through the cruise line.

If the Waimea Canyon is your top priority, you could reserve a rental car and drive the length of Waimea Canyon Drive (featuring two lookouts and a short nature trail), then proceed into Koke'e State Park where two more lookouts near the end of this road provide stunning ridgetop views down to the Na Pali Coast. You can also visit Waimea Canyon on a ship's shore excursion.

Beaches

Close to the cruise dock and good for swimming and beginner surfing is **Kalapaki Beach** (page 131), which fronts the Kauai Marriott Hotel. Along the east side of Kaua'i is the Coconut Coast, where **Lydgate Beach Park** (page 133) features excellent beach facilities and a swim-ming/snorkeling lagoon that is perfect for children.

North Shore beaches include several hard-to-reach spots such as Secret (Kauapea) Beach, which offers seclusion for sun-bathing but is not safe for swim-ming. **Lumaha'i Beach** (page 139) of *South Pacific* fame is another beautiful beach that is unsafe for swimming. **Hanalei Bay**'s two-mile beach is dotted with small beach parks and offers great swimming and body board-ing in summer, as well as a high surf in winter for experienced surfers. **Ha'ena Beach Park** and adjacent **Makua 'Tunnels' Beach** (page 139) also offer good summertime swimming and snor-keling (sea conditions permit-ting). **Ke'e Beach** (page 141) fea-tures a lagoon that's ideal for swimming and snorkeling in sum-mer when the seas are calm.

Good beaches on Kaua'i's sunny and sheltered south coast include **Po'ipu Beach Park**

(page 142) where a shallow, protected bay provides ideal swimming for children. You can also enjoy good surfing at Po'ipu Bay, especially along the shore break at Brennecke's Beach. **Salt Pond Beach** (page 143) is another south shore beach park that is ideal for children, which features a rock-enclosed swimming lagoon and where the windsurfing is excellent beyond the reef that partially protects the beach.

Surf Schools

The Beach Boys at Kalapaki Beach have been teaching beginner surfers ever since the old Kauai Surf Hotel opened in the late 1950s. Nakumoi Surf Co. beside Po'ipu Beach Park rents surfboards and bodyboards, and offers surfing lessons through Kaua'i Surf School. For information on all of Kaua'i's surf schools, call 808-821-1003 or visit surflessons@trykauai.com.

Snorkeling & Scuba Diving

On the Coconut Coast, Lydgate Beach Park's lagoon is an ideal place for children and beginners to snorkel. The North Shore's Anini Beach, Tunnels Beach and Ke'e Beach are all excellent in calm conditions. On the south shore, Po'ipu Beach offers good snorkeling in clear, calm waters along Nukomoi Point and at Koloa Landing, which is an inlet of lava rocks frequented by sea turtles that is good for snorkeling and diving. Another accessible diving site off Po'ipu is Sheraton Caverns, where ledges start at 30 feet (9 m) and descend to 60 feet (18 m), and where sea turtles, sharks, eels and an abundance of fish inhabit underwater caverns.

(Opposite) Watersports rentals are available at Kalapaki Beach. (Below) Divers explore an underwater cavern.

KAUA'I

There are plenty of surf, snorkel and scuba shops around the island. Snorkel Bob's is located in Kapa'a and Po'ipu, while Snorkel Depot is situated in Hanalei. Seasport Divers (www.seasportdivers.com / 800-685-5889) rents snorkel and scuba equipment, and offers daily boat/shore dives. The company has two locations: at Po'ipu on the south side (808-742-9303) and Kapa'a on the east side. Fathom Five dive shop in Koloa offers half-day boat dives and snorkeling trips (808-742-6991).

Kayaking

The Hule'ia, Wailua and Hanalei Rivers are ideal for kayaking, and kayak rentals are readily available. Island Adventures offers guided kayaking excursions of the Hule'ia River from Nawiliwili Small Boat Harbor. These excursions comprise a one-way paddle up the Hule'ia River followed by a short hike through the Hule'ia

National Wildlife Refuge to two hidden waterfalls. This tour can be booked with the cruise lines and includes a stop at Menehune Fishpond Overlook.

Numerous guided kayak outfitters operate on the Wailua River, including Ali'i Kayak Tours, located across from Kalapaki Beach in the Harbor Mall (1-877-246-ALI'I). Kayak Hanalei (808-826-1881) operates kayak and snorkel eco-tours at Hanalei Bay on the North Shore (www.kayakhanalei.com).

Golfing

Three of Hawai'i's top-ranked courses are found on Kaua'i – at Princeville Resort, Po'ipu Bay Resort and **Kaua'i Lagoons Golf Club**, which is a five-minute drive from the cruise dock at Nawiliwili Bay. Designed by

An aerial view of Nawiliwili Bay showing the cruise harbor and Kaua'i Lagoons Golf Club.

Jack Nicklaus, Kaua'i Lagoons Golf Club's Kiele course lies along 40 acres (16 ha) of tropical lagoons and ocean cliffs. The other 18-hole course at Kaua'i Lagoons is the Mokihana Course, a Scottish-style links.

The **Po'ipu Bay Resort Course**, designed by Robert Trent Jones, Jr. and featuring 11 water holes and 86 bunkers, is a stunning and unique venue for the PGA Grand Slam of Golf. The **Prince Course** has been rated the number one course in Hawai'i in *Golf Digest* and is considered a Robert Trent Jones, Jr. master-piece with its challenging hills and ravines.

For information on these courses, check with your cruise ship's shore excursion office, or call 1-800-634-6400 or 808-241-6000. Kaua'i has a total of nine golf courses, including **Puakea Golf Course** at the base of Mount Ha'upu, which was designed by Hawai'i's Robin Nelson.

Gardens

There are five botanical gardens on Kaua'i. Closest to the cruise port is **Smith's Tropical Paradise**, in Wailua River Marina State Park (see page 134). The National Tropical Botanical Garden administers the **McBryde Garden** and adjacent **Allerton Garden** near Po'ipu on the south coast (page 143), as well as the **Limahuli Garden** on the north shore (page 140). Another north shore garden open to the public is **Na Aina Kai** (page 138).

Hiking

Kaua'i's state parks contain dozens of hiking trails that range from easy to strenuous. One of the most scenic is the ancient Kalalau Trail along the Na Pali Coast. Starting at Ke'e Beach

Overlooks along the scenic Na Pali Coast can be enjoyed while hiking the Kalalau Trail.

Park, the first two miles of this 11-mile (18-km) trail trace a narrow cliff-side path to Hanakapiai Beach. To go beyond this point and hike the entire trail, sections of which are very challenging, requires an overnight camping permit.

Other trails on Kaua'i include those within Waimea Canyon State Park and Koke'e State Park. Hiking maps are available at the Koke'e Museum in the park. For information on Kaua'i's trail system, which is administered by the Division of Forestry and Wildlife, visit www.hawaiitrails.org or call 808-274-3433.

Shopping

Nearby **Anchor Cove** can be reached on foot (it's a 10- to 15-minute walk) or by catching the free shuttle. Anchor Cove offers a handful of shops selling Hawaiian souvenirs and good-quality clothing, as well as an ATM machine.

The **Aloha Center** at 3371 Wilcox Road (former location of the old Hale Kaua'i store) also can be reached on foot, and it features a fine arts and crafts gallery, information on island activities and tours, public phones, Internet access and an ATM. **Hilo Hattie**, located in Lihu'e, has a free shuttle at the pier, as do K-Mart and Wal-Mart, also in Lihu'e.

Coconut Marketplace is a plantation-style shopping mall featuring more than 60 unique shops and galleries, and 15 restaurants or snack bars in an Old Hawai'i setting. It is located eight miles (13 km) up the Coconut Coast from the cruise harbor, and the free shuttle takes you past Wailua Beach and the famous Coco Palms Resort (see page 135).

Galleries featuring the works of local artists include those at Kong Lung Center in Kilauea and at Kilohana Plantation near Lihu'e. The highest concentration of art galleries is located in Hanapepe

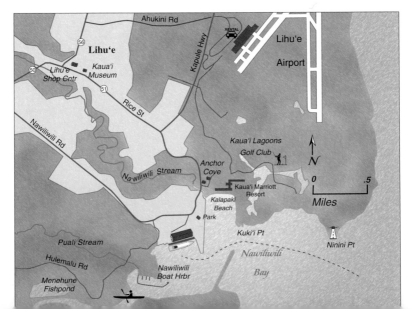

on the south shore. The Kaua'i Museum in Lihu'e houses a gift shop with quality crafts.

Lihu'e Attractions

Within walking distance (about 15 minutes) of the cruise dock is **Kalapaki Beach** – a quarter-mile crescent of fine sand that runs in front of the Kauai Marriott Resort. A sandy bottom and gentle wave action make this beach ideal for swimming and learning to surf. The Kalapaki Beach Boys provide surfing lessons and watersports rentals. Located right on the sands of Kalapaki Beach in front of the Marriott is **Duke's Kauai**, an open-air restaurant that is similar to Duke's Canoe Club in Waikiki. Duke's Kauai features a collection of Duke Kahanamoku memorabilia, including a 40-foot outrigger canoe and three of Duke's own surfboards. (For more on surfing legend Duke Kahanamoku, see page 93).

An overlook to the **Alakoko (Menehune) Fishpond**, which lies in a bend of the Hule'ia Stream, is located a one-mile (1.6-km) walk from the cruise dock. This ancient fishpond is a National Historic Landmark and is adjacent to the Hule'ia National Wildlife Refuge, which provides a protected habitat for Hawai'i's native water birds and plants. This is where the opening

(Below) Duke's at Kalapaki Beach. (Bottom) The view over Menehune Fishpond.

KAUA'I

Who Were the Menehunes?

Of the many legends recounted in ancient Hawaiian chants, one of the most indelible is that of the Menehunes – dark-skinned dwarfs of considerable strength. Legend asserts that these hobbit-like people were the original inhabitants of Kaua'i who built fishponds and other prehistoric structures. Lending credibility to these legends is the recent discovery of 12,000-year-old skeletons in a wet cave on the Indonesian island of Flores. While some anthropologists believe these small skeletons are simply the remains of early humans who suffered from microcephaly (a genetic disorder) or dwarfism, others speculate they may have belonged to a separate species. More detailed analysis will be needed to determine whether a race of little people actually existed.

scene in *Raiders of the Lost Ark* was filmed, in which Indiana Jones (played by Harrison Ford) swings from a vine into the water and swims to a waiting floatplane. According to legend, the fishpond's 900-foot (274-m) wall that cuts off a bend in the Hule'ia Stream was built by the Menehune (see box above) with rocks brought from the seashore by passing each one from man to man. Kayakers can enjoy paddling along Hule'ia Stream, which drains into Nawiliwili Bay. The 102-acre (41-ha) parcel of land encompassing the Alakoko

Fishpond was listed for sale in 2006 at a price of $12 million.

Visit the town of **Lihu'e** by taking the Hilo Hattie shopping shuttle. Two blocks south of Hilo Hattie, on Rice Street, is the Kaua'i Museum, the town's former library, which houses historic exhibits behind an impressive neo-classical facade.

Kaua'i's colonial era is showcased at the **Grove Farm Homestead** on the outskirts of town where tours of this former sugar plantation must be arranged beforehand. The homestead was established in 1864 by George Wilcox, whose nephew Gaylord Wilcox built Kaua'i's grandest plantation estate at **Kilohana** in 1935. A manor house designed in the English Tudor style that was popular in Hollywood at the time, Kilohana has been converted into shops selling Hawaiian clothing and galleries featuring original paintings, prints and sculptures by local artists. Occupying the mansion's original dining room overlooking the central courtyard is Gaylord's – one of Kaua'i's

Gaylord's at Kilohana.

finest restaurants – serving breakfast, lunch and dinner. Clydesdale-drawn carriage rides of the grounds and sugar cane field tours are also available.

Natural attractions in the area include **Wailua Falls**, its twin cascades featured in the TV show *Fantasy Island*. A steep trail leads from the roadside overlook to the freshwater pool at its base.

Coconut Coast

Stretching along the east side Kaua'i, 10 miles north of Lihu'e, is the Coconut Coast. Here you will find the island's largest concentration of shops, services and historic sites. The mouth of the **Wailua River**, Hawai'i's longest navigable river, was once a traditional gathering place of royalty. Numerous archeological sites are found in the area, including royal birthstones, petroglyphs, a place of refuge and the ruins of several *heiaus* (lava-walled temples).

On the south side of the Wailua River mouth is **Lydgate State Park**, which is ideal for families

(Above) Wailua Falls. (Below) The children's lagoon at Lydgate State Park.

and first-time snorkelers with its boulder-enclosed lagoon and lifeguard station. Park facilities include a picnic area and playground. Lydgate Park was transformed in 1964 when a lava-rock barrier and breakwater was built to create a shallow swimming and snorkeling lagoon that is perfect for children, with water that is flat calm and crystal clear.

This lovely lagoon was inspired by Albert Morgan, a native Hawaiian and community leader whose wife Helen liked to take their five children to Lydgate Park to play on the beach, but where there was no sheltered swimming. In 1958, the Morgans visited the Italian seaside town of Sorrento where they saw people swimming in protected areas of the bay. Upon returning home, Mr. Morgan formulated the idea of constructing something similar at Lydgate. The Hawaiian government responded positively to his proposal of constructing a children's wading pool and an adult swimming pool. Funds were raised, and a rock barrier was built using boulders donated by Lihu'e Plantation, which were lifted off the beach and positioned by a crane that had been floated into the bay. The lagoon was designed to allow fish to swim in and out, and there is a $1500 fine for spear-fishing them. The beach beside the lagoon is exposed to ocean swells and is not recommended for swimming.

Riverboat rides and kayaking tours are available at the mouth of the Wailua River, where a major attraction is the **Fern Grotto**. The Smith family has been running riverboat excursions on the Wailua River since the late 1940s. Their boat ride is a two-mile journey, during which passengers are enter-

(Left) A bend of the storied Wailua River.

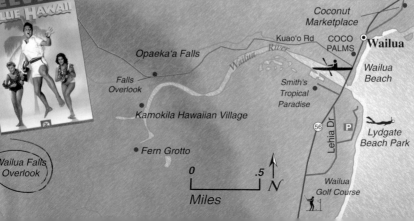

Hollywood's Tropical Back Lot

Dozens of movies have been filmed on Kaua'i, including scenes from *South Pacific* (1958), *Blue Hawaii* (1961) and *Raiders of the Lost Ark* (1983). Stephen Spielberg was on Kaua'i filming scenes for *Jurassic Park* when Hurricane Iniki struck in 1992. He and his film crew hunkered down at the Westin Kauai, which closed for repairs after the storm and reopened as the Kauai Marriott. Numerous television shows have also been shot on Kaua'i, including the popular miniseries *The Thorn Birds*, starring Richard Chamberlain.

tained with songs and stories of ancient Hawai'i. At the boat landing, a nature walk leads to the lush fern grotto where couples come to be wed and serenaded by Hawaiian singers.

Other Wailua attractions include the **Opaeka'a Falls**, which visitors can view from an overlook along Kuamoo Road, which traces the Wailua River's north bank. Across the highway from the Opaeka'a Falls parking lot is Poli'ahu Heiau, the site of a large war temple. A short drive from the Falls overlook is **Kamokila Hawaiian Village**, which was built on a terraced hillside in 1981 as a hands-on example of what daily life was like in the ancient fishing and farming village that once occupied this site. Open daily from 9:00 a.m. to 5:00 p.m., admission is $5 for adults and $3 for children. Outrigger canoe rides are available from the village to scenic spots along the Wailua River, including the Fern Grotto (www.kamokila.com).

Upon returning to the Kuhio Highway and proceeding a short distance up this coastal highway,

you will come upon Wailua's famous **Coco Palms Resort**, which is set in a grove of coconut palms and lagoons, and was once considered among the most beautiful hotels in Hawai'i. The wedding scene in *Blue Hawaii*, starring Elvis Presley, was filmed

(Below) Opaeka'a Falls.

here in 1961 and has since prompted thousands of couples to be wed here in a similar fashion. The history of this famous resort began in 1896 when William Lindeman planted some Samoa coconut trees. In the 1940s, the owners of the 47-acre site turned their home into the Coco Palms Lodge, which they sold in 1953 to Lyle and Grace Guslander, who then expanded the resort while retaining a Polynesian theme throughout. Mrs. Guslander proved to be a superb hotelier and promoter, whose dedicated staff and loyal clientele included local and international celebrities, all of whom enjoyed the resort's relaxed atmosphere. Larry Rivera, a well-known Hawaiian musician, was an entertainer at the Coco Palms in the 1950s and 60s, and he recalls luminaries such as Elvis Presley and Patty Page joining in with background vocals while he sang Hawaiian love songs in the lagoon-side bar.

The Coco Palms Resort closed in 1992 after its buildings were badly damaged by Hurricane Iniki, and is now being rebuilt (slated to open in 2008). The cottage where Elvis stayed will be preserved as a museum.

Meanwhile, the only way to visit the resort's grounds and view the coconut-fringed lagoons is by taking a Hollywood Movie Tour or by booking a 'Blue Hawaii' wedding package (see Weddings & Honeymoons in the Cruise Options section).

(Left) Christ Memorial Episcopal Church. (Below) Kilauea Point Lighthouse.

North Shore

Princeville Resort Golf Course.

Kaua'i's north coast, one of the most scenic in Hawai'i, starts at Kilauea Point and ends at Ke'e Beach, where the Na Pali Coast begins. This is is a windward coast of lush volcanic mountains, their bases fringed with turquoise surf and white-sand beaches.

Here the Kuhio Highway, which weaves past scenic look-outs and breathtaking beaches, is reduced to two lanes and one-lane bridges; the local style of driving requires everyone to slow down and yield to one another.

To reach **Kilauea Point Lighthouse**, take the detour off Kuhio Highway at Kilauea, an old plantation town. The turn-off is opposite the distinctive **Christ Memorial Episcopal Church**, constructed in 1941 of native lava rock and featuring beautiful

stained-glass windows. Follow Kilauea Road until you reach the National Wildlife Refuge at Kilauea Point. A viewing area beside the parking lot provides a good look at the lighthouse, which is being restored. This historic tower was activated in 1913 and houses the world's largest clamshell lens that can shine 90 miles out to sea, providing a beacon to ships bound for the Orient. In winter, humpback whales can be sighted off this rugged promontory, which is a sanctuary for nesting seabirds such as red-footed boobies, Laysan albatrosses, shearwaters and great frigate birds. Hawaiian monk seals sometimes haul out on Moku'ae'ae Islet at the base of the lava cliffs. A beautiful beach lies at the base of Kilauea Point.

KAUA'I

Near the town of Kilauea (just before its entrance if you are heading west) is the **Guava Kai Plantation**, said to be the world's largest guava orchard, where you can sample various guava products at the visitor center. Also near Kilauea is **Na Aina Kai**, a privately owned botanical garden featuring whimsical statuary and a children's garden with a maze.

The Kalihiwai turnoff leads to **Anini Beach Park** where there is excellent snorkeling along one of Hawai'i's longest reefs. The water is four feet deep on the landward side and plunges to greater depths on the seaward side. Beginner snorkelers should not venture beyond the reef.

The next turnoff is for **Princeville**, a resort community with condos, hotels, restaurants, vacation homes, tennis and one of Hawai'i's highest-rated golf courses.

Just past the Princeville turnoff is the **Hanalei Valley Lookout**, one of Kaua'i's most famous vistas of wetland taro fields, stretching in emerald green splendor across the floor of this beautiful river valley.

Next is the Hanalei Bridge – the first of several – and then the turnoff for famous Hanalei Bay, its pier featured in the movie *South Pacific*. Several beach parks lie along the shores of Hanalei Bay, its name meaning Crescent Bay. These offer great

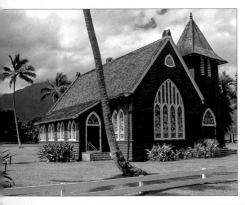

(Left) Wai'oli Huia Church.
(Below) Hanalei Valley.

swimming and body boarding in summer, and a high surf in winter for experienced surfers. Local outfitters include a kayak company that runs guided tours up the Hanalei River, which snakes through a wildlife refuge and is the only river on Kaua'i where commercial, motorized boats are banned. On the landward side of the highway that skirts Hanalei Bay is the **Wai'oli Huia Church**, built in 1912, and Wai'oli Mission House, built by missionaries in 1834. Wai'oli means 'joyful water' and is frequently heard in the Hawaiian hymns sung by the church's congregation each Sunday.

The next beach after Hanalei Bay is **Lumaha'i Beach** , which was immortalized in the movie musical *South Pacific*, filmed here in 1958, when Mitzi Gaynor tried to wash that man right out of her hair. A roadside overlook provides a view of this famous beach, which can be reached by a steep trail that is not easy to find. There are, however, several beautiful, safer and more accessible

(Top) Lumaha'i Beach. (Above) Snorkelers at Ha'ena Beach.

beaches a short drive west of Lumaha'i.

Ha'ena Beach is a stunning stretch of beach where expert surfers come in winter to ride the waves. The seas settle down in summer, when families come to swim and snorkel, under the watchful eyes of a lifeguard, and enjoy the facilities at Ha'ena Beach Park, including picnic tables, rest rooms and showers. At the far end of the bay, inside Ha'ena Point, is **Makua Beach**, which the locals call 'Tunnels' because of the sand-filled alleys that run through the shallow part of the reef, providing excellent snorkeling. This is also a popular surfing spot.

Nestled in the valley opposite Ha'ena Beach Park is **Limahuli Garden**, a breathtaking tropical garden that provides a glimpse of ancient Hawai'i when taro was widely cultivated. Towering above the garden's terraced green slopes is Mount Makana, cast as Bali Hai in the film *South Pacific*. Limahuli is part of the National Tropical Botanical Garden, whose director, Charles Wichman, donated 989 acres of land in this valley as a preserve where he and his fellow horticulturists nurture native plants that are extinct elsewhere on the islands. Guided and self-guided tours of the 17-acre public garden are available, the former requiring a reservation. The Garden is open to the public Tuesday through Friday, and on Sunday.

(Left) Limahuli Garden. (Below) Ke'e Beach seen from Kalalau Trail.

Ke'e Beach lies at the end of the road on Kaua'i's north shore and is a popular swimming/snorkeling beach with its sheltered lagoon and extensive reef lying at the base of mountains, which mark the start of the Na Pali Coast. Snorkelers can explore the reef's coral canyons and hikers can access the 11-mile (18-km) **Kalalau Trail**. The trailhead starts near the parking lot, and a short walk up the trail provides great views of the coast. Hanakapi'ai Beach, lying at the mouth of a stream-carved valley, is a two-mile (one-hour) hike from the trailhead but a person need hike only the first mile to enjoy some of the trail's most spectacular views before returning to Ke'e Beach. The trail beyond Hanakapi'ai is a strenuous backpacking expedition that requires a camping permit. The parking lot at Ke'e Beach Park is often full by mid-day, so try to get there as early as you can.

Ke'e Beach, often used for location shots in television and film productions, is part of the 230-acre (93-ha) **Ha'ena State Park**, six acres of which were once owned by Howard Taylor, brother of actress Elizabeth Taylor. While Taylor negotiated with the state for the sale of his beachfront property, he invited a group of hippies to live there. They built themselves tree houses that they raised off the ground to stay dry during winter's high surf. This haphazard cluster of counter-culture residents became known as Taylor Camp. When Taylor and the state settled on a sum after eight years of negotiations, the residents of Taylor Camp resisted relocation. They eventually left willingly and their tree houses were burned to make way for Ha'ena State Park, which was established in 1977.

South Coast

Motorists heading to Kaua'i's sunny south coast are treated along the way to a mile-long (1.6-km) section of road shaded by a leafy canopy of eucalyptus trees. This tunnel of trees marks the entrance to Kaua'i's historic sugar plantation region, where Hawai'i's first sugar mill was built at **Koloa** in 1835. Old Koloa Town was completely restored in the 1980s and features a variety of charming shops, art galleries

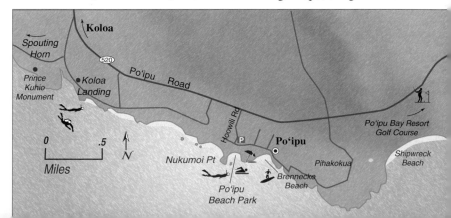

(Above) Po'ipu Beach Park.
(Below) Spouting Horn.

and eateries. Of historic interest is Koloa Church, built in 1854. Two miles (3 km) south of town is Koloa Landing, once the island's major port for Yankee whalers and inter-island steamers. Koloa Landing is located at the western end of Po'ipu – the island's largest resort community.

Some of Kaua'i's best beaches are found along Po'ipu's sheltered coves, which offer excellent swimming, snorkeling and surfing. **Po'ipu Beach Park** is an ideal family destination with activities for everyone. Small children can swim in the shallow waters of this sheltered cove, while surfers can head to the waves just beyond the lava rock barrier and snorkelers can check out the reefs along Nukumoi Point. Facilities here include restrooms and picnic pavilions, and rental of surf boards and snorkel gear.

Less than a mile west of Koala

Landing is a monument marking the birthplace of Prince Jonah Kuhio Kalaniana'ole, who was born March 29, 1871. A nephew of Queen Lili'uokalani, Hawai'i's last monarch, the Kaua'i prince was named heir to a no-longer-existent throne by his deposed aunt in 1899. **Prince Kuhio** was elected as a delegate to Congress in 1903, a position he served until his death in 1922. The last great Hawaiian *ali'i*, Prince Kuhio is honored each year on his birthday with an island-wide celebration of the arts.

West of Po'ipu is **Spouting Horn County Park**, where visitors can watch sea water explode 50 feet (15 m) skyward from a submerged lava tube each time a large wave rolls onto the rocky shoreline here. Nearby is the visitor center for the adjoining **McBride and Allerton Gardens**, managed by the National Tropical Botanical Garden, which offers self-guided and guided tours of these extensive collections of rare tropical flora. The Allerton Garden was originally planted in the 1870s by a grieving Queen Emma seeking solace here at her vacation home after the deaths of her husband, Kamehameha IV, and their only child, four-year-old Prince Albert. In 1938 Robert Allerton bought the property and spent the next 20 years collecting rare plants to add to this botanical showpiece, which features pools, statuary and garden 'rooms.'

Hanapepe is a bay-side town of shops and art galleries housed in historic buildings. It is also the location of **Port Allen**, a small-boat harbor where tour operators offer an array of catamaran and rigid-inflatable dinghy rides up Kaua'i's west side to the Na Pali Coast.

Nearby is **Salt Pond Beach Park**, a protected cove providing good swimming, snorkeling and beginner body boarding. The beach park facilities include a lifeguard, restrooms and showers. Salt is still made here in earthen pans filled with seawater, which, upon evaporating, produce a natural sea salt used for cooking or as an Epsom salt-like medicine.

Waimea

Waimea Bay is where **Captain Cook** first landed during his momentous visit in 1778, this historic event (see History section in Part I) commemorated with a statue of the great explorer looking out to sea. **Russian Fort Elizabeth State Park** stands on the east bank of the Waimea River's mouth. The remains of this incomplete boulder-built fort date to a short-lived Russian occupation of the site.

The Waimea River drains into Waimea Bay, and along its lower reaches is an ancient aqueduct called the **Menehune Ditch**, said to have been built by the Menehunes who were also credited with building the Menehune Fishpond near Nawiliwili Bay (see page 131). About 200 feet (61 m) of stone wall still remains at the Menehune Ditch, which diverted water from the Waimea River onto adjacent taro fields.

KAUA'I

'Grand Canyon of the Pacific'

Humorist Mark Twain would no doubt have been amused to learn that he is widely credited with describing Waimea Canyon as 'The Grand Canyon of the Pacific' despite the fact that he never set foot on Kaua'i. And he likely would have written an entertaining tale explaining how he came up with such an appropriate label.

Waimea Canyon

Over the millennia, Kaua'i's abundant rain and swollen streams have steadily eroded the island's central mountains into deep valleys, the most famous example being **Waimea Canyon**. This great gorge is 2,000 to 3,000 feet deep (610 to 914 m) and

Waimea Canyon Overlook.

resembles a miniature Grand Canyon. A ridgetop road travels the 10-mile (16-km) length of Waimea Canyon and has several overlooks that provide spectacular views of the canyon's chiseled depths. Often shrouded in mist, the canyon's rock strata form a layered landscape of earthen-hued reds and burnt oranges interspersed with patches of green vegetation.

The north end of the canyon abuts the cool forests of **Koke'e State Park**, where the ridgetop road continues to Koke'e Lodge & Museum and beyond to two spectacular lookouts with vistas of the Na Pali Coast. Kalalau Lookout (4,120 feet/1256 m) overlooks precipitous slopes plummeting to the sea below; Pu'u O Kila Lookout (4,176 feet) provides not only a view down amphitheater-headed Kalalau Valley to the Na Pali Coast but another view up across the Alaka'i Swamp to Mt. Wai'ale'ale (assuming there is no cloud cover). There are dozens of hiking trails in the Waimea Canyon and Koke'e State Parks, and detailed maps are available at the Koke'e Museum. A restaurant and gift shop are housed in the Koke'e Lodge.

Beyond Waimea the coastal highway continues to the west side of Kaua'i (the hottest and driest part of the island) where it terminates at the Pacific Missile Range Facility – a U.S. military training facility built originally by NASA in 1960 to track the Mercury spacecraft. The clear skies here are ideal for high-altitude studies of the earth's atmosphere and for amateur stargazing.

Lying 17 miles across Kaulakahi Channel is the 'forbidden island' of **Ni'ihau**. This small, arid island has been privately owned since 1864 when it was purchased from the Hawaiian kingdom by an extended Scottish family comprised of the Sinclairs, the Robinsons and the Gays, who arrived in Hawai'i via New Zealand. They established a cattle and sheep ranch on Ni'ihau and also purchased an acreage near Hanapepe on Kaua'i, which is today the Gay and Robinson

Kalalau Lookout in Koke'e State Park overlooks the Na Pali Coast.

sugar plantation. There is no public access to Ni'ihau, which has about 250 Hawaiian-speaking residents. The islanders are known for their excellent shell work, especially for the Ni'ihau leis that are threaded with rare tiny shells found only on the beaches of Ni'ihau.

Polihale State Park lies at the end of a five-mile (8-km) dirt road extending from the Kaumuali'i Highway, its large beach backed by sand dunes rising to 60 feet (18 m). The water is unsafe for swimming but beachcombers can view the sea cliffs of the Na Pali Coast. Just north of Polihale is a sacred site (Polihale Heiau) from which the ancient Hawaiians believed souls of the dead departed into the setting sun.

The Na Pali Coast viewed from a passing cruise ship.

Na Pali Coast

Mother Nature has worked on the **Na Pali Coast** for thousands of years, eroding its volcanic mountains into knife-edged ridges that rise from the ocean's edge in vertical lines, their sheer slopes covered in varying shades of velvety green. Hawaiians once lived in isolated villages along this rugged coast, traveling by canoe along its surf-lapped shores where tour boats (and locals who never tire of revisiting this remote coastline) visit hidden beaches and sea caves. The region's last residents departed in the early 1900s but the legends live on, including that of the Valley of the Lost Tribe. When archeologists exploring the hanging valley above the twin beaches of Honopu found several skulls believed to have belonged to a pre-Polynesian race, a myth was born and continues to be told,

despite the fact that later studies determined that these people were in fact early Hawaiians.

The Na Pali Coast is a prime area to view spinner dolphins, green sea turtles and (from mid-January to mid-April) Pacific humpback whales. Snorkeling and picnic lunches on remote beaches are usually part of a full-day catamaran or ocean raft excursion, which you can book through the cruise line's shore excursion office. These excursions include transportation to and from Port Allen, a half-hour drive from the cruise dock.

If you are on an NCL cruise and your ship departs Kaua'i at mid-day, you will be treated to a ship-board view of the Na Pali Coast. If your ship departs Kaua'i late in the day, it is not likely that you will be cruising past this stunning coastline. In that case, consider taking a boat excursion or helicopter ride to view Na Pali. Another way to see part of this

Passengers enjoy the Na Pali Coast from their cruise ship.

coast is to rent a car and drive to Ke'e Beach, where you can park your vehicle and hike the first mile or two of the Kalalau Trail.

Kaua'i's Ali'i

Kaui's royalty were the first Hawaiians to officially greet James Cook when he made his historic landfall at what he called the Sandwich Islands. When Captain Vancouver returned to the islands in 1792, he met the young Prince Kaumuali'i and was singularly impressed with the boy's refined manners and alert intelligence. Years later when the promising prince became Kaua'i's king, his grace and charm served his people well.

Although Kamehameha the Great had tried to invade Kaua'i, only to have his fleet repelled by stormy seas in Kaua'i Channel, the great conqueror eventually signed a peace treaty with Kaumuali'i instead. When Kamehameha I died in 1819, his son and successor Liholiho (Kamehameha II) wanted reassurance of Kaumuali'i's continued loyalty, so he journeyed to Kaua'i to meet King Kaumuali'i, who was brought back to Honolulu as a sort of royal hostage. There he met the dowager queen Ka'ahumanu – favorite wife of the late Kamehameha the Great – who was so enamored with the king's handsome and gentlemanly disposition that she married him.

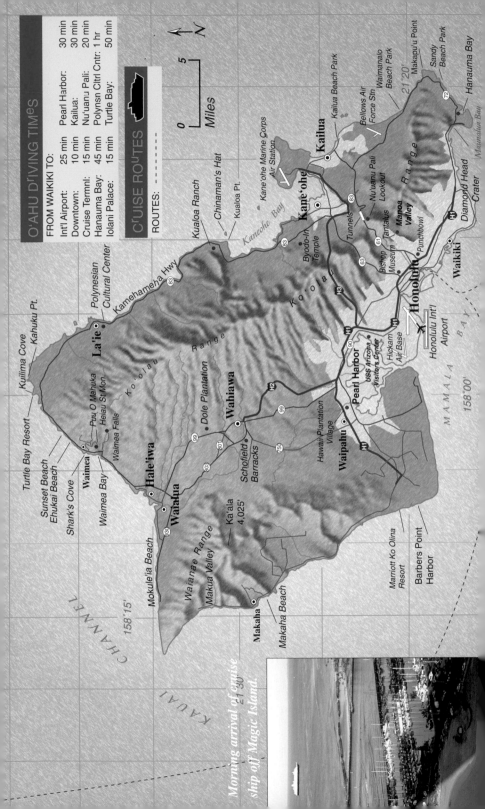

CHAPTER Two

O'AHU

O'ahu means 'gathering place' and Honolulu is indeed the hub of the Hawaiian Islands. A major sea port and vibrant metropolis, Honolulu is the state capital and economic engine of Hawai'i. The city is also of historic importance, containing the only royal palace on American soil, the world's foremost museum on Polynesian culture, and the oldest Chinatown in America. Nearby is Pearl Harbor, where the USS Arizona Memorial stands as a poignant monument to America's military sacrifice in World War II.

O'ahu's north shore is where you will find Hawai'i's famous surfing beaches. Even more famous is the south shore's Waikiki Beach, a storied stretch of sand anchored at one end by volcanic-formed Diamond Head – a landmark recognized the world over. In the 'must see' world of travel, O'ahu tops the list.

A Few Fast Facts

O'ahu, third-largest of the Hawaiian Islands in size, is the most populated. Nearly three-quarters of Hawai'i's total population lives on O'ahu, and about half of the island's 885,000 residents live in Honolulu, which lies at the base of the Ko'olau Range. O'ahu's highest peak is Mt. Ka'ala (4,040 ft/1,231 m), which is part of the western Wai'anae Range.

MUST SEE: 👁

Waikiki Beach (page 174) still stunning after all these years
Pearl Harbor (page 188) a national landmark with three World War II visiting sites
North Shore (page 201) the world's best surfing beaches

Getting Around Independently

The cruise port is located at Honolulu Harbor, which lies between the airport (5 miles/8 km to the west) and Waikiki (3 miles/5 km to the east). The main cruise pier – 10/11 – is located right beside the Aloha Tower. Pier 2 is located a half mile east of the Aloha Tower. (See map page 166.)

Most of the downtown attractions are within walking distance or a short taxi ride from the cruise port. Waikiki (3 miles / 5 km away) can be reached by taxi, bus or trolley. The Aloha Tower's Cruise Concierge desk is located under the Boat Days Bazaar arch on Pier 11 where staff can assist with car rentals, trolley shuttle tickets and booking local excursions.

If you are going directly from the airport to the cruise port or vice versa, you can arrange transfers in advance through the cruise line. Taxicabs are another option. Fares are set by law, and are posted in a visible spot near the taxi's meter. At Honolulu Airport, you can find taxi dispatchers stationed at the center median fronting the terminal baggage claim areas. Approximate taxi fares: airport to cruise port $15-$20; airport to Waikiki $25-$35; cruise port to Waikiki $15; cruise port to Pearl Harbor $25.

Several dozen companies provide shuttle service between the airport and Waikiki; it is best to make arrangements with one of them beforehand. Island Express Transport offers a shuttle service between the airport and Waikiki ($10 per person), from Waikiki to the cruise pier ($10 per person), and from Waikiki to Arizona Memorial at Pearl Harbor ($9 per person). For reservations, visit their website at www.islandexpresstransport.com or call 808-944-1879.

Airport Waikiki Express, operated by Roberts Hawai'i Tours, runs a shuttle every 20 to 30 minutes between the airport and Waikiki, which costs $8 per person and allows two bags per person, with a $3 charge for extra luggage, golf bags, car seats, strollers, etc., and a $12 charge for surf boards. Call 808-539-9400.

Honolulu Harbor's Aloha Tower is a distinctive landmark.

The Bus, O'ahu's efficient public transit, provides service between the airport, the cruise port and Waikiki. Because your luggage must fit underneath your seat or on your lap, the bus is a practical option only if you're arriving by ship at the cruise port for a day-long visit, or if you have checked into a hotel in Waikiki and want to visit the local and island attractions without renting a car, hiring a taxi or booking a tour. Bus routes are extensive and buses run frequently. Fares are $2 per adult, $1 per youth (six to twelve years old), and free for children under six sitting in an adult's lap. Exact change is required. Timetables are available at the Ala Moana Center, street level facing Kapiolani Boulevard (www.thebus.org).

The major **rental car** companies operate from the airport, with drop-off locations in Waikiki. If you are arriving by air in Honolulu and rent a car at the airport, be aware that traffic is heavy during Honolulu's morning and afternoon rush hours. Downtown Honolulu is best explored by car on Saturday or Sunday when offices are closed and street parking is widely available. On weekdays, you can park your rental car in one of the centrally located municipal lots. Many of the streets in Waikiki are one-way, with traffic flowing east on Kalakaua Avenue and west on Ala Wai Boulevard. Car rental

(Below) Pali Highway leads from Honolulu to Nu'uanu Lookout.
(Bottom) Kualoa Point lies along O'ahu's scenic east coast.

O'AHU

companies at or near Honolulu International Airport include Avis, Budget, Dollar, Hertz, National, Alamo, Enterprise and Thrifty.

The **Waikiki Trolley** runs open-air buses throughout down-town Honolulu and Waikiki. The Red Line Trolley (also called the Honolulu City Line) runs between the Aloha Tower Marketplace and Waikiki, depart-ing every 35 minutes from 11:20 a.m. to 6:00 p.m. daily. Route maps are available at various kiosks and hotel activity desks; all routes originate or include a stop at the Royal Hawaiian Shopping Center.

Turtle Bay Resort is located on O'ahu's north shore, next to surfing and snorkeling beaches.

Shore Time Suggestions

If you are a first-timer to Hawai'i and are arriving by ship in Honolulu with only a day to spend in port, the place to see is Waikiki (pages174-183). The downtown historic sights and port-area attractions are also well worth visiting (pages 167-174). Pearl Harbor (pages 188-197) requires at least half a day.

You can book tours to these destinations, as well as day-long coach tours of the island, which offer an overview of O'ahu and its numerous attractions, through the ship's shore excursion office. This should be done well in advance of arriving in O'ahu as the tours often sell out.

If you are staying on O'ahu for a few nights, a day-long circle drive east of Waikiki by rental car

is a recommended option (pages 198-201), as is a visit to the Bishop Museum (page 187) and the Polynesian Cultural Center (page 203); please note, both of these venues require a half day. You can complete the drive to O'ahu's north shore (pages 201-210) and back in a day, but a more relaxing alternative would be to spend a night at the Turtle Bay Resort (pages 165, 203-204) before returning to Waikiki.

If your cruise originates and/or terminates in Honolulu, try to stay for at least two or three nights to thoroughly enjoy O'ahu's many attractions. If your cruise is a round-trip itinerary from Honolulu (i.e. an NCL America cruise), try to tag a few days to each end of your cruise. This extra time will allow you to recover from a full day of air travel to Honolulu and be relaxed when you board your ship; it also allows you to avoid hurrying back to the airport after disembarking at the end of your Hawai'i cruise.

SHIP-TO-SHORE EXCURSIONS

Whether you are spending a few days on O'ahu or your ship is pulling into port for the day, you can reserve most local tours beforehand through the cruise line's shore excursion office. It is possible to book a local tour once you have arrived, but the savings gained by booking directly with a local operator are usually minimal. In some instances, however, a recommended tour might not be available through the cruise line, thus requiring you to reserve directly with a local operator.

The cruise lines offers several sightseeing and cultural tours of O'ahu, including day-long coach tours with stops along the way, such as one for lunch. Or you can choose from other excursions that focus on specific places of interest, such as Pearl Harbor, the Bishop Museum or Honolulu's famous landmarks.

The following is a sampling of O'ahu shore excursions available through the cruise lines. Times are approximate. For general information on shore excursions, please refer to the Cruise Options section in Part I. **More detail on the attractions listed below can be found within this chapter.**
• Pearl Harbor & USS Missouri (6.5 hrs)
• Pearl Harbor & Honolulu City Tour (4.5 hrs)
• Pali Lookout & Bishop Museum (4 hrs)
• Diamond Head, Makapu'u Point & Pali Lookout (3.5 hrs)
• Grand Circle Island Tour (7 hrs)
• Deluxe Grand Circle Island Tour (9 hrs)
• Valley of the Temples, North Shore & Hale'iwa (5.5 hrs)
• Atlantis Submarine (4 hrs)
• Meet the Dolphins at Sea Life Park (5.5 hrs)
• Shopping in Waikiki & Aloha
• Stadium Flea Market (6 hrs)
Note: This is a general list of ship-organized shore excursions and will vary with each cruise line. For more detail, consult your shore excursions booklet (supplied by the cruise line) or log onto your cruise line's website.

Beaches

Waikiki is the beach everyone wants to experience when visiting O'ahu, its setting unsurpassed and its sands lapped by gentle waves that are ideal for swimming and learning to surf (see page 177). There are, however, other excellent, less-developed beaches around the island that can be reached by rental car or the bus. These include **Ala Moana Beach Park**, just west of Waikiki, where locals go to enjoy the soft sand and clear waters; facilities include lifeguards, concessions and plenty of parking.

Good beaches east of Waikiki include **Hanauma Bay** (page 198), which is famous for its snorkeling. Further east is **Sandy Beach Park**, one of O'ahu's best surfing and boogie boarding beaches (pages 199-200). **Makapu'u Beach** (page 200) is another favorite with experienced boogie boarders.

The best swimming beaches on O'ahu's east coast are **Waimanalo Beach Park** (page 200), **Lanikai Beach** (page 200) and **Kailua Beach** (page 200-201). Waimanalo is also ideal for beginner bodysurfers.

O'ahu's **north shore** is best known for its spectacular surfing beaches – Sunset, Banzai Pipeline (Ehukai Beach Park) and Waimea

Waimanalo Beach with Manana (Rabbit) Island lying offshore.

Bay. These beaches are calm enough for swimming during the summer months but are suited only to veteran surfers during the winter months. You can enjoy swimming and snorkeling year-round at **Kuilima Cove** beside the Turtle Bay Resort (page 204).

Snorkeling & Scuba Diving

The most popular snorkeling spot on the island is **Hanauma Bay** (page 198) where you can view hundreds of species of fish a short distance from shore. Divers head to the outer reef where depths plunge to 70 feet (21 m).

You can find good snorkeling in **Waikiki** at **Sans Souci Beach** and in the waters off the adjacent **Natatorium**. Magic Island at **Ala Moana Beach Park** is another good place for snorkeling. East of Diamond Head in **Maunalua Bay** are several dive sites, including Turtle Canyon with its abundance of green sea turtles.

On the north shore, Kuilima Cove beside Turtle Bay (page 204) is ideal for beginner snorkeling. Shark's Cove and Three Tables are popular for cavern dives, but only in summer.

O'ahu's west coast offers excellent snorkeling but only when sea conditions are calm (see page 211). The sunken minesweeper *Mahi Wai'anae* lies 50 feet (15 m) beneath the surface in the waters just south of Wai'anae.

You can rent snorkeling equipment at numerous locations, including Snorkel Bob's (700 Kapahula Avenue) where you can conveniently return gear to any of the company's other inter-island locations.

Golf Courses

There are more than two dozen golf courses on O'ahu, and most are open to the public. Golf and transportation packages from Waikiki are widely available. **Turtle Bay Resort's Arnold Palmer Course**, situated along the spectacular North Shore of O'ahu, is one of the top-rated golf courses in Hawai'i. Another challenging course is **Ko'olau** (a 20-minute drive over the Pali Highway from downtown Honolulu), which is considered one of the toughest courses anywhere due to its massive scale and tropical terrain. Also recommended are Coral Creek Golf Course and Makaha Resort & Golf Club. For a description of these and other courses, visit www.bestplaceshawaii.com/tips/10_best/golf_courses.html). To arrange a tee time, visit teetimeshawaii.com, or call Stand-by Golf at 888-645-2665 or Mickey Golf Tours at 888-732-1516 (or 737-0034).

Hiking on O'ahu

The **Diamond Head State Monument Trail** (see page 184) is the most accessible hiking trail for visitors staying in Waikiki. However, there are numerous nature trails on O'ahu, several of these situated in Honolulu's back yard, where valley floors give way to mountain slopes, their steep trails ascending to ridge tops and hidden waterfalls. In addition to great views, these

The view toward Waikiki from atop Diamond Head.

trails present the opportunity to view native wet forest plants and various bird species.

The **Hawaii Nature Center** at 2131 Makiki Heights Drive provides information about local hikes, such as the Manoa Cliff/Pu'uohia Trails, which begin at the end of Round Top Drive and skirt **Manoa Valley** and **Tantalus Crater**. On the other side of the Manoa Valley is the Wa'ahila Ridge Trail, which starts at Wa'ahila Ridge State Recreation Area parking lot and ends at a ridge junction, with views of Waikiki and of Manoa and Palolo valleys. (See map, page 166.)

The Manoa Valley, location of the University of Hawai'i and long-established neighborhoods with lovely old homes, has a popular trail ascending to the base of **Manoa Falls**, a 100-foot (30.5-m) waterfall and pool. This three-quarter-mile (1.2 km) uphill trail starts at the end of Manoa Road and traces a stream to the base of Manoa Falls; allow two hours for the round trip. Situated near the trailhead is the Lyon Arboretum, its gardens displaying varieties of indigenous and exotic plants.

Other trails in the Honolulu area include those along the ridges (Wiliwilinui, Hawai'iloa and Kuli'ou'ou) east of Diamond Head. The Koko Crater Trail, its trailhead located within the Koko Crater Botanic Garden, provides summit views of O'ahu's windward side and across Maunalua Bay to Diamond Head.

More good trails are located in the Pacific Pallisades area above Pearl Harbor, and others are found along the windward coast, starting in the south with the **Makapu'u Lighthouse Road**, which takes about 45 minutes to

Makapu'u Point marks the south end of O'ahu's windward coast.

hike to the summit for splendid views (but no access to the lighthouse). Near the north end of the windward coast is the popular Sacred Falls Trail, which is closed during danger periods because the steep, narrow canyon is prone to flash floods during heavy rains. In 1999, seven bathers were killed and dozens injured by falling rocks and boulders while lounging in the pool at the base of this 80-foot waterfall.

The Hawaii Audubon Society (Suite 505, 850 Richards Street, Honolulu, HI 96813-4709, Telephone 808-528-1432) publishes a detailed map of O'ahu's hiking trails, entitled Hidden Treasures of O'ahu. **For general hiking tips, see page 23**.

Shopping

The **Ala Moana Shopping Center** is the largest shopping venue in Hawai'i. Located in between the cruise port and Waikiki (see map, page 166), the center provides a $2 shopping shuttle that runs regularly between the center and several locations in Waikiki. The center is said to be the world's largest outdoor shopping mall, with more than 200 stores set amongst koi ponds in open-air walkways.

The **Victoria Ward Centers**, across from Kewalo Basin, can be reached by bus or the Waikiki Trolley, and is a growing shopping/dining district where shops

(Top & middle) International Marketplace. (Bottom) Rainbow Baazar, Hilton Hawaiian Village.

featuring Hawaiian-made products include Native Books/Na Mea Hawai'i.

There are two **Hilo Hattie** stores in Honolulu: one is at the Ala Moana Shopping Center and the other (the Flagship Nimitz Store) is located west of the cruise port. A free 10-minute shuttle runs between the flagship store and several Waikiki hotels, with optional drop-offs at the Aloha Tower marketplace and the Ala Moana Shopping Center. The shuttle runs from 8:30 a.m. to 5:00 p.m., with pick-ups and drop-offs at such hotels as the Hilton Hawaiian Village, Sheraton Moana Surfrider and Aston Waikiki Beach (beside the Waikiki Marriott). Hilo Hattie was the stage name of a popular singer and dancer of the 1950s, and her namesake chain of stores – founded in 1963 – is a well-known manufacturer of Hawaiian products.

Right in Waikiki, shopping venues include the **Rainbow Baazar** at the Hilton Hawaiian Village and the shopping complex at the Hyatt Regency Waikiki, which features an inner court waterfall. **The Royal Hawaiian Shopping Center**, which stands on grounds once belonging to The Royal Hawaiian hotel, is an extensive complex of shops and restaurants. Across the street is the **International Marketplace**, an open-air bazaar

that many people associate with Waikiki's early days of tourism. Recent plans to replace this island-style marketplace with an upscale retail center have been re-evaluated, and a more modest renovation is now being planned.

Scattered throughout Waikiki are **ABC convenience stores**, which are good for buying inexpensive souvenirs, such as Kona coffee and macadamia nuts, and beach accessories, such as sunscreen and roll-up beach mats. Sidney Kosasa, who grew up working in his parents' grocery store in Honolulu, opened his first ABC outlet on Waikiki Beach in 1964. Today there are 38 ABC stores in Waikiki, open daily from 6:30 a.m. to 1:00 a.m.

Polynesian art is sold in galleries throughout O'ahu.

O'AHU

Where to Stay

Most visitors bypass the hotels in downtown Honolulu and head straight to Waikiki Beach. Accommodations in Waikiki range from luxury ocean-view suites to modest units in budget-priced hotels that are located a block or two from the beach. Several of Waikiki's beachfront hotels are famous landmarks worth taking a stroll through or visiting for lunch. Better yet, stay at one of these unique properties and enjoy the best of Waikiki.

Hilton Hawaiian Village (www.hilton.com), wholly owned and operated by Hilton Hotels Corporation, is located at the far western end of Waikiki Beach, away from the hustle and bustle yet within easy walking distance of Waikiki's main attractions. Many guests never leave the 22-acre (9-ha) village with its array of restaurants, lounges, shops and other attractions. The expansive grounds feature tropical foliage and exotic wildlife, including South African penguins. The resort's Rainbow Bazaar has dozens of restaurants and shops (including an ABC store) as well as a Thai Temple and a replica Japanese pagoda.

Each of the resort's six guest towers is unique. The beachfront Ali'i Tower is the most exclusive, housing the resort's luxury accommodations. The Rainbow Tower, also on the beach, is where the resort's waterfront restaurants are located. This tower opened in 1968, its facade at either end decorated with one of the world's largest ceramic-tile mosaics, incorporating more than 16,000 tiles. The Tapa Tower, built on the site of a previous tower, opened in 1982 and is set

The Rainbow Tower at Hilton Hawaiian Village in Waikiki.

O'AHU

back from the beach, its ocean-view rooms providing a sweeping view of the village and the water-front. In 1999, a geodesic dome at the resort's entrance was torn down and construction begun on the Kalia Tower, which now houses the **Bishop Museum Collection** in the Hawaiian Arts & Culture Center. This collection is worth seeing if you haven't the time to visit the Bishop Museum in downtown Honolulu, and is open from 10:00 a.m. to 5:00 p.m. daily. There is a small admission charge for adults; children under 12 are admitted free.

The village's beach, the widest on Waikiki, was enhanced during the resort's construction when workers blasted and dredged the shoreline and added 30,000 cubic yards of sand, as well as palm trees for shade. You can book surfing lessons at the Beach Activities Center, as well as a variety of boat excursions that depart from the Port Hilton Dock, including sunset sails and dinner cruises. Atlantis Submarines operates from this dock and transfers passengers by boat to its high-tech submarine for a 45-minute dive that includes viewing a World War II oil tanker.

The **central section** of **Waikiki Beach,** stretching from the Outrigger Reef Hotel to the Moana Surfrider Hotel, is dominated by Sheraton properties. One notable exception is the luxury Halekulani Hotel (www.haleku-lani.com), a five-diamond hotel that ranks as one of the world's leading resorts.

(Above) Tiki displayed outside Tapa Tower. (Below) South African penguins at the Hilton.

O'AHU

The Royal Hawaiian

(www.sheraton.com/hawai'i) was built in 1927 by the Matson Steamship Co. and became known as the Pink Palace of the Pacific, accommodating the rich and famous of that era who would arrive from San Francisco by steamship. Now a Sheraton property, the Royal Hawaiian remains an elegant enclave of palm-filled gardens and pool-side umbrella tables, and is still frequented by celebrities who are among the guests at this grand hotel.

The hotel's Spanish-Moorish design is not exactly Hawaiian, but this style was very popular in California in the 1920s due in part to the Rudolph Valentino movies everyone was watching. The site of the hotel was once a coconut grove where Queen Ka'ahumanu (favorite wife of King Kamehameha) had a summer residence. Today the grounds contain a lovely tropical garden.

Sheraton Moana Surfrider

(www.sheraton.com/hawai'i) is the oldest hotel on Waikiki Beach. Known as 'The First Lady of Waikiki', the hotel held its grand opening in 1901 and is now listed on the National Register of Historic Places. Its Banyan wings were added in 1918, creating a courtyard around an historic banyan tree where a veranda restaurant serves elegant meals and afternoon tea. Beginning in 1935, the famous radio show 'Hawai'i Calls' was broadcast from the Banyan Court each week. The show, which lasted 40 years, was carried by hundreds of radio stations in the mainland U.S. and attracted a worldwide audience at its peak of popularity in the 1950s.

The Moana's 75-foot-tall banyan tree was planted in 1904 and was one of the first to be placed on the City and County of Honolulu's Exceptional Tree List

in 1979. Protected by state law, this huge banyan – with a canopy extending 150 feet (46 m) across – requires a permit for a team of arborists to trim its branches and check its root system.

Many famous names are associated with the Moana, including the American novelist James Jones, who penned *From Here to Eternity* (1951) while staying in Room #424 of the Banyan Wing. Another wing was added to the hotel in 1952, and the tower was completed in 1969.

The **eastern end** of **Waikiki Beach** consists of **Kuhio Beach County Park**; hotels along this stretch are separated from the beach by Kalakaua Avenue, Waikiki's main thoroughfare. Adjacent to Kuhio Beach is Queen's Surf Beach and Kapi'olani Park (see page 182), which is an inviting green space that lies at the base of Diamond Head crater (see page 183).

(Opposite) The Royal Hawaiian.
(Above and below) The Moana's banyan tree and grand entrance.

Marriott Waikiki Beach Resort (marriottwaikiki.com) offers an excellent location at the Diamond Head end of Waikiki Beach, next to Kapi'olani Park. Recently refurbished, the Marriott's rooms are decorated with vibrant colors in a Hawaiian motif. This hotel is in the heart of the action, and is within easy walking distance of restaurants and night clubs. Norwegian Cruise Line has a service center in the lobby where NCL guests can arrange pre- or post-cruise tours and obtain advice on local restaurants and attractions. NCL passengers enjoying a pre-cruise stay at the Marriott can also pre-book their shore excursions here and pre-check-in for their cruise, thus circumventing the lines at the cruise terminal on embarkation day.

Turtle Bay Resort (www. turtlebayresort.com) on the north shore is a 35-mile (56-km) drive from Honolulu Airport. The perfect place to unwind before boarding your ship in Honolulu, this independent luxury hotel occupies Kuilima Point and is flanked by fine beaches. The resort grounds also contain 42 beachfront cottages, all elegantly appointed. Two championship golf courses, a horseback riding stable, tennis courts, Hans Hedemann Surf School and 12 miles of ocean-front hiking trails are among the attractions of this

(Opposite) Waikiki Beach viewed from James Jones's room at the Moana. (Right) Waterfront dining at the Royal Hawaiian.

laid-back resort. You can enjoy swimming and snorkeling at adjacent Kuilima Cove with its crescent beach of white sand. Each Friday, the resort stages a Polynesian revue called 'Legends of the North Shore' featuring traditional dances from various Pacific island groups. A pre-show luau buffet is served on the lawn terrace overlooking Kuilima Cove.

Where to Dine

Cruise Port Area
Aloha Tower has an array of restaurants, ranging from waterfront dining to fast-food outlets. Chinatown, a short walk away, is where you will find a good selection of Asian restaurants, particularly along Nu'uanu Avenue. On the edge of Chinatown, at the corner of Merchant Street and Nu'uanu Avenue, is Murphy's Bar & Grill, Honolulu's oldest pub, serving lunch and dinner daily. The Ala Moana Shopping

O'AHU

Center (reached by shuttle from the cruise port) houses a selection of restaurants and a food court.

Waikiki Beach

Waikiki's most appealing restaurants are those within a shell's throw of this famous beach. Hilton Hawaiian Village offers elegant dining at **Bali by the Sea**, serving Pacific Rim cuisine in an open-air setting. The Village's **Rainbow Lanai** is more casual and ideal for families, with tables overlooking the beach and an ornamental pond bordering this outdoor restaurant.

For superb French cuisine, **La Mer** at the luxury Halekulani Hotel offers elegant oceanfront dining. The hotel's poolside pavilion, **House Without a Key**, is a casual yet classy place to enjoy a breakfast buffet, lunch or cocktails at sunset while being entertained by live Hawaiian music and hula dancing.

Next door, Sheraton Waikiki's **Ocean Terrace** offers a buffet and a la carte menu with nightly entertainment at the main pool stage from 6:00 p.m. to 8:00 p.m. This is a great spot to enjoy a casual dinner as the sun sets and surfers haul their boards up onto the beach while a Hawaiian band performs beside the torch-lit swimming pool. Sea turtles often swim off the seawall in front of the terrace.

The Outrigger Waikiki is home to **Duke's Canoe Club**, a popular seafood restaurant named for Duke Kahanamoku, Olympic swimming champion and Hawai'i's Father of Surfing. This oceanfront restaurant occupies the site of the original Outrigger Canoe Club and is reminiscent of 'old Waikiki' with its palm-thatched roof, koa wood paneling and extensive collection of Duke memorabilia, which includes surf boards and framed photographs. You can enjoy live Hawaiian

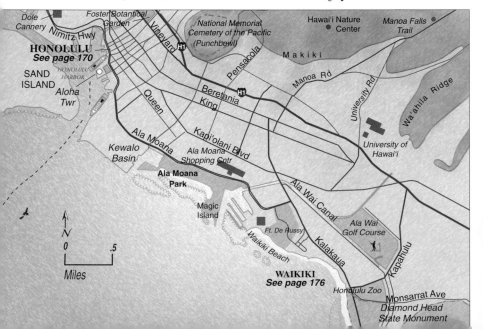

entertainment in the Barefoot Bar while sipping a tropical cocktail and watching waves lap the shore where Duke himself once surfed. Duke's is open for breakfast, lunch and dinner, and offers a children's menu. Also in the Outrigger Waikiki overlooking the beach is **Hula Grill**, an excellent eatery serving Hawaiian seafood.

You can enjoy an old Hawai'i ambiance at the **Banyan Court** in the Moana Surfrider (see page 162-163). This verandah restaurant is a lovely place to enjoy a leisurely breakfast as the early morning surfers take to the water. Sunday brunch and afternoon tea are also served here.

Tiki's Bar & Grill is the place to soak up Waikiki's upbeat atmosphere while enjoying excellent regional cuisine created by Fred DeAngelo, one of Hawai'i's most highly regarded chefs. This

A mural at Pier 10/11 depicts the arrival of a Matson steamship.

popular restaurant is located on the second storey of the Aston Waikiki, next door to the Marriott. The decor is retro-Hawaiian with indoor and outdoor seating. Patrons seated on the outdoor deck overlooking Kalakaua Avenue can watch the people strolling up and down the beachfront promenade.

Honolulu Harbor & Downtown Attractions

Honolulu Harbor is a major commercial harbor, handling the bulk of Hawai'i's exports and imports. This natural harbor was formed by the stream that flows down the Nu'uanu Valley into a small ocean basin where the freshwater outflow cut several channels through the surrounding coral reef. The early Hawaiians established a village here on the waterfront, but Waikiki was the preferred location, where outrigger canoes could beached. When ships of the fur trade began calling on the Hawaiian Islands in the

late 1700s, they sought a sheltered anchorage with deep water, which they found at the port that had been created by Nu'uanu Stream. They called the harbor Fair Haven, and its name later

Honolulu's downtown is within walking distance of the port.

translated into Hawaiian as Honolulu, which means 'protected bay.'

The city of Honolulu was officially named in 1859, taking its name from the harbor. Situated at 'the Crossroads of the Pacific,' Honolulu had grown from a small seaside town of grass huts to a port city with wharves, warehouses and shops. Local merchants prospered servicing the trading ships that pulled into port, and sandalwood was sold at lucrative prices by Hawaiian royalty and loaded in large quantities onto ships bound for China. When the North Pacific whaling fleet began arriving annually for repairs and supplies, teams of Hawaiian men would wade out from shore to catch the ships' lines and tow the whalers to their moorings.

As steamships began delivering Hawai'i's first tourists, their arrival was greeted with much fanfare. Flower leis were draped over the shoulders of disembarking passengers, and festivities included music by the Royal Hawaiian Band, the tossing of colorful streamers and the swaying symmetry of grass-skirted hula dancers. The entire town got caught up in the excitement of Boat Days, with people leaving work for a few hours to join in the fun. This all ended when the jet plane replaced the passenger ship as the main mode of travel to Hawai'i. Until now, that is. The recent renaissance of ship travel has created a modern revival of that bygone era when the harbor was the heart of Honolulu.

Aloha Tower Marketplace

Aloha Tower, once the center of activity whenever a steamship pulled into port, has regained its place of prominence with the opening of the adjacent marketplace in 1994. A Guest Services Kiosk is located in the Boat Day Promenade and provides information on local tours and transportation, and about the complex's 70 shops and restaurants. ATMs are situated throughout the marketplace.

The historic Aloha Tower is a Honolulu icon, completed in 1926 to greet Hawai'i's early tourists who arrived by steamship. Built to a slender height of 184 feet and topped with a domed cupola, the Aloha Tower was for decades the tallest building in Honolulu – and in all of Hawai'i. The E. Howard Clock Company of Boston built the seven-ton clock and installed it between the ninth floor office and the tenth floor observation deck. The massive clock's four faces are illuminated at night and are visible for several miles out to sea. Etched between each clock face and cupola balcony are the letters A-L-O-H-A. Visitors are welcome to climb the stairs to the observation deck, which is open daily from 9:00 a.m. to 5:00 p.m.

Marine life thrives in the waters of Honolulu Harbor, and food dispensers are located on the sea walls of the Aloha Tower Marketplace so that visitors can feed the fish and observe them as they swim to the surface for food.

The **Hawai'i Maritime Center** (a nautical museum that opened in 1989) is located next to the Aloha Tower Marketplace at Pier 7, where the four-masted *Falls of Clyde* is permanently moored.

NCL's Pride of Hawai'i departs Honolulu Harbor.

Falls of Clyde is moored beside the Hawai'i Maritime Center.

This restored sailing ship, built in Glasgow, Scotland, served as a Matson Navigation Company cargo and passenger liner from 1898 to 1920, and is now on the National Register of Historic Places.

Also berthed at the maritime complex, when not out at sea, is the *Hokulea*, a double-hulled sailing canoe that made a famous voyage in 1976 as a re-enactment of the ancient Polynesians' seagoing migrations. The *Hokulea* is often joined by another replica canoe, the *Hawai'iloa*, both of which are sailed by the Polynesian Voyaging Society. King Kalakaua's Boathouse once stood on stilts at Pier 7, which is where Duke Kahanamoku, Hawai'i's most famous surfer, set his first world swimming record in 1911. The Center is open daily from 8:30 a.m. to 8:00 p.m., and there is a small admission fee.

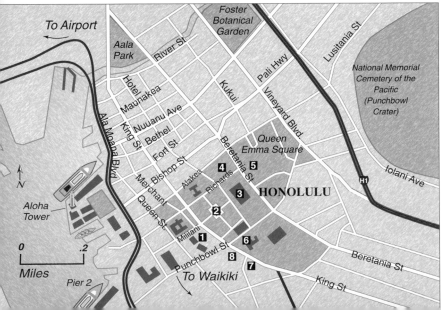

Downtown Sights 👁

Honolulu's historic core is a short walk from the cruise port where the **King Kamehameha Statue 1** is a good starting point for a self-guided tour. This statue of Kamehameha the Great, who united the islands under one kingdom, stands in front of Ali'iolani Hale, a government office building that was begun in 1872 during the reign of Kamehameha V. Originally commissioned as a palace, it was redesigned to house the State Judiciary.

The statue of Kamehameha was erected in 1883 as part of King Kalakaua's coronation celebrations. An American sculptor working in Florence was commissioned to create the statue, which portrays a young Kamehameha with outstretched arm – his pose similar to that of a famous classical statue of Augustus Caesar. After the King Kamehameha statue was bronzed in Paris, it was loaded onto a ship that was lost at sea near the Falkland Islands en

(Right) King Kamehameha statue. (Below) Iolani Palace.

route to Hawai'i. The original statue was eventually recovered (it stands near Kamehameha's birthplace on the big island of Hawai'i) but not before an exact replica was made and shipped to Hawai'i for its unveiling in Honolulu. The statue is draped with dozens of long colorful leis each June 11 in celebration of King Kamehameha Day, a state holiday.

The grounds of **Iolani Palace** – **2** the only one on American soil – are directly opposite the King

Notable buildings include the Hawai'i State Capitol (above), Washington Place (below) and Kawaiaha'o Church (bottom).

Kamehameha statue. Built in 1882, the Iolani Palace was home to the last reigning monarch, Queen Lili'uokalani, who ascended to the throne in 1891 and was overthrown by republican forces in 1893. The grounds and palace gift shop are open to the public but you must arrange tours of the palace interior, including the throne room, by advance reservation (522-0832).

3 The **Hawai'i State Capitol**, completed in 1969, stands on the far side of the Iolani Palace grounds. The building's architectural elements of cones, pillars and a reflecting pool are meant to represent Hawai'i's volcanoes, palm trees and surrounding seas. Across Richards Street from the **4** Capitol is the **Hawai'i State Art Museum**, which opened in 2002 and displays Hawaiian paintings, ceramics and sculpture. Opening hours are 10:00 a.m. to 4:00 p.m., Tuesday to Saturday.

Across the street from the Capitol, next to the eternal flame War Memorial on Beretania **5** Street, stands **Washington Place**. This pillared mansion was built by a sea captain named John Dominis whose son married the future Queen Lili'uokalani, Hawai'i's last monarch. When the Queen was deposed in a bloodless coup in 1893, she withdrew from the palace to her private residence at Washington Place. She was later arrested and charged for complicity in a counter-revolution when a cache of weapons was unearthed in her back garden. Eventually returning to Washington Place, she resided there until her death in 1917 at the age of 78. Washington Place was the official residence of Hawai'i's governor until 2003, when a new governor's mansion was built behind it.

Other buildings of note in the immediate vicinity of Iolani Palace are the State Archives, **6** Hawai'i State Library and **Honolulu Hale** (**City Hall**). Across from city hall, on King **7** Street, is the **Hawai'i Mission Houses Museum** – a complex of wooden, brick and coral stone buildings that the early missionaries built and occupied. They are now a registered National Historical Landmark.

8 Nearby is **Kawaiaha'o Church**, where royal weddings and inaugurations were once held. Construction of this church (which is the fifth to bear the name Kawaiaha'o Church) was begun in 1836 and completed in 1842. The previous structures, smaller and less permanent, were built of grassy materials while the current structure is made of coral blocks cut from nearby reefs. A special koa-wood pew was installed for the personal use of Queen Lili'uokalani, a devout Christian.

The tomb of King Lunalilo is held in the family mausoleum, which was built after his death inside the entrance to the church yard. Elected to the throne in 1873, Lunalilo was not a direct descendant of Kamehameha the

(Above, right) Lunalilo mausoleum. (Right) Murphy's pub.

Great, his ascension marking the end of the Kamehameha dynasty. During his life, Lunalilo felt slighted by members of the Kamehameha clan and did not want to be buried with them at the Royal Mausoleum in Nu'uanu Valley, so his dying wish was respected.

Chinatown

Merchant Street, the oldest thoroughfare in Honolulu, leads west from the King Kamehameha statue to Chinatown, where modern office towers give way to brick-

fronted buildings of the whaling era. Places of interest include Murphy's Bar & Grill, at the corner of Merchant and Nu'uanu streets, where such notables as Mark Twain and Robert Louis Stevenson once quaffed an ale. Nu'uanau Avenue is lined with art galleries and restaurants, and is home to lively street festivals throughout the year. The heart of Chinatown is the corner of Hotel and Maunakea. Flower shops are numerous along Maunakea, between Hotel and Beretania, and this is where the locals buy their fresh flower leis from a wide, well-priced selection. One block west of Maunakea, along Beretania, takes you to River Street, where a waterside walkway meanders to the northern outskirts of Chinatown. Here lies the **Foster Botanical Garden**, which contains a beautiful selection of rare and exotic plants, including 26 specimens designated as exceptional trees. Admission is $5 ($1 for children). Nearby is a Buddhist temple and across the river, along College Walk, is a Japanese Shinto shrine. (Please note: Some caution is advised when walking around Chinatown late at night.)

Waikiki Beach – The Story of Waikiki

One of the world's most famous resorts began quietly enough. Initially the two and a half miles of beach stretching eastward from downtown Honolulu was a place for Hawaiian royalty and wealthy families to relax at their elegant beach house estates. There were few facilities for visitors, just a handful of guest houses and hotel bungalows that served the first trickle of tourists to arrive at the islands by steamship from San Francisco. Some arrived by private yacht, like Robert Louis Stevenson, who checked his family into one of the beach bungalows at the Sans Souci, a hotel built in 1884 and named for Frederick the Great's palace.

Royal Hawaiian and Moana hotels, Waikiki Beach, 1940.

When the famous author wasn't being entertained at King Kalakua's beach house, he could be seen writing in the shade of a banyan tree.

Waikiki's bucolic atmosphere began to change with construction of the Moana Hotel. The first grand hotel to be built at Waikiki, the Moana's doors opened in 1901. Located on the tram line from Honolulu, three miles away, 'The First Lady of Waikiki' was an instant success. Dinner dances at the hotel's Banyan Court were the centerpiece of Waikiki nightlife, as was the pier and open-air pavilion off the beach in front of the hotel, where couples would stroll in the moonlight as the surf gently lapped the shore and where beachboys strummed their ukuleles. Among those who enjoyed dancing at the Moana to the music of band leader and songwriter Johnny Noble was the young Prince of Wales, who would later become King of England and, upon his abdication, Duke of Windsor.

Much of the area surrounding Waikiki was swampland and taro fields until construction of the Ala Wai Canal in 1921. This alleviated the mosquito problem, but some swampy areas remained. The architect of the Royal Hawaiian Hotel had been warned of this, and during construction of the hotel – just up the beach from the Moana – some of its supporting columns began to sink into the soft ground. A retired navy engineer was called in to stabilize the foundation with a system of jacks and bridge-type girders.

Tourist Booklet Cover, 1894.

With its grand opening in 1927, the Royal Hawaiian became the premier hotel in Waikiki, its famous guests including Mary Pickford, Douglas Fairbanks,

President Kennedy acknowledges the crowds lining Kalakaua Avenue in June, 1963.

Henry Ford, Shirley Temple and President Franklin D. Roosevelt. Following Japan's attack on Pearl Harbor, the U.S. Navy leased the Royal Hawaiian and turned it into a rest-and-relaxation center for servicemen on leave. In the early days of the war, barbed wire was stretched along Waikiki Beach in case of an enemy invasion, and blackout restrictions were enacted.

Following World War II, the introduction of jet travel brought tourists to Waikiki in ever-increasing numbers. One by one, private homes and guest houses were torn down to make way for modern hotel towers. In 1954, Henry J. Kaiser and his partner Fritz Burns set their sights on Waikiki, devising a resort master plan that called for a collection of skyscraper hotels, guest houses, oceanfront cottages, swimming pools, gardens and convention facilities. To obtain the 20 acres required for the Hawaiian Village resort, they purchased an ocean-front parcel of eight acres from the John Ena Estate as well as the neighboring Niumalu Hotel (which was torn down), along with some adjacent, privately owned lots. The Ocean Tower (now the Alii Tower) was completed in 1957, and that same year a geodesic dome designed by Buckminster Fuller and made of aluminum (the first of its kind) was erected at the corner of Kalia Road and Ala Moana Boulevard at the entrance to the Village. In 1961, Conrad Hilton purchased Kaiser's interest in the resort, which was renamed the Hilton Hawaiian Village.

Meanwhile, in 1959 Matson Steamship Co. sold its Waikiki hotels to the Sheraton hotel chain, which eventually sold them to Kyo-ya Co. Ltd., a subsidiary of a Japanese conglomerate founded by the industrialist Kenjo Osano. Since 1974, Kyo-ya has owned all of the former Matson hotels. Sheraton manages these proper-

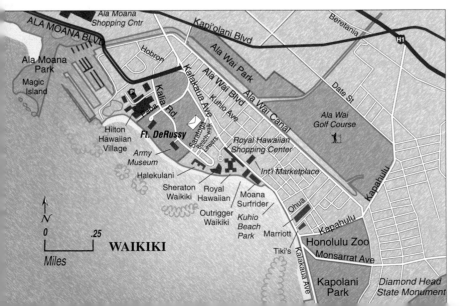

ties, which is one of several brands of Starwood Hotels & Resorts Worldwide.

When silent-screen stars Mary Pickford and Douglas Fairbanks visited Honolulu by steamship, they described Waikiki in their syndicated travel column as "the most beautiful place in the world." Some might say that Waikiki's beauty has faded over time, its lovely strand now overshadowed by a concrete jungle of highrise hotels. However, a revitalization project undertaken in the 1990s has resulted in widened pedestrian walkways, a reduction in car traffic and the staging of beach park events that bring locals and tourists together.

Today, Waikiki has much to offer – famous hotels, award-winning cuisine, exciting night life, international shopping and a beach that continues to delight visitors.

Beach Activities

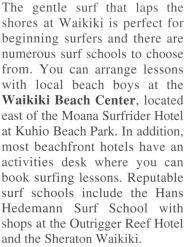

The gentle surf that laps the shores at Waikiki is perfect for beginning surfers and there are numerous surf schools to choose from. You can arrange lessons with local beach boys at the **Waikiki Beach Center**, located east of the Moana Surfrider Hotel at Kuhio Beach Park. In addition, most beachfront hotels have an activities desk where you can book surfing lessons. Reputable surf schools include the Hans Hedemann Surf School with shops at the Outrigger Reef Hotel and the Sheraton Waikiki.

Outrigger canoe rides and cata-

maran rides depart from the Port Hilton Dock in front of the Hilton Hawaiian Village. For body surfing and boogie boarding, a good spot is The Wall at Kuhio Beach near the eastern end of Waikiki.

Lu'aus and Night Life

Local musicians playing slack-key and steel guitar can be heard up and down Kalakaua Avenue and Waikiki Beach each evening. Beachfront venues include the Sheraton Moana Surfrider's Banyan Court and the Ocean Terrace at the Sheraton Waikiki.

Most cruise lines offer their guests the opportunity to attend a shoreside lu'au during their cruise, usually when the ship is overnighting at Maui. However, if you're interested in attending a pre- or post-cruise lu'au on O'ahu, there are several venues to choose from. The Royal Hawaiian Hotel hosts its Royal

Lu'aus feature Polynesian dance.

Waikiki at sunset.

O'AHU

Luau every Monday evening on the Ocean Lawn, with Waikiki Beach and Diamond Head providing a romantic backdrop. The Polynesian Cultural Center, a 45-minute drive from Waikiki, hosts an alcohol-free lu'au on Monday through Saturday evenings (coach tours can be taken from Waikiki). Another popular lu'au is held at Paradise Cove, near Ko Olina Resort, on the island's west shore.

Dinner shows abound in Waikiki, including a Polynesian extravaganza at the Sheraton Princess Kaiulani Hotel. The legendary entertainer Don Ho, known for his signature tune 'Tiny Bubbles' was performing nightly at the Waikiki Beachcomber Hotel until ill health forced the 75-year-old to undergo heart surgery in December 2005. The message to his fans from his hospital bed was, "I'm ready to go another 50 years." Mr. Ho passed away in 2007. Two other nightly shows – Blue Hawai'i and The Magic of Polynesia – are also staged at the Beachcomber. Blue Hawai'i features music of Elvis Presley.

Historical Walking Tours

The Waikiki Historic Trail marks places of historic interest throughout Waikiki with surfboard-shaped information panels. The Native Hawaiian Hospitality Association offers free two-hour,guided tours of Waikiki's historic sites each Tuesday, Thursday and Saturday, starting at the Royal Hawaiian Shopping Center (near the Fountain Courtyard on Kalakaua Avenue) at 9:00 a.m.

Sheraton Hotels & Resorts offers historical tours at all four of its Waikiki properties. The Sheraton Moana Surfrider, Waikiki's oldest hotel, hosts tours

Sheraton Waikiki's Ocean Terrace

several times a week (call 808-922-4422 for more information). The Moana Surfrider's second-floor Historical Room is open to the public and contains a collection of Hawaiian memorabilia.

The Royal Hawaiian also provides tri-weekly tours, as does the Sheraton Princess Kailulani, built in 1955 and named for one of Hawai'i's most beloved princesses, who lived on this site in a two-storey frame house when it was part of her family's royal estate. She would spend hours sitting on a stone bench with Robert Louis Stevenson, who penned the poem 'Island Rose' in her honor. The hotel's lobby contains portraits and memorabilia of 19th-century Hawaiian royalty. The Sheraton walking tour takes participants to each hotel and shares stories of Waikiki's past. (For more information, call 808-922-5811.)

Waikiki Attractions 👁

The **U.S. Army Museum of Hawai'i**, located at Fort DeRussy (immediately east of the Hilton Hawaiian Village) is open Tuesday to Sunday, from 10:00 a.m. to 4:45 p.m. Exhibits cover Hawai'i's military history from Kamehameha I to American campaigns in the Pacific. Fort DeRussy occupies prime waterfront and accommodates vacationing military personnel at its Hale Koa Hotel.

Overlooking Kalakaua Avenue, at the western end of Kuhio Beach, is a statue of the famous surfer **Duke Kahanamoku**, who is credited with introducing surfing to the world. He was also a strong swimmer and, after setting a world swimming record in Honolulu Harbor in 1911, Duke

Duke Kahanamoku statue.

won gold and silver medals the following year at the Stockholm Olympics. He competed in four Olympic Games and retired from competitive swimming at the age of 42. Serious surfers objected to his statue being positioned with its back to the water, as one of the rules of safe swimming and surfing is to always face seaward so you can see a big wave coming.

Near the Duke Kahanamoku Statue are the **Kahuna Stones**, considered a source of *mana* (spiritual power) by the ancient Hawaiians. When Kalakaua Avenue was renovated in recent years, the Kahuna Stones regained their place of prominence and respect. Also near the Duke Kahanamoku Statue is the **Kuhio Beach Hula Mound** where a free, hour-long torch lighting and hula show is staged nightly at 6:30 p.m. (6:00 p.m. November through January).

Saint Augustine Catholic Church, at the corner of Ohua Avenue and Kalakaua Avenue, houses the Damien Museum. Open weekdays from 9:00 a.m. to 3:00 p.m., this museum contains exhibits on the legendary Father Damien, who sacrificed his own life to nurse and comfort leprosy sufferers quarantined on Molokai in the 1870s.

Kapi'olani Regional Park

This urban park lies at the southeastern end of Waikiki Beach and is the location of several attractions, including the **Honolulu Zoo** and the Waikiki Shell. The park's name means 'arch of heaven' in reference to the rainbows that frequently appear overhead, their presence considered symbolic of royalty by the ancient Hawaiians. King Kalakaua donated the park land to the city in 1877, requesting that the park be named for his wife Queen Kapi'olani, a statue of whom stands near the **Kapi'olani Bandstand** where the Royal Hawaiian Band performs on Sunday afternoons and Friday evenings. Various Polynesian-themed shows are staged throughout the day at the **Waikiki Shell Amphitheater** (10:30 a.m., 12:30 p.m. and 2:30 p.m.), and the nightly show (7:00 p.m. to 8:30 p.m.) features hula and the Samoan fireknife dance. A two-mile-long jogging path encircles

Honolulu Zoo's monkey exhibit.

O'AHU

the park, which contains sports fields, tennis and volleyball courts, picnic tables and a playground. The **Honolulu Zoo** occupies the north end of Kapi'olani Park, its main entrance located near the junction of Kalakaua and Monsarrat Avenues. Animals living here include an elephant, giraffe, Galapagos tortoise and Nile crocodile. The extensive use of slope-top berms that hide fencing give the grounds the open, natural appearance of a tropical grassland. Every Saturday and Sunday local artists hold an outdoor art show – called Art at the Zoo Fence – along the Monsarrat Avenue fence of the zoo.

Queen's Surf Beach borders Kapi'olani Park's ocean side. The waters off this beach lie within the Waikiki Marine Life Conservation District, established in 1988. The **Waikiki Aquarium** is located at the south end of this beach, and features exhibits of colorful corals and reef fish, as well as tanks holding sharks, turtles and other marine life, including monk seals.

Nearby is the Waikiki War Memorial Natatorium, a tidal-fed saltwater swimming pool built in 1927 as a living memorial to the 102 Hawaiian servicemen killed in World War I. Buster Crabbe once trained here for the Olympics but the neglected pool was closed some time ago.

The Diamond Head trail leads through a short tunnel to the crest of the crater.

Diamond Head

There are no active volcanoes on O'ahu but you will find many extinct craters, the most famous being Diamond Head. Rising 761 feet (232 m), this famous tuff cone was formed about 100,000 years ago by a violent volcanic explosion of steam, which occurred when sea water entered an underground crack filled with superheated magma. The exploding steam blasted through coral reef and drove a massive cloud of limestone, ash and hard lava into the air. Eons later the crater that was formed by this eruption became the site of an ancient Hawaiian burial ground.

The Hawaiians called it Le'ahi, meaning 'brow (of the) ahi', because the crater's profile resembled the brow of this fish. Early 19th-century British sailors named the distinctive landmark

O'AHU

Diamond Head for the diamond-like calcite crystals in the crater's rock fragments. During World War II, Diamond Head was fortified and Fort Ruger was built at the northern end of the crater floor. In 1968, when development along Waikiki Beach threatened to spread up the slopes of Diamond Head, it was designated a national natural landmark.

The Diamond Head State Monument Trail, leading from the crater floor to its crest, is a popular hike and one best pursued early in the morning before the heat and the crowds intensify. Open from 6:00 a.m. to 6:00 p.m., the trail is accessed from a parking lot that is reached (from Waikiki) by taking Monsarrat Avenue to Diamond Head Road, where a sign will guide you to the park entrance (entry fee is $1 per person). The .7-mile (1.1 km) ascent to the summit involves climbing several flights of cement stairs and walking through a short, dark tunnel. The panoramic views at the top take in Koko Head to the east, and Waikiki and downtown Honolulu to the west. On the first Saturday of each

(Above) Ghandi Statue. (Below) Aerial view of Diamond Head.

month, volunteer leaders of The Clean Air Team conduct a three-hour, two-mile walking tour of Diamond Head. Participants meet at the Mahatma Ghandi Statue in front of the Honolulu Zoo at 9:00 a.m. ($10 per adult, free for kids, call 948-3299).

Honolulu's Outlying Attractions

Punchbowl Crater

A scenic drive leads to the summit of this 500-foot (152-m) hill overlooking downtown Honolulu. An extinct volcano, its bowl-like crater contains the National Memorial Cemetery of the Pacific. Buried here are the remains of soldiers from locations around the Pacific Theater. The cemetery first opened to the public in 1949 with services for five war dead, one of them a civilian named Ernie Pyle who was a noted war correspondent. The cemetery would eventually contain the graves of over 13,000 soldiers and sailors who died during World War II.

Back in prehistoric times,

National Memorial Cemetery of the Pacific in Punchbowl Crater.

Punchbowl Crater was an altar for human sacrifices. During the reign of Kamehameha the Great, two cannons were mounted at the crater's rim to salute important arrivals in Honolulu Harbor. During World War II, tunnels were dug for the placement of shore batteries. Today Punchbowl is a major tourist destination, drawing more than five million visitors each year. A lookout on the seaward edge of the cemetery provides a sweeping view of Honolulu and the harbor.

Royal Mausoleum

When the young son of King Kamehameha IV and Queen Emma died in 1862 (see next entry, Queen Emma Summer Palace), plans were made to build a royal mausoleum at this location. Upon its completion in 1865, the remains of previous monarchs, with the exception of King Kamehameha I, were transferred here from the first royal mausoleum at Iolani Palace. This

O'AHU

sacred burial ground is open Monday through Friday.

Queen Emma Summer Palace

This summer retreat of Queen Emma, consort of Kamehameha IV, was bequeathed from her uncle John Young II (whose father, a British sailor, had been an important advisor to Kamehameha the Great). The New England-style house, set on two acres of manicured grounds, contains Victorian furnishings and Hawaiian artifacts. Personal mementos include the wooden cradle and clothes of Queen Emma's only child (named Albert after Queen Victoria's consort), who died when he was just four years old, on August 27, 1862.

Prince Albert was the last child

born to a reigning Hawaiian monarch, and his tragic death from a mysterious brain disease plunged his parents and the Hawaiian people into a state of intense sorrow. His grief-stricken father died a year later from chronic asthma, worsened by heavy drinking. Queen Emma remained an influential figure in Hawaiian affairs of state, and her death in 1885 was marked by a three-hour-long funeral procession along King Street and up Nu'uanu Valley to the Royal Mausoleum, where her remains were interred alongside those of her husband and son. The Palace (admission is charged) also features a gift shop managed by the Daughters of Hawai'i.

Nu'uanu Pali Lookout

This historic lookout stands atop the cliffs of the Ko'olau Mountain Range and was the site of a famous battle in 1795 in which Kamehameha the Great's warriors drove their enemies to

(Left) Queen Emma Summer Palace. (Below) Pali Lookout.

their deaths. Kamehameha's decisive victory here clinched his conquest of O'ahu and led to the eventual unification of all Hawaiian islands under his rule. This historic lookout provides sweeping views of O'ahu's windward coast and is open daily from 9:00 a.m. to 4:00 p.m. There is no admission and parking is free. Trade winds can funnel through this area, creating blustery conditions at the lookout.

Bishop Museum

The world's foremost museum of Polynesian culture was founded in 1889 by Charles Reed Bishop in memory of his wife Bernice Pauahi Bishop. Bishop, an American banker, served as a minister to King Lunalilo. His Hawaiian wife, who was a great granddaughter of Kamehameha the Great, inherited from her cousin Princess Ruth vast land holdings - one-ninth of all the land in the kingdom. With this wealth, Bernice established the Kamehameha Schools for Hawaiian boys and girls. Her husband later used funds from his late wife's estate as well as his own funds to establish and maintain the Bishop Museum.

Exhibits include Polynesian art, ceremonial regalia and Kamehameha the Great's famed feather cloak. The museum (open daily; $15 adult admission, $5 for children 4 to 12) houses a planetarium and a new Science Adventure Center with hands-on exhibits for children that includes a walk-through volcano and a wave-making tank.

(Above) The old road below Pali Lookout leads to Maunawili trail. (Below) Bishop Museum.

*USS Arizona Memorial
*USS Bowfin Submarine
  Museum & Park
*Battleship Missouri Memorial

Hawaiians once dived for pearls in this large natural harbor. Today, people come by the thousands to view a memorial built over the *USS Arizona*, its sunken hulk lying on the sea floor where it remains a tomb for the 1,177 men who perished aboard the stricken battleship.

December 7, 1941 – the day described by President Franklin D. Roosevelt as one that will live in infamy – began like any other in the Pacific paradise of Hawai'i. The bulk of the U.S. Pacific fleet was moored in Pearl Harbor, where seven of the fleet's eight battleships were tied alongside at Battleship Row on Ford Island. Naval aircraft stood in rows at various stations, while those of the U.S. Army Air Corps were parked in groups,

unarmed, as a defence against possible sabotage on the ground.

War was raging in Europe but the United States and Japan (which had joined Nazi Germany in the Axis Alliance) were still engaged in diplomatic negotiations. However, unbeknownst to the U.S. government, Japan was planning a surprise attack. Its target: Pearl Harbor. Its goal: immobilize the Pacific Fleet. Its objective: gain a quick and decisive victory so that Japan could carry out its military expansion in Asia and the western Pacific without interference from the United States.

A fleet of 33 warships and six aircraft carriers had left northern Japan on November 26, 1941, bound for the Hawaiian Islands. Their route was north of the usual shipping lanes and on December 7, in the pre-dawn darkness, the fleet reached its launch position

Aerial view of Pearl Harbor looking north to Ford Island.

230 nautical miles north of O'ahu. On the other side of the island, five midget submarines – each carrying two crewmen and two torpedoes – were launched from larger mother submarines about 12 miles outside the entrance to Pearl Harbor, with orders to sneak inside before the air strike began.

At 6:40 a.m., the crew of the destroyer *USS Ward* sighted the conning tower of one of these midget subs, opened fire and sank it. Minutes later, a signal indicating the approach of aircraft from the north was picked up at a mobile radar station near Kahuku Point on O'ahu's north shore. Senior officers, when notified, believed these aircraft to be either from the carrier *Enterprise* or an expected flight of B-17 bombers from the mainland, so no action was taken.

By 7:55 a.m. the first wave of Japanese fighters and bombers filled the skies over O'ahu as they flew in formation across the

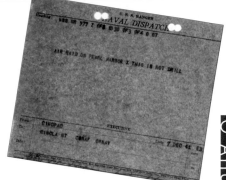

The naval dispatch alerting the world of the Japanese attack.

island toward Pearl Harbor and other military installations. Their leader radioed the coded messages "To, to, to" and "Tora, tora, tora" to the Japanese fleet, notifying them that the attack had begun and the enemy had been taken completely by surprise. Ten minutes later, a bomb slammed through the deck of the *USS Arizona*, setting off a huge explosion in its forward ammunition magazine that ripped apart the

Japanese photo of torpedoes about to strike Battleship Row.

PEARL HARBOR

At 8:06 a.m., the USS Arizona explodes after being hit by a 1760-pound armor-piercing bomb. In less than nine minutes the ship sinks with 1,177 of its crew.

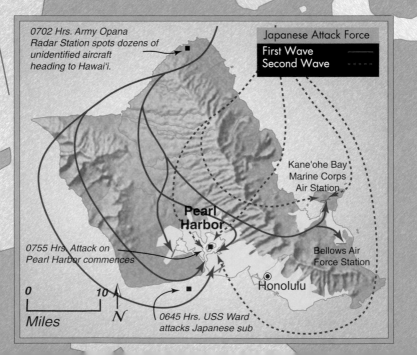

0702 Hrs. Army Opana Radar Station spots dozens of unidentified aircraft heading to Hawai'i.

Japanese Attack Force
First Wave
Second Wave

Kane'ohe Bay Marine Corps Air Station

Pearl Harbor

Bellows Air Force Station

0755 Hrs. Attack on Pearl Harbor commences

Honolulu

0
10

Miles

N

0645 Hrs. USS Ward attacks Japanese sub

UNDER ATTACK

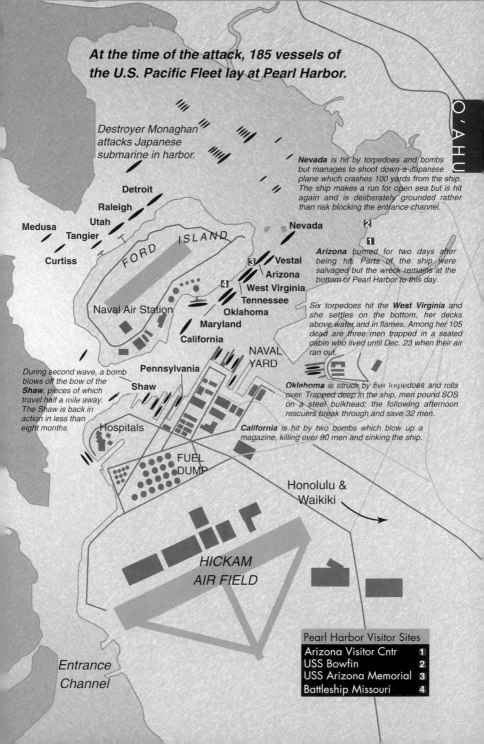

At the time of the attack, 185 vessels of the U.S. Pacific Fleet lay at Pearl Harbor.

Destroyer Monaghan attacks Japanese submarine in harbor.

Nevada is hit by torpedoes and bombs but manages to shoot down a Japanese plane which crashes 100 yards from the ship. The ship makes a run for open sea but is hit again and is deliberately grounded rather than risk blocking the entrance channel.

Medusa
Detroit
Raleigh
Utah
Tangier
Curtiss

FORD ISLAND

Nevada

2

1

Vestal
Arizona
West Virginia
Tennessee
Oklahoma
Maryland
California

3
4

Naval Air Station

Arizona burned for two days after being hit. Parts of the ship were salvaged but the wreck remains at the bottom of Pearl Harbor to this day.

Six torpedoes hit the **West Virginia** and she settles on the bottom, her decks above water and in flames. Among her 105 dead are three men trapped in a sealed cabin who lived until Dec. 23 when their air ran out.

During second wave, a bomb blows off the bow of the **Shaw**, pieces of which travel half a mile away. The Shaw is back in action in less than eight months.

Pennsylvania
Shaw

NAVAL YARD

Oklahoma is struck by five torpedoes and rolls over. Trapped deep in the ship, men pound SOS on a steel bulkhead; the following afternoon rescuers break through and save 32 men.

Hospitals

California is hit by two bombs which blow up a magazine, killing over 90 men and sinking the ship.

FUEL DUMP

Honolulu & Waikiki →

HICKAM AIR FIELD

O'AHU

Pearl Harbor Visitor Sites	
Arizona Visitor Cntr	**1**
USS Bowfin	**2**
USS Arizona Memorial	**3**
Battleship Missouri	**4**

Entrance Channel

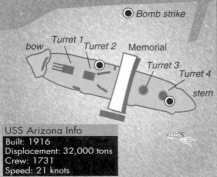

Ford Island

● Bomb strike

bow   Turret 1   Turret 2   Memorial

Turret 3

Turret 4

stern

USS Arizona Info
Built: 1916
Displacement: 32,000 tons
Crew: 1731
Speed: 21 knots

Broken in two, Arizona sinks.

battleship, sending it to the bottom in minutes. Others followed. The *USS Oklahoma* was hit by torpedoes and capsized, with over 400 men trapped inside. The *Utah* also capsized, with more than 50 crew on board. The *California* and *West Virginia* sank at their moorings. The *Maryland, Pennsylvania* and *Tennessee* all took direct hits.

The *Nevada* tried to run out to sea but, after taking several hits, was forced to beach itself rather than sink and block the harbor

entrance. Black smoke filled the air as burning oil spewed across the water. Crewmen leapt from doomed battleships and swam through oil and flames to Ford Island. A second wave of attack planes picked their way through the dense smoke and anti-aircraft fire, destroying the *USS Shaw* and *Sotoyomo*, and inflicting heavy damage on the *Nevada*. Oahʻu air fields, stations and barracks were also hit in both waves of attack.

When the two-hour-long attack was over, American losses were staggering: nineteen naval vessels sunk or severely damaged, including eight battleships; 188 aircraft destroyed; 2,280 military personnel killed and 1,109 injured; 68 civilians killed. The Pacific fleet was crippled and the destruction wrought upon the U.S. Navy was the worst in its

Hit by nine aerial torpedoes, the West Virginia burns. Amazingly, the battleship survived to fight to the end of the war.

history. The Japanese lost 29 planes and 55 airmen, along with all five midget submarines and nine of the 10 crewmen. The 10th crewman escaped his sub when it ran aground on O'ahu's northeast coast. He was washed up on shore and captured, becoming America's first prisoner of war in a conflict that would last for the next three and a half years.

Japan's leaders believed the United States would be completely demoralized by the crushing defeat of its navy at Pearl Harbor, but this infamous attack had the reverse effect. It galvanized the American people as never before. The following day, President Roosevelt addressed the nation and informed the world that the United States of America had declared war on Japan. Charges of negligence were laid against the army and navy commanders responsible for Pearl Harbor's defence but this did not divert attention from the country's call to arms and ultimate victory.

All of the ships damaged at Pearl Harbor – except the *Arizona, Utah* and *Oklahoma* – were salvaged and later saw action. The *Arizona*'s superstructure and three gun turrets were salvaged, but the hull and deck were left lying in 40 feet (12 m) of silty water. After the war, President Eisenhower approved the creation of a memorial to be erected over the *Arizona*. The chosen architect, Alfred Preis, designed a simple white structure that straddles the submerged battleship. The slight sag in the middle represents initial defeat, while

the two ends stand erect to symbolize strength and resilience.

One of the gun turret's circular mounts protrudes above the water's surface beside the memorial, as does a flagpole flying the Stars and Stripes, which is mounted on the ship's severed mainmast. Inside the memorial is a marble tablet inscribed with the names of the men entombed in the sunken hull below. Those veterans who survived the attack can, if they wish, be laid to rest with their fellow crew members.

Oil still seeps from fuel bunkers lining the outer hull, and visitors are invited to drop anthuriums and plumerias into an open well of the memorial where they float delicately on the oil-stained water. About a quart of oil leaks daily from the *Arizona* and does little harm to the harbor's ecocsystem. However, about a half million gallons of oil remain inside the fuel bunkers. Should one of these bunkers collapse, a major spill would result. Underwater archeologists regularly inspect the wreck to monitor its rate of corrosion. Meanwhile, there is no attempt to stop the slowly escaping oil because many consider it a poignant symbol of the tragedy that unfolded here more than 60 years ago.

(Top to bottom) Memorial viewed from the water. Along its causeway. Marble tablet bearing names of entombed men. Another tablet with names of veterans later laid to rest here.

(Above) Arizona's protruding turret. Nearby black-and-white moorings bear the names of the ships tied up on the day of the attack. (Right) A quart of oil a day still seeps from the Arizona.

A national historic landmark, the memorial was transferred from the Navy to the National Park Service in 1979 and a visitor center was completed the following year. The complex, located on the eastern shoreline of Pearl Harbor, contains a museum, bookstore and small snack area. The lawn behind the center provides an excellent view of Ford Island and Battleship Row. A 23-minute documentary film about the Pearl Harbor attack is shown to visitors, after which they board a Navy shuttle boat for the short ride to the Memorial.

All visitors return to the center on the same shuttle boat that took them there. Security is tight, with no bags of any description – including purses and camera bags

– are allowed at the Memorial. A storage facility is located near the Visitor Center where, for a nominal fee, you can check everything but your wallet and camera. The visitor center is open daily from 7:30 a.m. to 5:00 p.m., except for Thanksgiving Day, December 25 and January 1. There is no charge to visit the Arizona Memorial but donations are accepted. The Arizona Memorial is an extremely popular venue and the line-ups are typically shorter first thing in the morning or late in the afternoon.

If you're driving from Waikiki, take the H1 freeway past the airport. When you reach the Pearl Harbor exit, do not take it. Take the next exit, called 'Arizona Memorial, Stadium,' which will take you past the Navy base (on the left) and the Pacific Fleet headquarters (on your right). Exit left at the 'Arizona Memorial' sign. You can also take public buses (#20 and #42) from Waikiki. A private firm (VIP Tours) offers round-trip shuttles between Waikiki and Pearl Harbor, with pre-arranged pick-up and drop-off at your hotel (reservations should be made the day before).

Two other visitor attractions are located at Pearl Harbor – the **USS Bowfin Submarine Museum & Park** and the **Battleship Missouri Memorial**. Both are run by non-profit organizations and charge admission. The **USS Bowfin Submarine Museum and Park** is next to the USS Arizona Memorial Visitor Center. There is a $4 admission charge to view the museum and an additional $6 to tour the WWII submarine ($3 all-inclusive

USS Missouri, the 'Mighty Mo.'

admission for children ages 4 to 12; children under 4 are not allowed on board the sub). Tickets for the **Battleship Missouri Memorial** are also sold here ($16 adult admission; $8 per child) and a shuttle takes you across the bridge to Ford Island where the *Missouri* is permanently docked at the most seaward end of Battleship Row.

The *Bowfin* was launched on December 7, 1942 (exactly one year after the Pearl Harbor attack) and completed numerous successful patrols. Designated a National Historic Landmark in 1986, the *Bowfin* offers visitors the opportunity to see firsthand what life was like aboard for the sub's 80-man crew. The museum's exhibits include a Poseidon C-3 submarine missile – the only one of its kind on public display.

The *USS Missouri* (Mighty Mo) opened as a memorial and museum in January 1999. This famous battleship, built at New York Naval Shipyard, was commissioned on June 11, 1944. Following sea trials and battleship practice, the *Missouri* headed to San Francisco via the Panama Canal for final fitting out as fleet flagship before steaming toward Japan via Hawai'i. The *Missouri* saw plenty of action, including the invasion at Iwo Jima and the Okinawa campaign, followed by strikes on Hokkaido and northern Honshu.

With news of Japan's unconditional surrender after the dropping of a second atomic bomb, *Missouri* entered Tokyo Bay under the command of Admiral Halsey and prepared for the formal surrender ceremony. On September 2, 1945, General Douglas MacArthur, Supreme Commander for the Allied Powers, was received onboard, along with other high-ranking military officials, followed by a party of Japanese emissaries. A few minutes later, on the ship's 01 verandah deck, General MacArthur officially accepted Japan's surrender. The ceremony was broadcast around the world and marked the end of WWII.

Forty-three years later, the decommissioned *Missouri* returned to Pearl Harbor where she serves as a memorial and museum, which opened to the public on the 54th anniversary of the great battleship's launching.

Pearl Harbor is one of the largest and finest natural harbors in the East Pacific Ocean. A pioneer survey of the harbor was made in 1793 by one of Captain Vancouver's officers who discovered a large coral reef blocking the entrance channel. Thus, the only way a ship could enter this nearly land-locked harbor was by warping. In 1890, when Hawai'i was annexed by the United States, Pearl Harbor became a naval base after the entrance was cleared and the harbor dredged to accommodate large ships. Today, Pearl Harbor is home to the chief U.S. Pacific naval bases as well as Hickam Air Force Base and headquarters for the U.S. Pacific Command. *(Websites: nps.gov, ussmissouri.com, bowfin.org.)*

Hawai'i's Plantation Village is located on the northwest side of Pearl Harbor. It contains more than 30 authentic plantation homes from the 1800s and early 1900s, when immigrants from various countries, including Japan, the Philippines and Portugal, came to Hawai'i to work and settle, contributing to the state's cultural diversity.

The Arizona Memorial shuttle-boat dock and visitor center.

O'AHU

Attractions East of Honolulu

A circle drive east of Waikiki is a pleasant, day-long outing. If you plan to snorkel at Hanauma Bay, you should proceed in a counter-clockwise direction and try to be there by 8:00 a.m. (before the parking lot is full and no further admissions are allowed until the early arrivals start leaving later in the day). The scenic drive along the coastal side of Diamond Head is often as quick a route as the main highway (which can become clogged with traffic). This pleasant seaside route winds through an upscale residential district.

Along the way is **Maunalua Bay**, where you can arrange to parasail, jetski, scuba dive, wake-board, waterski or take a glass-bottom boat ride at Hawai'i Water Sports Center, located at Koko Marina.

Hanauma Bay State Beach Park is in danger of being loved to death. A flooded, volcanic crater, Hanauma Bay attracts an abundance of fish whose high concentration has made this nature reserve (established in 1967) the most popular snorkel site on O'ahu. The bay's white sandy bottom, clear waist-deep water and multitude of colorful fish makes it the perfect snorkel-ing beach. By the 1990s, the park was receiving three million visitors a year, their overwhelming presence a growing threat to the bay's fragile ecosystem. In 2002, new regulations were introduced

Snorkelers of all ages enjoy the natural beauty of Hanauma Bay.

to limit visitors and protect the reef through strict guidelines for visitors, such as no feeding of the fish and no walking on the reef.

A nine-minute educational film must be viewed before you are allowed access to the beach, which is a short walk or tram car ride down the hillside from the Marine Education Center. Tour buses are no longer allowed into the park; their passengers view the bay from a nearby overlook. Only 300 cars are allowed into the parking lot at one time, which opens at 6:00 a.m. Once the lot is full, which it often is by 8:30 a.m., you must wait until others leave before you can enter. Admission to the park is $5.00 (children are admitted free), and you can rent snorkel gear for $6.00. There are no food stands, so bring a bagged lunch if you plan on staying the day.

Halona Blow Hole is a lava tube that shoots sea water skyward when large waves rush in.

The lookout for the blow hole is accessed from a roadside parking lot. To the right of the lookout, when looking seaward, is a pocket beach where the famous beach scene in *From Here to Eternity*, starring Burt Lancaster and Deborah Kerr, was shot. To the

(Below) The beach featured in From Here to Eternity. (Bottom) Sandy Beach.

(Above) Waimanalo Beach.

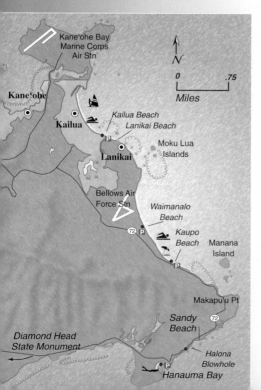

left is a view of **Sandy Beach Park**, famous for its high-risk boogie boarding and bodysurfing in conditions suitable only for experts.

Makapu'u Point marks the beginning of O'ahu's windward side, where Makapu'u Beach is popular with experienced boogie boarders. Nearby is **Sea Life Park**, which specializes in interactive experiences with dolphins and other marine life. Visitors can wade into a pool filled with Hawaiian brown stingrays or climb down a ladder into a coral reef tank for a close view of feeding fish and reef sharks.

Waimanalo Beach County Park is a lovely stretch of sand that is good for swimming and boogie boarding, and is ideal for learning to body surf with its gentle surf and weak currents. The sandy bottom means you can walk out to the waves, which rarely exceed three feet (1 m). Locals gather here on weekends to picnic in the shaded area near the beach.

Lanikai Beach, backed by luxury homes, is widely touted as one of the best beaches on O'ahu. There are, however, no facilities and access is off residential streets where parking is limited. A number of celebrities reportedly own homes along this exclusive stretch of sand.

Just north of Lanikai is two-mile-long (3.2-km) **Kailua Beach Park**, a stunning beach with park facilities that include

O'AHU

a large parking lot, restrooms, showers, a picnic area and lifeguards. A good swimming beach, Kailua is perfect for sailboarding and kite boarding with its smooth waters and steady breezes. Sailboards, kite boards, boogie boards, kayaks and snorkel gear can be rented here. Lessons are also available, as are guided kayaking adventures to secluded beaches.

O'ahu's North Shore & Attractions Along the Way

Called 'the country' by Honolulu residents, the island's north shore is an hour's drive from Waikiki – if you make no stops along the way. This is the quiet part of the island, except for the crash of surf during the winter months when world-class surfers ride the waves at Sunset Beach, Banzai Pipeline and Waimea Bay. There are two main routes to the north shore – the coastal highway that runs along the east coast or the high-

(Above) Kailua Beach. (Below) Lanakai Beach. (Bottom) Aerial view of these east coast beaches.

O'AHU

way that runs through the middle of the island, thus allowing travelers to complete a circle drive there and back.

Leading northwest from Honolulu over the Ko'olau mountains are the Likelike Highway (63) and the Pali Highway (61), the latter with Nu'uanu Pali Lookout at its crest. Both highways connect with the coastal highway.

Bydo-In Temple, nestled in the Valley of the Temples, is worth a stop while traveling the Kahekili Highway (83). This replica of the 900-year-old Bydo-In of Uji, Japan, was built in 1968. The temple's landscaped gardens create a sublime setting in which to contemplate the teachings of Buddha. Two miles (3.2 km) up the highway, where it hugs the shores of Kaneohe Bay and its ancient fishponds, is Kualoa Ranch – a 4,000-acre working cattle ranch where horseback riding and narrated tours take visitors into Ka'a'awa Valley, where *Jurassic Park* and other Hollywood movies have been filmed.

Beach parks dot the windward coast, where many of the tiny offshore islands are seabird sanctuaries. Near the north end of the island is **La'ie**, a rural community surrounded by sugar cane fields and home to one of O'ahu's most popular attractions – the

(Top) The scenic drive north.

(Middle) Bydo-In Temple.

(Bottom) Mokoli'i Island, a.k.a.
Chinaman's Hat.

Polynesian Cultural Center. Founded in 1963 by the Church of Jesus Christ of Latter-day Saints, and staffed with international students from adjacent Brigham Young University-Hawai'i, this 42-acre site is the place to immerse yourself in Hawaiian culture and enjoy an authentic lu'au with music, dancing and a stage show featuring 100 performers. Eight nations of Polynesia are represented at the Center, their re-created villages bordering a man-made lagoon, where visitors are transported from village to village by canoe. Each afternoon at about 2:30 there is a waterborne parade called Rainbows of Paradise in which the performers are transported by double-hulled canoe.

University students are ready to greet visitors to the Polynesian Cultural Center.

The college students employed at the center act as hosts and entertainers, their tuition covered by a work-study agreement between the university and the Polynesian Cultural Center, which has enabled over 13,000 BYU-Hawai'i students to work their way through school. Visitors can experience first-hand the daily activities of the early Polynesians as they mingle with their student hosts and partake in various activities. The center also features museum stores offering works by Polynesian artists, and a missionary complex built in the 1850s style. The center is open Monday through Saturday, and tickets range from basic admission to all-day packages that include the evening lu'au, which serves non-alcoholic beverages. (www.polynesia.com)

Down the road from the Center is the Hawai'i Temple, an imposing white structure built in 1919 by the Church of Jesus Christ of Latter-Day Saints. Often called the Taj Mahal of the Pacific, its gardens and visitor's center are open daily to the public.

Kahuku Point is the northernmost point of O'ahu, backed by coastal plains where sugar plantations once thrived. A hotel first opened on nearby Kuilima Point in 1972. Called Del Webb's Kuilima Resort Hotel, it is now the luxury **Turtle Bay Resort**

O'AHU

(see pages 152 & 165). The green sea turtles for which Turtle Bay is named are not as abundant as they once were, but you can still see them surfacing for air on calm days, especially early in the morning when they come in-shore to feed. In winter, the waves breaking off Kuilima Point attract world-class surfers. Just around the point is **Kuilima Cove,** where the sheltered waters are ideal for swimming and snor-keling. The scenic 17th green of the resort's Arnold Palmer Course is near Kahuku Point.

The North Shore's famous surfing beaches line the coastline between Sunset Point and Waimea. This is where the world's best surfers ride waves up

(Top left) Kuilima Cove. (Left)
Kuilima Point. (Opposite)
Arnold Palmer Course's 17th
hole near Kahuku Point.

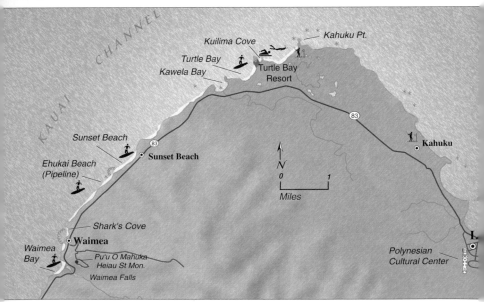

Kuilima Cove
Kahuku Pt.
Turtle Bay
Kawela Bay
Turtle Bay Resort
CHANNEL
KAUAI
83
Kahuku
Sunset Beach
83
Sunset Beach
Ehukai Beach
(Pipeline)
N
0   1
Miles
Shark's Cove
Waimea
Waimea
Bay
Pu'u O Mahuka
Heiau St Mon.
Polynesian
Cultural Center
Waimea Falls

to 25 feet (7.6 m) in height. These beaches are unsafe for swimming in winter and even beachcombing can be dangerous when waves breaking on the beach are powerful enough to knock people down and drag them out to sea. The parking lots at **Sunset Beach** and **Banzai Pipeline (Ehukai Beach Park)** are across the road from the beaches; at **Waimea Bay Beach Park**, the parking lot is adjacent to the beach. Winter waves crashing ashore here are

known to roll right up to the restrooms, some 100 yards from the beach.

Sunset Beach, site of the World Cup of Surfing each winter, is calm and good for snorkeling in summer. Neighboring **Ehukai Beach** is the site of the famous **Banzai Pipeline,** where winter waves take on a tubular shape; expert surfers will momentarily disappear inside these barrel waves.

Shark's Cove is located next to the Pupukea Marine Life Conservation District and is ideal for snorkeling in the summer months when the water is calm. Divers also take advantage of the sandy beach's water entry and the opportunity to explore the sea caves around Kalalua Point.

(Left) A north shore surf shop.
(Below) The summertime surf break off Kuilima Point.

(Above and right) Waimea Bay.
(Bottom right) In summer, kids
enjoy leaping from Jump Rock.

In summer, from July through September, the waters of **Waimea Bay** are fairly calm and families come here to swim, favoring the far side of Pinball Point. Jump Rock is a popular place for kids to leap into the water during the summer, unlike the winter when the seas around this rock outcropping are horrendous. The largest surfable waves in the world (30 or more feet/9 or more meters) roll into Waimea Bay during the winter months.

You can reach an overlook that provides a stunning view of **Waimea Bay** by taking the narrow winding road that ascends the hillside off Pupukea Road up to the **Pu'u O Mahuka Heiau State Monument**. This is the site of an ancient *heiau*, the largest on O'ahu, and has been designated a national historic landmark.

(Top) Pu'u o Mahuka Heiau.
(Left) Captain George
Vancouver.

Overgrown paths lead from the main altar area to several hilltop viewpoints above the Waimea River, where it enters the ocean at Waimea Bay.

A bronze plaque beside the *heiau* makes reference to an incident that took place in May of 1792 when the British supply ship *Daedalus*, under the command of Lieutenant Richard Hergest,

stopped here on its way to the Pacific Northwest to rendezvous with Captain Vancouver's ships. Onboard the *Daedalus* was an astronomer named William Gooch who was to join Captain Vancouver's expedition. While their ship was anchored at Waimea Bay, tragedy befell Hergest and Gooch. In a foolhardy fashion, they ventured ashore unarmed to collect water, despite warnings from a young Hawaiian man accompanying them that no chief was present to restrain the crowd should any misunderstandings arise.

While the two Englishmen wandered away from the watering place to visit the nearby village, one of their crew collecting water became involved in a fracas and was killed. Afraid that Hergest and Gooch would exact revenge, the guilty Hawaiians seized the two English officers upon their return, stripped them of their clothes and marched them up the hillside to Pu'u O Mahuka Heiau, where they were murdered and dismembered, their body parts shared among seven chiefs. Captain Vancouver later tried three of the men accused of this crime onboard his ship the *Discovery* while at anchor off Waikiki. The three were found guilty and put to death by their own chief. Their public execution took place in a double canoe alongside the ship with a pistol shot to the head.

The **Waimea Valley Park** is an historic nature park featuring hundreds of species of documented tropical plants and a trail leading to Waimea Falls, a 45-foot (14-m) cascade.

Hale'iwa, the service center of the North Shore surfing community, is an historic town of boutiques, art galleries and eateries that was founded in 1832 by the Protestant missionaries John and Ursula Emerson. They built the Queen Lili'uokalani Church, which still stands, as does the structure of their original adobe home across from Matsumoto's Shave Ice. The town's white sand beach is good for swimming year-round.

(Top right) Pineapple plants are on display at Dole Plantation.
(Right) Visitors pose in front of a banyan tree in Waimea Valley.

Dole Plantation, located on O'ahu's central plateau of sugar cane and pineapple fields, is a fun place to pause in your tour of O'ahu's countryside and become acquainted with anything and everything about pineapples. The

visitor pavilion and immediate grounds are open daily from 9:00 a.m. to 5:30 p.m. General admission is free, providing access to the pineapple gardens, where you can stroll the paths leading past various signposted varieties of pineapple. There is a fee to ride the Pineapple Express Train on a two-mile (3.2-km) 20-minute narrated tour. There is also a fee to explore the Pineapple Garden Maze, described as the world's largest maze with its 1.7 miles (2.7 km) of paths. Visit

www.dole-plantation.com for tips on buying and serving fresh pineapple, and instructions on how to grow your own pineapple – a process that takes two years!

Schofield Barracks are named for General John M. Schofield, who visited Hawai'i in 1873 to ascertain the strategic potential of Pearl Harbor as an American naval base. Scenes in *From Here to Eternity,* starring Burt Lancaster and Montgomery Clift, were filmed at these military barracks. The barracks are home to the **Tropic Lightning Museum**, opened in 1957 to house and exhibit artifacts of the 25th Infantry Division from 1941 to the present. The museum is open Tuesday to Saturday, from 10:00 a.m. to 4:00 p.m.

(Left) The Pineapple Express Train and visitor pavilion (below) at Dole Plantation

O'AHU

O'ahu's West Coast

This less-visited side of O'ahu is not well known to tourists but is very popular with professional surfers who come to ride the waves at **Makaha Beach**. There are few tourist facilities along this arid stretch of coastline, although a five-diamond Marriott Resort stands near the south end, not far from Kolaeloa (Barbers Point) Harbor. Nearby is Hawaiian Waters Adventure Park.

(Top) Aerial view of Barbers Point. (Above) Green sea turtles.

The west coast is abundant with marine life, such as sea turtles, spinner dolphins and, in winter, humpback whales. **Wild Side Specialty Tours** operates dolphin-watching boat charters out of Wai'anae Boat Harbor, their marine biologist crews providing passengers with the opportunity to snorkel with sea turtles or swim with dolphins without disturbing them. For more information call 808-306-7273 or visit www.sailhawaii.com

Kahe Point Beach Park is a good place to snorkel, although the swimming is not good due to the rocky shoreline here. Also good for snorkeling is the small cove by the Marriott Ihilani Resort at Ko Olina, where an extensive reef has massive fan, antler and lobe coral heads, and is home to green sea turtles and a variety of fish species. This cove, protected by large boulders, is part of the Lanikuhonau historic site where three natural lagoons were considered sacred pools by Hawaiian royalty who would bathe here while partaking in religious rites.

MAUI Driving Times

FROM KAHULUI AIRPORT TO:

Cruise dock:	10 min
Haleakala:	2 hrs
Hana:	2hrs 30 min
'Iao Valley:	25 min
Ka'anapali:	50 min
Kapalua:	1 hr
Kihei:	25 min
Lahaina:	45 min
Wailea:	40 min
Wailuku:	10 min

FROM KAPALUA WEST MAUI AIRPORT TO:

Lahaina:	10 min
Haleakala:	3 hrs
Maui Ocean Ctr:	40 min
Kapalua	15 min
'Iao Valley:	1 hr
Wailea	50 min

CRUISE ROUTES

ROUTES: - - - - -

N

0   5
Miles

Moloka'i Is.

Lanai Is.

Kaho'olawe Is.

PAILOLO CHANNEL

Honolua Bay

Kapalua
Napili

Kahana

Ka'anapali

West Maui
Airport

Lahaina

AUAU CHANNEL

Waihe'e Pt

Wailuku

Kahului

Maui Tropical
Plantation

'Iao
Needle

Maui
Ocean
Center

Honoapiilani Hwy

McGregor
Point

Ma'alaea Bay

Kihei

Wailea

Makena

Makena
State Park

Molokini V

ALALAKEIKI CHANNEL

KEALAIKAHIKI CHANNEL

20°50'

20°40'

Ho'okipa
Beach

Kahului Airport

Lower Pa'ia

Pa'ia

Makawao

Pukalani

Haleaka/a Hwy

Kula Hwy

Kula Lodge

Waiakoa

Rice Park
Lookout

Science
City

Pu'u Ula'ula
10,023'

Polipoli Spring

Tedeschi
Winery

156°20'

Waipilo Bay

Jaws

Kaumahina
State Wayside

Wailua

Ke'anae

Pua'aka'a
State Wayside

Visitors
Center

Haleakala
National Park

Kipahulu Valley

Kahuna Garden

Hana Hwy

Hana

'Ohe'o Gulch
(Seven Pools)

Charles Lindbergh
Grave

CHAPTER THREE

MAUI

Two centuries ago, when the great conqueror Kamehameha brought Maui to its knees, the island was on the verge of having nothing. Today Maui is the island that has everything – the most swimming beaches, the best whalewatching, and a wide assortment of resorts and restaurants. Maui also has excellent snorkeling and is one of the world's premier windsurfing destinations, so it's not surprising that Maui has been called The Best Island in the World.

Dubbed the Valley Isle, Maui consists of two mountain masses connected by an isthmus and a fertile valley. Natural wonders include Haleakala National Park, which contains one of the world's

Ka'anapali Beach, West Maui.

largest dormant volcanoes. Maui also features one of the most scenic coastal drives anywhere – the famous Hana Highway, which winds along a cliff-edged coastline. Major towns include the old whaling port of Lahaina, a national historic site and tourist hub with an array of shops, restaurants and charter boats that depart daily on snorkeling and whale-watching excursions.

MUST SEE: 👁

Lahaina (page 238) an old whaling port and national historic site
Ka'anapali (page 241) Maui's most famous stretch of sand
Haleakala Volcano (page 250) sublime views from the summit
Hana Highway (page 254) stunning coastal scenery

MAUI

MAUI

A Few Fast Facts

Maui is the second largest island of the Hawaiian chain. The island's 120,000 residents (about 10% of Hawai'i's total population) are vastly outnumbered by the 2.3 million visitors their island receives annually. The island's principal port is Kahului, which borders Wailuku (the county seat of Maui). Together, Kahului and Wailuku form the island's largest population center of about 41,000 residents. Maui's chief industry is tourism and its major crops are sugarcane and pineapples. The county of Maui also includes the nearby islands of Kaho'olawe, Lana'i and Moloka'i.

Kaho'olawe Island

This barren, uninhabited island has served as a prison and, starting in 1941, was used as a bombing range. By the 1980s, Kaho'olawe had become symbol-ic of the native Hawaiians' growing movement to reclaim their culture. Outrage at the disregard shown for the ancient sites dotting Kaho'olawe resulted in numerous protest demonstrations, after which the island was returned to state control in the early 1990s for the restoration of its altars and ancient house sites.

Lana'i Island

When Jim Dole, who pioneered Hawai'i's pineapple industry, purchased the entire island of Lana'i in 1922, it became the world's largest pineapple plantation. The last crop of pineapples was grown on Lana'i in 1993 and the island (97 percent of it) is now owned by David Murdock, chairman and chief executive of Dole Food Co. Inc., who has transformed Lana'i into an elite tourist resort offering secluded beaches

The Experience at Ko'ele golf course on the island of Lanai.

and pastoral scenery. You can visit Lana'i by ferry boat on a 45-minute crossing from Lahaina or take a guided boat excursion.

Moloka'i

This island lying off Maui's northwest coast is largely rural and its scenery includes a spectacular 15-mile (24-km) stretch of coast on its north side where sea cliffs – the tallest in the world – rise as high as 3,000 feet (914 m) from the foaming sea at their base. This mountainous wall also separates Kalaupapa Peninsula from the rest of the island and is accessible only by way of a 2,000-foot (610-m) pass. It was here on this isolated point of land that a government leper colony was established in 1860 and where Father Damien selflessly ministered to the sufferers who were quarantined here.

The rest of the island supports cattle ranches and pineapple plantations but the poor soil is unsuitable for cultivating sugar cane. The majority of the island's 7,500 inhabitants are of Hawaiian descent and strive to preserve their ancestors' rural way of life, which is why Moloka'i has been dubbed 'Most Hawaiian Isle.' In 2003, Holland America Line announced it was canceling all scheduled calls to Moloka'i following a request from a Hawai'i State Senator to do so until a community meeting could determine the impact of large numbers of cruise passengers arriving at the small island. Although a court ruling had allowed HAL's ships to continuing calling on Moloka'i, the cruise company complied with the community's wishes. Most cruise passengers now view Moloka'i's scenery from the air, on helicopter tours from Maui.

Halawa Bay on the spectacular north coast of Moloka'i.

Maui's Cruise Ports

Kahului (on the north side of the island) and **Lahaina** (on the west side of the island) are the ports of call for cruise ships visiting Maui. Lahaina is a tendering port but Kahului is a deepsea port, built to handle the shipment of bulk sugar, pineapple and other freight. Norwegian Cruise Line's round-trip Maui cruises use Kahului for a base port. (**For NCL passengers embarking and disembarking on Maui, see 'Where to Stay' on page 232.**)

Getting Around Independently

If your ship is docking in **Kahului**, your best option for exploring the island independently is to rent a car at Kahului Airport (the island's major airport) which is about five miles (8 km) from the port. If your ship is anchoring off **Lahaina**, you can rent a car at Kapalua West Maui Airport, which is 15 miles away.

Overnight parking is available at both ports. When reserving a car, be sure that you have made pick-up arrangements for the correct location: Kahului Airport if your ship is docking in Kahului Harbor; Kapalua West Maui Airport if your ship is anchoring at Lahaina.

Shore Time Suggestions

Besides renting a car or taking an organized shore excursion while docked in **Kahului**, other shore-side options include taking the shopping shuttle to the Queen Ka'ahumanu Center, or walking to Kanaha Beach Park, which is about two miles (3 km) away. Another option is to book through your cruise line (if available) the shuttle to Lahaina (45 minutes each way) or the morning shuttle to Ka'anapali Beach, where you can spend several hours doing whatever you like before catching

A ship's tender heads ashore at the port of Lahaina, Maui.

the afternoon shuttle back to Kahului. Buses operated by Maui Public Transit depart for Maalea / Lahaina and Kihei / Wailea outside the Wal-Mart off Dairy Road, about two miles (3 km) from the cruise port. The one-way fare is $1 or $2 (depending on the route) and the buses run Monday through Saturday.

In **Lahaina**, which is compact and ideal for walking, you could easily spend a half-day at the town's shops and historic sites. A free shuttle runs between Lahaina and Whaler's Village in Ka'anapali every 20 minutes until 2:30 p.m. The bus, which costs $1,

leaves hourly for Ka'anapali from behind the Wharf Cinema Center on Front Street, departing at 25 minutes past the hour and returning at five minutes to the hour. Taxis are metered and the one-way fare to Whaler's Village is about $10.

SHIP-TO-SHORE EXCURSIONS

Helicopter tours are a good way to see Maui's spectacular north shore of sea cliffs and waterfalls, where the Hana Highway winds like a ribbon along the edge of the coast. Some tours include flights over the lunar-like landscape of Haleakala's volcanic crater while others head across Pailolo Channel to Moloka'i Island, where the island's splendid scenery includes sea cliffs that are the highest in the world.

The following is a sampling of Maui shore excursions available through the cruise lines. Times are approximate. For general information on shore excursions, please refer to the Cruise Options section in Part I. **More detail on attractions listed below can be found within this chapter**:
• Haleakala Crater (5 hrs)
• Maui Ocean Center & Iao Valley (3.5 hrs)
• Maui Tropical Plantation & Iao Valley (3.5 hrs)
• Motorcoach drive along the Hana Highway (8 hrs)
• Historic walking tour of Lahaina (3 hrs)
• Kahakuloa Valley (4 hrs)
• Atlantis Submarine (4 hrs)
• Molokini Snorkel (5 hrs)
• Whale Watching (3 hrs)
• Helicopter Tours (2 - 4 hrs)
• Championship Golf (5 - 6 hrs)
• Evening Lu'au (4 hrs)
• Sunset Sail (2 hrs)
• Rainforest Hike (4 hrs)
• ATV Ranch Adventure (4 hrs)
• Zipline Adventure (3 hrs)
• Horseback Riding (3 hrs)
• Bicycling Haleakala (8 hrs)
• Learn to Surf (5 hrs)
• Learn to Windsurf (3.5 hrs)
• Kayak & Snorkel (3 hrs)
• SCUBA diving (5 hrs)
Note: This is a general list of ship-organized shore excursions and these will vary with each cruise line. For more detail, consult your shore excursions booklet (supplied by the cruise line) or log onto your cruise line's website.

(Above) D.T. Fleming Beach.
(Below) Kamehameha Iki Beach.

Beaches

Maui's beaches regularly appear on Dr. Beach's list of 10 best American beaches **(see page 21)**, and several have won top honors. The leeward side of the island is where most of Maui's best swimming and snorkeling beaches are located, including famous **Ka'anapali Beach** (see page 241) which claimed Dr. Beach's first-place ranking in 2003. This three-mile-long beach has good swimming, snorkeling and other watersports. A beach walk connects the hotel resorts, where day trippers can retreat from the sun for lunch or some shopping at Whalers Village.

Kahekili Beach Park lies opposite the train stop at the north end of Ka'anapali. Also known as Old Airport Beach, this is a great place for small children with its calm water and beach park facilities. The beach here is protected by an extensive reef structure that also makes it a prime snorkeling and diving location, especially for introductory dives.

More award-winning beaches lie north of Ka'anapali Beach, in the Kapalua resort area (see page 244). **Kapalua Beach** and **Napili Beach** are both ideal for swimming, and Kapalua Beach (Dr. Beach's first choice for 1991) also offers excellent snorkeling. **D.T. Fleming Beach Park** was named Best Beach on Dr. Beach's 2006 list, and its amenities include lifeguards, showers, picnic facilities, trees for shade and ample parking. In summer the swimming is good, but the surf and currents pick up in winter when bodyboarding and surfing are popular here.

The best swimming beach near **Lahaina** is Pu'unoa Beach (also called **Baby Beach**), which is a 20-minute walk from the tender dock north along Front Street. Just past the Seamen's House & Hospital is a crossroad called Kenui Street that leads down to the beach. Directly south of Lahaina's small boat harbor is the beach at **Kamehameha Iki Park**, suitable for swimming and popular with surfers.

More good beaches lie south of Lahaina. Those stretching the length of **Kihei** are backed by low-rise hotels, while the secluded pocket beaches in **Wailea** (see page 247) are backed by luxury resorts. The parking lot between the Grand Wailea and The Four Seasons provides access to **Wailea Beach**, where there are public restrooms and showers.

Wailea Beach, Dr. Beach's 1999 winner, is ideal for children with its shaded areas, gentle waves and a shallow sandy bottom that slowly drops off to deeper water. The snorkeling here is good and conditions are suited to beginner bodysurfers.

South of Wailea, just beyond the end of Wailea Alanui Road, is a beautiful stretch of sand called **Big Beach**. Located within **Makena State Park**, Big Beach is good for bodysurfing, board surfing and swimming if the seas are calm. A point of land at the base of Pu'u Ola'i separates Big Beach from secluded Little Beach, which attracts nude sunbathers (although this is illegal in Hawai'i).

In the Hana area is beautiful **Hamoa Beach** (see page 259), made famous by James Michener

Lahaina's Baby Beach.

MAUI

who considered it Hawai'i's most 'South Pacific' beach. This pocket beach faces Alenuihaha Channel, so it rarely receives a direct ocean swell. However, any surf breaking offshore rolls onto the beach and, depending on the direction of the swell, often produces good opportunities for bodyboarding.

Surfing & Bodyboarding

The surf break in front of Lahaina is one of the best places on the island to learn to surf. Experienced surfers head to Honolua Bay where they can be viewed from D.T. Fleming Beach Park. On winter days, when the surf exceeds 15 feet (4.5 m) at Jaws (off Maui's north coast), some of the world's best surfers are towed out to sea by jet skis to tackle the waves that form near Kapukanulua Point. This is a remote surfing spot, accessed off the Hana Highway by a dirt road requiring a four-wheel drive.

The bodyboarding is good at Kamaole III Beach Park in Kihei, at D.T. Fleming Beach in Kapalua, and at Wailea Beach.

Snorkeling & Scuba Diving

Most of Maui's shore-accessed snorkel sites lie off the west shore. Beginners can wade into the water at Honolua Bay (a marine preserve), Kapalua Bay and at Black Rock on Ka'anapali Beach (see photo, page 213). You can also snorkel at the three Kamaole Beach Parks in Kihei, at Wailea Beach, and at Ahihi Bay (a marine reserve) near the island's southern tip. Experienced snorkelers often head to South Maui's Makena Landing / Five Caves (Graves) and the marine reserve at La Perouse Bay.

Some of the best snorkeling on Maui requires boat access. At Ma'alea and Lahaina Harbors you can arrange snorkel expeditions to Molokini, Turtle Arches and Coral Gardens; several of these can be booked in advance through your cruise line.

Pacific Whale Foundation operates snorkel tours out of Lahaina and Ma'alaea, as does

The surf break off Lahaina is ideal for beginners.

Maui Dive Shop (1-800-542-3483; www.mauidiveshop.com), which offers snorkel and dive rentals, SCUBA instruction and boat charter service. Maui Dive Shop locations include the Lahaina Cannery Mall, Whalers Village in Ka'anapali and The Shops at Wailea. You can rent gear at Snorkel Bob's near Lahaina Cannery Mall on Front Street in Lahaina.

Molokini Island, a submerged crater lying three miles off Maui's south coast, contains a host of snorkel sites in its remarkably clear waters, where visibility exceeds 100 feet (30 m). Numerous tour boats from Ma'alaea, Lahaina and Kihei bring snorkelers (and scuba divers) to Molokini but the crater area, with its abundant fish life, is large enough to accommodate dozens of snorkelers at one time. Shaped like a crescent moon, Molokini is protected as a state bird sanctuary and a Marine Life Conservation District. The best

(Above) Snorkelers explore the reefs in Honolua Bay. (Below) Molokini crater off South Maui.

snorkeling for beginners is from the shoreline out to about 35 feet of depth. Intermediate snorkelers will enjoy the reefs at the mouth of the crater while advanced snorkelers will want to explore the back side of the crater, which is also a superb wall dive with its 350-foot vertical drop. Other dive sites are Honolua Bay, Kapalua Bay, Black Rock, Wailea Beach, Five Caves/Graves, Ahihi Strip and La Perouse Bay.

Windsurfing & Kiteboarding

With its ideal combination of steady trade winds and consistent surf, Maui offers excellent wind-surfing and kiteboarding along the north shore, from Kahului Bay to Ho'okipa Beach Park. One of the best places to learn either sport is **Kanaha Beach Park** near Kahului Bay (see page 235). Spreckelsville, up the coast from Kanaha, is good for intermediate and advanced windsurfers, while Ho'okipa Beach Park is strictly for the experts – and spectators.

Maui has instituted an 11 o'clock rule for windsurfers and kiteboarders, which allows swimmers and fishermen exclusive

access to Maui's nearshore waters prior to 11:00 a.m. After this time, which is when the local winds usually reach full strength, windsurfers and kiteboarders have shared access to local waters.

Kihei and Ka'anapali on West Maui are also popular windsurfing and kiteboarding beaches, especially when the wind is blowing from the south.

Outrigger Canoe Rides

At the Fairmont Kea Lani in Wailea, instructor Kimokeao Kapahulehua offers lessons in a 45-foot (14-m) canoe while sharing his knowledge about early Polynesian seafarers and teaching the traditional names for each part of the canoe. For registration, call 808- 875-4100.

The Kihei Canoe Club, which meets at the north tip of South Kihei Road at 7:30 a.m., welcomes visitors who want to join one of their experienced crews of paddlers on a one-hour, mile-long voyage in a six-person canoe. Basic instruction is provided, and interested guests need only be punctual. A small suggested donation is appreciated. For more information, call 808-879-5505.

Whalewatching

Humpback whales can be sighted in Hawaiian waters from mid-December to mid-April, and the interconnecting channels that lie off Maui's west coast (called the

(Left) A windsurfer at Ho'okipa.
(Opposite) Kihei Beach.

Lahaina Roads in the days of whaling ships) are a sanctuary for the humpback whales that arrive here each winter to mate, birth and nurse their young. Their numbers have been increasing annually, and each February the Pacific Whale Foundation (PWF), founded by Greg Kaufman in 1980 and based in Kihei, conducts an annual whale count. Volunteers arrive from across the United States to assist with the effort, positioning themselves at a dozen counting stations along Maui's south and west shores, extending from the Ritz Carlton at Kapalua to Pu'u Ola'i, the cinder cone at the south end of Makena Bay.

The PWF is headquartered in Ma'alaea, and admission is free to its interpretive whale center. The PWF also stations a naturalist from 8:00 a.m. to 2:00 p.m. daily at the McGregor Point Lookout's free Whale Information Station. Although humpback whales can be sighted from shore, you might get a closer look from a whale-watching vessel (although sightings are not guaranteed).

A variety of whalewatching boat excursions depart from Ma'alaea and Lahaina harbors, weather permitting. The PWF,

(Left) A humpback calf does a back flip in Ma'alaea Bay.
(Below) An adult humpback slaps the water with its fins.

which has been offering whale-watching cruises since 1980, operates high-tech sailing catamarans out of Ma'alaea and Lahaina harbors. Profits from their cruises support the foundation's education programs and conservation work. (For details, visit www.pacificwhale.org or call 1-800-WHALE11 or 808-249-8811.) You can book some of these whalewatching tours through your cruise line.

The skippers of whalewatching boats must follow strict guidelines when approaching a humpback, such as maintaining a boat speed of less than 13 knots, never leaving the helm, posting a lookout and staying 100 yards (90 m) away from a whale. Despite these precautions, there were a record seven boat collisions with whales during the 2005/06 breeding season. On March 9, 2006, a PWF vessel, the 65-foot *Ocean Spirit*, while on an educational whalewatch cruise carrying about 70 schoolchildren, collided with a humpback calf that suddenly surfaced beneath the vessel. The baby whale was bloodied from injuries to its pectoral fin and head but appeared to be swimming normally when observed later in the day by NOAA Fisheries staff. The skipper of the *Ocean Spirit*, which sustained a damaged rudder in the accident, was following whalewatching guidelines.

Several factors were involved in this accident. Male escort whales were nearby at the time, so the mother and calf may have been under pursuit and trying to evade aggressive suitors. In fact, mothers with calves often swim toward boats when male whales are pursuing them. Also, with several hundred calves being born in Hawaiian waters each year,

Numerous boat excursions are available in Lahaina Harbor.

navigating among them is akin to "driving in a school zone" according to marine biologist David Schofield of the NOAA. Calves need to surface more often (every three to five minutes) than adult humpbacks, which surface every seven to 15 minutes.

Marine Eco Tours

The warm clear waters off west Maui offer excellent visibility and the opportunity to sight dolphins and sea turtles. Boat excursions are available from Lahaina Harbor and Ma'alaea Harbor, including those run by the Pacific Whale Foundation. Atlantis Submarine operates out of Lahaina, as does the *Reefdancer*, a semi-submersible glass-bottom boat. Places visited include Molokini and Lanai, where spinner dolphins are regular sights along the island's south shore.

Golf Courses

Maui's most prestigious golf courses lie along the west side of the island. **Kapalua Bay Resort**, 10 miles (16 km) north of Lahaina, is surrounded by three challenging courses, including its famous **Plantation Course**. Designed on a grand scale by Ben Crenshaw and Bill Coore, the Plantation Course hosts the PGA Tour's season-opening Mercedes Championships (808-669-8877).

Robert Trent Jones, Sr. designed the Tournament North Course (par 71; 6,136 yards) at **Ka'anapali**. With huge rolling greens and unpredictable winds, this course is more challenging than the slightly shorter Resort South Course, which was designed by Arthur Jack Snyder

North Course at Ka'anapali.

and features natural canals, undulating greens and coconut tree boundaries. Lessons, putting greens and a driving range are also available at Ka'anapali (808-661-3691).

There are three courses at **Wailea Golf Club**, the most challenging being the Gold Course, which opened in 1993. It was designed by Robert Trent Jones, Jr., and hosts the Champions Skins Game. A year later the Jones-designed Emerald Course opened. The Blue Course, designed by Arthur Jack Snyder, opened in 1972. The beautiful ocean views at Wailea include wintertime sightings of humpback whales, whose aquatic acrobatics have slowed down play on the course as distracted golfers keep taking their eye off the ball. For tee times, call 808-875-7450 (www.waileagolf.com).

Maui also has some excellent public courses. **The Dunes** at Maui Lani, near Kahului, is a unique course designed by Robin Nelson and featuring holes that wind up, down and around 60-foot-high (18 m) sand dunes. The **Elleair Maui Golf Club** in Kihei, designed by Bill Newis and featuring expansive views, is considered one of the best public courses in Hawai'i.

You can reach Stand-by Golf, Hawai'i's last-minute discount tee service, at 888-645-2665. The cruise lines usually feature several courses in their all-inclusive golf programs.

Kapalua's Plantation Course.

Hiking

Maui's premier hiking venue is **Haleakala National Park**, which contains more than 30 miles (48 km) of high-altitude hiking trails that range in difficulty from easy to extremely strenuous. Park rangers lead guided hikes for which there is no charge. Prepare for a range of air temperatures by dressing in layers.

Polipoli Spring State Recreation Area, which is located at 6,200-feet elevation in the Kula Forest Reserve and reached by a steep, narrow 10-mile road, contains a dozen hiking trails – including the moderate-rated Redwood Trail, which descends 1.7 miles (2.7 km) from the camping/picnicking area through stands of California redwoods and other conifers.

The **Kipahulu** section of Haleakala National Park is locat-

Iao Valley (above) and Haleakala National Park (below) feature hiking trails.

ed 10 miles (16 km) south of Hana and has rainforest trails leading to coastal viewpoints, freshwater pools and waterfalls.

Several state parks offer hiking, including **Wai'anapanapa State Park**, where a coastal trail leads to nearby Hana. The most accessible state park trails are situated in the **Iao Valley State Monument** at the end of Iao Valley Road, which encompasses six acres of nature trails.

The five-mile (8-km) **Lahaina Pali Trail**, which opened to the public in 1997, connects Lahaina with Ma'alaea and was once part of an ancient trail system. The trail climbs to 1,600 feet (488 m) and is hot and arid but offers panoramic views of the coastline. Hikers can park at the unpaved parking areas at either end of the trail.

Waihe'e Ridge Trail in West Maui (see page 246) is another very good hike. For information on Maui's hiking trails, visit www.hawaiitrails.org or call 808-873-3509.

Bicycling

You can rent bicycles all over the island, which features numerous bike lanes and roads with designated shoulders, although traffic can be heavy along the main coastal roads. The most popular cycling route is the downhill ride from the 10,000-foot (3000-m) summit of Haleakala, which most people do on mountain bikes provided by a tour operator. Cyclists are transported to the top of the mountain to embark on the 38-mile (61-km) downhill ride back down to the north coast.

Local art on display beneath the Banyan Tree in Lahaina.

Shopping

In **Kahului** the best shopping is at Queen Ka'ahumanu Center (Maui's largest shopping complex), which you can reach by a shuttle (nominal charge) from the cruise port.

In **Lahaina**, the shops and art galleries are concentrated on Front Street and most are within walking distance. A free shuttle runs every 30 minutes to Hilo Hattie beside the Lahaina Center. Lahaina Cannery Mall is a 30-minute walk from the pier or a $1 bus ride. (Taxi service is $6 each way).

Every Friday night the town's art galleries host Art Night in Lahaina, with guest artists in attendance to discuss their work with visitors who are served *pupu* (appetizers) and wine.

A similar art event is held every Wednesday evening in the galleries located in Shops at Wailea. A free guide to Maui's numerous artists and galleries, called Art Guide Maui, is available island-wide at galleries and specialty stores (www.artguide-maui.com).

Each of the major resort areas has a shopping section, including Whalers Village at Ka'anapali (which you can reach by a free shuttle from Lahaina or a $1 bus ride).

Lu'aus and Hula Shows

To book a lu'au (including transfers) contact your ship's shore excursion office. NCL offers its passengers the Pacific Paradise Lu'au, held at the Maui Prince Hotel on Makena Bay at the south end of the Wailea resort area. Drums of the Pacific Lu'au is held at the Hyatt Hotel on Ka'anapali Beach. The Wailea Marriott hosts a waterfront lu'au on Monday, Tuesday, Thursday and Friday, 5:00 p.m. to 8:00 p.m.

Pacific Paradise Lu'au.

If your ship is overnighting at Lahaina, you may want to attend the **Old Lahaina Luau** held on the waterfront opposite Lahaina Cannery Mall. This authentic lu'au receives rave reviews and has been attended by Robin Williams, Billy Crystal and Jason Alexander. Advance reservations are recommended (1-800-248-5828; www.oldlahainaluau.com).

Also held in Lahaina is the theatrical stage show **Ulalena**, whose singers, dancers, acrobats, drummers and other musicians retell Hawai'i's mythical and historical past by blending authentic chants and hulas with contemporary sounds and rhythms. Produced by Roy Tokujo and staged in the Maui Theatre at 878 Front Street, the music for this spellbinding production was composed by Montreal musicians Michel Cusson and Luc Boivin, who have also contributed to Cirque du Soleil productions. Performances of Ulalena are staged at 6:30 p.m. Tuesday through Saturday. For information or reservations, call 877)-688-4800 or 808-661-9913 (www.mauitheatre.com) or book tickets through your cruise line.

You can see free hula shows at Lahaina Cannery Mall on Saturdays and Sundays at 2:00 p.m. and at Lahaina Center on Wednesdays at 2:30 p.m. and Fridays at 6:30 p.m. when the *keiki* (children) perform.

At Ka'anapali, free hula shows are staged in Whalers Village on Mondays and Wednesdays at 6:30 p.m., and at Ka'anapali Beach Hotel at 6:30 p.m. nightly. The Ka'anapali Beach Hotel also showcases Rudy Aquino, who performs nightly with his group, Lanui, from 6:00 to 9:00 p.m. in the hotel's courtyard.

Dining

There is a plethora of restaurants on Maui, including modest establishments such as **Ruby's** in Kahului for good family dining and **Aloha Mixed Plate** near Mala Wharf in Lahaina for a Hawaiian fast-food lunch.

If you're spending a day at Ka'anapali, try the **Hula Grill** for lunch or dinner. Located in Whalers Village and reminiscent of a 1930s Hawaiian beach house, this beachfront bistro serves regional seafood and is famous for its **Barefoot Bar**, where diners can sink their toes in the sand beneath the shade of palm-thatched table umbrellas.

The upscale resort area of Wailea in South Maui is where you will find cuisine created by

some of the world's finest chefs. Highly touted are **Nick's Fishmarket** at the Fairmont Kea Lani and **Ferraro's Restaurant** at the Four Seasons Resort. Kapalua, north of Ka'anapali in West Maui, offers fine dining at **The Banyan Tree** in the Ritz-Carlton Kapalua. For a memorable lunch on the green, try **The Plantation House Restaurant** at Kapalua or **The Sea Watch** at Wailea.

Mama's Fish House is considered one of the island's best for fresh seafood. This local favorite is perched on a cliff overlooking Kuau Cove, just east of Pa'ia, near the start of the Hana Highway. Reservations are recommended for lunch and dinner, while light fare is available throughout the afternoon in the elegant bar lounge (579-8488).

In Hana, the best place to dine is at the **Hotel Hana-Maui's** elegant open-air dining room overlooking Hana Bay, which serves locally caught fish and organic produce grown in the area. Breakfast, lunch and dinner are served daily, and mid-afternoon

(Above) Waterfront dining in Lahaina. (Below) Hulu Grill at Whalers Village in Ka'anapali.

snacks are available in the **Paniolo Bar**, where live music and hula are performed nightly, Thursday through Sunday. For reservations call 800-321-HANA or visit www.hotelhanamaui.com.

Where to Stay

"I went to Maui to stay a week and remained five," wrote Mark Twain in 1866. "I never spent so pleasant a month before, or bade any place good-bye so regretfully."

Maui's tourist appeal continues to grow, and passengers embarking and/or disembarking in Honolulu can extend their Hawaiian vacation with a pre- or post-cruise stay on Maui. Accommodations are plentiful, ranging from modestly priced condo-hotels to lavish resorts.

Popular resort areas include Kihei, where low-rise condo hotels line the beaches and family restaurants are plentiful. The **Mana Kai Maui** overlooks an excellent swimming beach at the

(Top to bottom) The open-air lobby of the Fairmont Kea Lani; Polo Beach lies in front of the Kea Lani; balconied suites overlook the Kea Lani's grounds.

south end of Kihei and offers condominuiun and hotel room units ($100-$300). South of Kihei is the upscale resort area of Wailea, featuring such luxury hotels as the Four Seasons and Grand Wailea. Also located in this exclusive neighborhood is **The Fairmont Kea Lani**, overlooking quiet Polo Beach. Accommodations consist of one-bedroom suites and private villas with patios and splash pools. Hawaiian activities include outrigger canoe rides, an evening torch lighting ceremony and a childrens program. (www.fairmont.com/kealani; $385-$2800)

The Ka'anapali area, two miles north of Lahaina, was Hawai'i's original master-planned destination resort. One of the first hotels built here at Black Rock was the **Sheraton Maui Resort**, its grounds featuring tropical gar-

(Right) A cliff diver at the Sheraton Maui Resort (below).

dens and man-made lagoons with waterfalls. Each evening at sunset a Hawaiian cliff diver performs a torch-lighting ceremony before ascending Black Rock to toss his blazing torch into the sea and perform a swan dive against an orange sky. The hotel's general manager, Gerald Bahouth, first worked here more than 30 years ago when his father was the resident manager. One evening the scheduled cliff diver took ill, so 14-year-old Gerald – who spent

(Above) Grounds of the Sheraton Maui. (Below) View from Black Rock along Ka'anapali Beach.

his days leaping off Black Rock – was called upon to perform the ceremony. His debut performance earned him a summer job of back-up diver. (www.starwoodhotels.com; $360-$980)

Other hotel resorts in Ka'anapali include the Westin and Hyatt Regency. Low-rise hotels include the **Ka'anapali Beach Hotel,** which has earned the well-deserved label of 'Maui's Most Hawaiian Hotel.' The staff at this modest hotel are schooled regularly in Hawaiian culture and are encouraged to interact with guests, who can partake in a variety of free Hawaiian activities daily. The hotel staff present nightly hula shows and host a complimentary childrens program. The man behind all this aloha is Mike White, who grew up on Oahu and became the hotel's general manager in 1986. White's decision to preserve Hawaiian culture at this hotel initially seemed impractical from a business standpoint, but his initiatives have earned him widespread respect from his employees and the local community, as well as accolades from repeat guests. (www.kbhmaui.com)

North of Ka'anapali is the Kapula resort area where accommodations range from the opulent Ritz-Carlton to more modestly priced properties, such as the **Napili Surf Beach Resort** ($200-$300) where one-bedroom kitchen units overlook lovely Napili Beach.

Central Maui

Kahului and bordering Wailuku form the commercial center of Maui. Historic landmarks include **Ka'ahumanu Congregational** (1837), Maui's oldest church, named after Queen Ka'ahumanu. Also of historic interest is the **Bailey House Museum**, an early missionary home built of lava rock and native hardwoods, containing 19th-century Hawaiian furnishings and artwork.

Located a 20-minute walk from the cruise port in Kahului Bay is **Kite Beach** and adjacent **Kanaha Beach Park**, where conditions are ideal for novice windsurfers and kiteboarders. The onshore breeze always brings beginners safely back to shore, and the nearshore, reef-protected waters remain fairly flat. The NE trade winds blow from 13 to 25 knots along this section of coastline, where they are funneled across Kite Beach into the valley that bisects the island. Near Papa'ula Point, where an approach to Kahului Airport crosses overhead, no kiteboarding is allowed.

Ka'ahumanu Congregational is Maui's oldest church.

Beach park facilities at Kanaha include a grassy area for rigging windsurfers. Windsurfing School of Maui (WSM) is conveniently located on the road leading to Kanaha Beach, where you can book lessons or rent equipment (www.wsmaui.com). Lessons and equipment are also available at Maui Windsurf Company (800-872-099), located in the Maui Mall. Occupying the same building is the Kiteboarding School of Maui (www.ksmaui.com). NCL offers windsurfing lessons as a shore excursion.

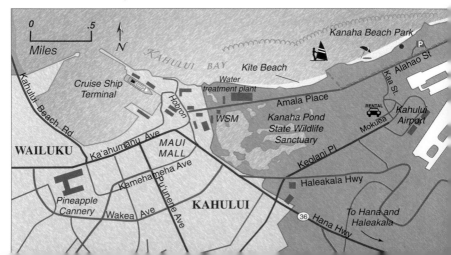

Across the road from Kite Beach is **Kanaha Pond State Wildlife Sanctuary**, a former royal fish pond used by migratory birds and the endangered Hawaiian stilt and coot. The sanctuary's observation pavilion is on the south side of the pond.

Iao Valley

The rising sun often bathes this lush valley with morning light, thus its name Iao, meaning 'supreme light.' Rising abruptly from the valley floor at the head of this amphitheater-shaped valley is the **Iao Needle**, a pinnacle of volcanic rock isolated by erosion from the adjacent ridge. According to an ancient myth, the needle was created by the demigod Maui who turned his daughter's unsuitable lover into a pillar of stone.

Hawaiians called the Iao Needle *kuka emoku* ('standing on a boundary'), aptly describing a landmark that was likely used as a lookout. In 1790 a bloody battle took place in this valley when Kamehameha the Great invaded Maui and staged an assault backed by a large brass cannon that he had acquired in trade. As the Maui defenders retreated into the valley, Kamehameha opened fire on them with his cannon, followed by a pursuit in which his

(Above) Kanaha Beach. (Left) Iao Needle is a Maui landmark.

warriors slaughtered so many men it is said their bodies filled the valley stream, stopping the flow of water.

Today the valley is a tranquil place where park visitors can view the Needle from railed stairs and footbridges. You can also hike further up the valley along nature trails lying within the six-acre Iao Valley State Park. On the way to the state park is the Hawai'i Nature Center, which features the Interactive Nature Museum and Rainforest Walk.

Maui Ocean Center

A person could spend hours scuba diving in local waters before seeing half of the marine life featured in the Maui Ocean Center. This aquarium is one of several that is owned by Coral World International, founded in the mid-1970s by the Israeli billionaire businessman Morris Kahn and the late David Fridman, a world-renowned reef biologist.

Kahn was inspired to build the company's first aquarium at Eilat on the Red Sea after puncturing his eardrum in a diving accident. He envisioned a land-based observatory that provided an opportunity for people without the skills and equipment required for scuba diving to experience an up-close encounter with the underwater world. At Maui Ocean Center, which opened in 1998, the various indoor and outdoor exhibits feature sea turtles, hammerhead sharks, living coral reefs and tropical fishes. The highlight for most visitors is walking through a huge water tank via a clear, 54-foot acrylic tunnel (meant to simulate a walk on the ocean floor) with sharks, rays and other fishes swimming all around you. Admission is $22 for adults and $15 for children. For more info, visit www.mauioceancenter.com.

Visitors linger in the undersea tunnel at Maui Ocean Center.

West Maui

Lahaina

Lahaina is a lively port, with town activities centered around the huge banyan tree beside the old courthouse. An historic whaling port, Lahaina is now a center for whalewatching throughout the winter when humpback whales frequent local waters. Charter boats offering whalewatching, snorkeling and other eco-adventure tours fill the small-boat harbor, and the town's heritage buildings house a wide selection of shops and restaurants as well as museums.

For a time, Hawai'i's king held court in Lahaina. New England missionaries also settled here, establishing a school called Lahainaluna on a hillside overlooking the town (the oldest American school west of the Rocky Mountains) and Hawai'i's first newspaper, Lama Hawai'i (The Hawaiian Luminary) was published at Lahainaluna. David Malo was the first to graduate from Lahainaluna High School in 1831 at the age of 38. He was representative of a new group of highly educated Hawaiians who worked tirelessly to protect the interests of his people. Malo and others pressured the Hawaiian king (Kamehameha III) to accept the principle of representative

(Left) Kerne Erickson's vintage postcard art is sold in local shops. (Below) Until sunk as a dive site, the Carthaginian was a familiar sight in Lahaina harbor.

government. The legislature met in Lahaina until 1844, after which sessions were held in Honolulu. Malo's gravesite is about 50 yards (46 m) above the large, whitewashed 'L' that's visible on a slope above Lahaina.

The huge New England whaling fleet began descending annually on the tiny island kingdom of Hawai'i after two New Bedford whaling ships took, in 1819, an offshore whale that yielded more than 100 barrels of oil. Lahaina became a major port for the whaling ships, whose crew came ashore looking for everything the missionaries disapproved of. When a law was passed forbidding local women from swimming out to the ships, angry crew lobbed cannonballs at the town, prompting the construction of a fort on the waterfront to maintain law and order, and serve as a prison for drunken and rowdy sailors. The discovery of petroleum in 1859 made whale oil obsolete and brought an end to Hawai'i's profitable place in the whaling industry.

An historic trail runs from one end of town to the other and most points of interest are marked with an interpretive plaque. A walking map is available at the visitor center in the

(Top, right) Lahaina's Front Street. (Middle, right) Ruins of the old fort.

1 **Old Lahaina Courthouse** and detailed maps are displayed in wooden kiosks throughout town.

Historic sites include the **2** **Pioneer Inn**, its original west wing built in 1901 to accommodate inter-island ferry passengers. Famous guests who have stayed here include Spencer Tracy while filming *Devil at Four O'clock*.

Behind the Courthouse is the **3** **Banyan Tree**, brought here from India in 1873. Eight feet tall when planted, the tree now stands 50 feet in height and its branches span about 200 feet, casting shade over nearly two-thirds of an acre. Each May, the International Festival of Canoes is held beneath the Banyan Tree, where master carvers use mallets, chisels and adzes to create a finished canoe from enormous logs of albicia wood. These logs are harvested in Puna on the Big Island, then brought to Kamehameha Iki Park where, using power tools, the carvers shape the logs and hollow them out before moving them beneath the Banyan Tree. The canoes must be built within a two-week window, thus justifying the use of power tools to speed up the process while creating a traditional Polynesian craft.

The **Baldwin House**, on Front **4** Street, is the oldest surviving building In Lahaina and is now a museum. Originally the home of

(Top to bottom) Lahaina's Old Courthouse Visitor Center; Pioneer Inn; Banyan Tree; Seamen's Hospital.

Reverend Dwight Baldwin, it was built with coral, stone and wood in 1834. At the far end of Front Street, heading toward Ka'anapali, is the privately owned **Seamen's Hospital** building. **5** It was constructed in the 1830s to house King Kamehameha III's court and was later used as a hospital for whalers.

The arts and skills of ancient Hawaiians are displayed in Hale Kahiko, a free exhibit at the **Lahaina Center** on Front Street where visitors can stroll through a replica 1,000-square-foot village of thatch-roof *hale kahiko* (ancient houses).

Taking a ride on the historic **Lahaina-Ka'anapali & Pacific Railroad** (called the Sugar Cane Train) represents a step back in time to Maui's plantation days. The one-hour ride from Lahaina to Ka'anapali and back is along tracks once used to transport sugarcane to the mill for processing (808-667-6851; www.sugarcane-train.com).

Locals enjoy a game of chess on the Lahaina seawall.

Ka'anapali

It was the stunning three-mile stretch of beach that sealed Ka'anapali's fate to become one of Hawai'i's most popular resorts. This is a former plantation region, where a train once offloaded shipments of sugarcane at a wharf near Black Rock, and where a nearby camp was home to immigrant families who worked the cane fields. Following WWII, the place was all but deserted. Then, in the early 1960s, a development company

The Sugar Cane Train.

decided to build Hawai'i's first planned resort. A small airport was constructed and the brush was cleared to create golf courses and beachfront hotels.

Today Ka'anapali Beach is a world-famous tourist destination and the action here is non-stop. Visitors can enjoy many water-sports activities, including snorkeling, windsurfing, parasailing and kayaking. Hotel resorts line the beach, and shops and restaurants are located at **Whalers Village**, which also houses a free museum displaying artifacts from the golden era of whaling (1825-1860). The shuttle from Lahaina disembarks passengers at Whalers Village, where parking is also available.

The **Ka'anapali Beach Walk** runs south from Black Rock, past hotel resorts and beach activity kiosks. Historic sites located along the Ka'anapali Beach Trail are marked with a lava-rock monument shaped like Pu'u Keka'a (Black Rock). Free 90-minute tours (reservations required) take place every Tuesday and Friday at 9:00 a.m., departing from the Royal Lahaina Resort at the north end and terminating at the Hyatt Regency Maui at the south end. For self-guided tours, a walking map is available at the Ka'anapali Beach Resort Assn. office (2530 Keka'a Drive; 808-661-3271).

(Top to bottom) Whalers Village; Ka'anapali Beach Trail; Ka'anapali Beach viewed from Black Rock.

Black Rock

In ancient Hawai'i, Pu'u Keka'a (Black Rock) was a sacred spot, where the souls of the dead leaped from earth to their ancestral spirit land. According to legend, no one dared leap from Pu'u Keka'a for fear they would never return. This myth was shattered by King Kahekili, who lived in Ka'anapali for most of his rule from 1750 to 1794, and was known for his fearless athletic feats. One day Kahekili leaped from Pu'u Keka'a and swam back to shore unscathed, earning the respect of his warriors, and the title 'King of the Spirit Leap.'

A staff member of the Sheraton Maui enacts the traditional leap from Black Rock every evening at sunset. Attired in the traditional *malo* (loincloth) of an ancient Hawai'ian warrior, the diver lights the torches set on the crest of the rock, then makes the ceremonial offering of the flower lei, lifting it to the sky in all four directions before tossing it onto the water far below and diving in afterwards.

During daylight hours, the snorkeling is excellent along the underwater lava rock ledge skirting Black Rock where sea turtles frequent the overhang.

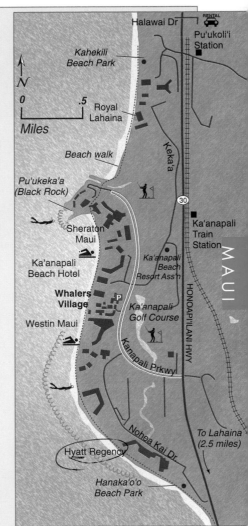

A cliff diver performs the nightly torch lighting at Black Rock.

Kapalua

Lava-rock peninsulas shelter the five bays of Kapalua, another planned resort of beautiful beaches and golf courses on West Maui's northwest side about five miles north of Ka'anapali. When the Maui Land & Pineapple Co. began planning the Kapalua Resort in 1975, it set aside Stable Beach at Honokahua Bay as a beach park and renamed it for David Thomas Fleming (1881-1955) who had been the manager of nearby Honolua Ranch when it was converted to a pineapple plantation. Meanwhile, the beach at Kapalua Bay, which locals had been calling Fleming's Beach, was restored to its original name of Kapalua Beach.

Kapalua Beach is an ideal beach for swimming and snorkeling, and features public restrooms and showers. If the parking lot is full, an excellent and quieter alternative is **Napili Beach**, just around the point from Kapalua Beach. Napili Beach is also sheltered from the surf and offers good swimming and snorkeling. Enter along Napili Place and park under the trees near the Napili Surf Beach Resort.

Another excellent beach in the Kapalua area is **D.T. Fleming Beach Park**, which is popular with locals and visitors alike. The swimming is good from May to September and, because the

(Left) Kapalua Beach and neighboring Napili Beach (below).

MAUI

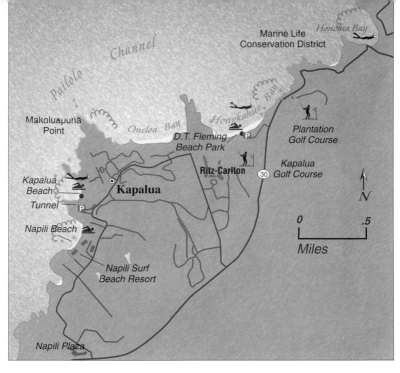

beach has a steep bottom, the waves are often good enough for bodysurfing. In winter, northwest swells wash onto the beach and at times there are rip currents and backwash. Lifeguards are always on duty here. The **Ritz-Carlton Kapalua** overlooks the south end of the beach where, during the five-diamond hotel's construction in the early 1990s, an ancient burial site was discovered. The Honokahua Preservation Site was established and the hotel's construction site moved up the hill behind it.

A mile past D.T. Flemming Beach Park is **Honolua Bay** (see

D.T. Fleming Beach Park.

photo, page 221), which is a nature reserve and prime snorkel and dive site, with good surfing during the winter.

It is possible to drive right around the top end of west Maui but the curves in the road get sharper and eventually the asphalt narrows to one lane. Vehicles slow to a crawl in a places but the challenging drive is well worth the spectacular cliff-top vistas that await. Scenic places along this remote and rugged coastline include **Kahakuloa Valley**, where residents of the local village have cultivated taro for hundreds of years. Kaukini Art Gallery is a popular stop a few miles south of Kahakuloa. Further south, opposite Waihe'e Point, is a turn-off leading inland on Maluhia Road to the trailhead for **Waihe'e Ridge Trail**, which starts at 1,000 feet (305 m) elevation and climbs the windward slope of west Maui through guava thickets and scrub forest. Views along the way include Waihe'e Gorge and Makamakole Gulch. If the weather is clear, you will be rewarded with panoramic views of West Maui upon reaching the summit (2,563 feet). The trail is 2.5 miles long and of moderate difficulty.

(Left) A narrow highway skirts the headlands north of Kapalua. (Below) Kahakuloa Valley.

MAUI

South Maui

Resorts and beaches line the leeward coast of South Maui, from
Kihei's Sugar Beach at the north
end to Makena State Park's magnificent Big Beach at the south
end. In between is the planned
resort of **Wailea**, where luxury
hotel resorts have been designed
to blend with a pleasing landscape of undulating golf links and
scalloped shorelines, and where
pocket beaches present ideal set-
tings for swimming and snorkeling in sheltered waters. A public
beach walk connects the quiet
beaches and luxury waterfront
resorts of Wailea, winding past
bordering gardens that feature
rare native flora and historic
points of interest. All beaches
have public access, and several
parking lots are located nearby.

(Top and middle) Wailea beach
walk. (Bottom) The Wailea
Marriott hosts a regular lu'au
in its oceanfront gardens.

Renaissance
Wailea Resort
PA, Showers/
Restrooms
WAILEA
Marriott
Wailea
Shops at   Grand
Wailea   Wailea
PA, Showers/
Restrooms
Four
Seasons
Fairmont
Kea Lani Maui   PA - Public Access

Makena

0   .5

Miles

Keawala'i
Church
Malu'aka
Beach
Maui
Prince
Oneuli
Beach
Makena-La Perouse
Bay State Park

Oneloa (Big)
Beach   *Big Beach*

'Ahihi-Kina'u
Natural Area
Reserve

KEAWALA'I
FOUNDED 1832

Maui Prince, the southern-most resort in the area, is at the south end of Malu'aka Beach. To the north, is **Makena Landing**'s popular snorkeling spot called Five Graves. Nearby is **Keawala'i Church**, a stone structure built in 1855. Part of the church's Sunday sermon is delivered in Hawaiian, along with some of the hymns.

Makena-La Perouse Bay State Park lies south of Makena Bay, just beyond the end of Wailea Alanui Road. A prominent feature of this extensive wildland park is a red cinder cone called Pu'u Ola'i. Stretching south-ward from this red-colored hill is Big Beach, from which a path leads over Pu'u Ola'i to secluded Little Beach, which attracts nude sunbathers.

Ahihi-Kina'u

The coast beyond Big Beach becomes increasingly rugged, with the rocky shorelines of Ahihi Bay and La Perouse Bay offering excellent snorkeling and scuba diving. Black lava rock from Haleakala volcano lies alongside the road, which ends at La Perouse Bay – named for the French explorer who anchored here in 1786.

East Maui

Upcountry

Maui's eastern half is dominated by sprawling Haleakala volcano. Several roads lead up the mountain's western flank, where sugarcane and pineapple fields lying at its base gradually give way to tall eucalyptus and jacaranda trees. This upcountry area of Maui is one of grassy ranchlands and flower farms that thrive in the highland climate and rich volcanic soil. Among the crops grown here are giant strawberries and sweet Kula onions.

A handful of small towns dot the upcountry, its hub being **Makawao**. Founded by *paniolo* (cowboys) in the 1800s when cattle were first introduced to the island, Makawao is nestled in the rolling hills just off Haleakala Highway. Baldwin Avenue is lined with fine-art galleries and restaurants and is fronted with hitching posts. This 'wild west' town hosts an annual 4th of July parade and rodeo, but you're less likely to see cattle stampeding through town than you are bicyclists coasting through on their ride from Haleakala's summit.

Just past Makawao, the Kula Highway branches off from the Haleakala Highway and climbs to about 3,000 feet. Attractions along this road include the **Rice Park lookout** where picnickers can enjoy panoramic views. From here a short detour up Kekaulike Avenue leads to **Kula Botanical Garden**, which features nature walks amid its collection of native plants. Further along the Kula Highway is the Ulupalakua Ranch, home to **Tedeschi Winery**, Maui's only vineyard. Tedeschi first introduced a pineapple wine (Maui Blanc) in 1977, followed by a grape wine (Maui Brut). Wine tastings and purchases are available in the King's Cottage, built in 1874 for King Kalakaua and his wife Queen Kapiolani, who frequently visited the ranch.

An upcountry orchid farm.

Haleakala National Park

Haleakala volcano is 10,023 feet (3,055 m) high and has been dormant since the mid-1700s. Its crater, one of the largest in the world, is an erosional depression that is 2,720 feet (829 m) deep, with a circumference of 21 miles (34 km). It was formed by the erosional forces of water, wind and possibly glaciers. Two valleys with amphitheater-like heads slowly converged at the mountain's summit where they formed a huge basin (the crater). Subsequent lava flows created cinder cones, the tallest of these standing 500 feet (150 m) from the crater floor.

The park is home to rare Hawaiian forest birds as well as the nene (Hawaiian Goose) and the rare silversword plant. The park encompasses 36 miles (58 km) of hiking trails, including the Sliding Sands Trail, which descends to the crater floor. The crater, barren but starkly beautiful, resembles a lunar landscape and was used to train some of NASA's Apollo astronauts for moon landings in the 1960s.

Several private operators offer tours within the park, including half-day trail rides into the crater and downhill biking on the park road. The latter involves motor transportation to the summit, followed by a bicycle ride back down the mountain, either as a group riding single file or independently (depending on the tour booked).

Haleakala is considered sacred ground by the Hawaiian people, whose ancestors venerated the sun for its life-giving force. They believed that Pele, the goddess of fire, created the row of 16 cinder cones that extends from Haleakala's summit down its eastern flank into the ocean off the tip of Haneo'o near Hana. Along this sacred alignment of hills they built over 300 *heiaus* (temples of worship), the highest

Sunrise at Haleakala

MAUI

concentration in the Hawaiian archipelago.

Today visitors by the hundreds drive to the summit of Haleakala in the pre-dawn darkness to pay homage to the sun rising over Maui. As the first rays of light shine across the massive crater, warming the pink sky, the panoramic view is stunning. The island of Maui lies at your feet and across the water are the distant volcanoes of Mauna Kea and Mauna Loa on the Big island, their peaks poking through the clouds.

Haleakala commands respect from all who visit. Few fail to be humbled by the immensity of the volcano's crater and eroded valley, which form a vast cinder desert. Time on top of Haleakala is measured not in years, not in centuries, but in eons, back to when Haleakala first began forming on the ocean floor.

The sunrise views will vary with the amount of cloud cover that morning. The time of sunrise

and sunset changes throughout the year and is anywhere from 5:30 to 7:00 each morning and evening. To check on the exact time of sunrise and sunset for the day you will be visiting, visit the National Park Service website at nps.gov/hale or call the National Weather Service (877-5111) for a taped message. The weather is unpredictable at the summit,

(Top) Cyclists prepare for their descent. (Right) Silversword plant. (Below) A cinder cone along Sliding Sands Trail.

MAUI

MAUI

where conditions are often wet and windy. There are no weather predictions available for sunrise, but the sunset viewing conditions are more foreseeable.

It takes about 1.5 hours to drive from Kahului to the summit and there is a $10 entrance fee per vehicle to the park (which is valid for seven days and includes entry to the Kipahulu section of the park, which is accessed along the highway past Hana). The road leading up to Haleakala's summit is not lit and there is no food, clothing or gasoline for sale in the park, which is open all the time. (The Kula Marketplace, next to the Kula Lodge just before Haleakala Crater Road, is open daily from 8:00 a.m. to 7:00 p.m. and food items sold here include ready-made box lunches.)

The Haleakala Visitor Center does not open until 7:30 a.m., so early-morning visitors must be prepared to brave the elements and should dress accordingly. The weather is unpredictable and temperatures at the summit range between 32° and 65° F. (sometimes dipping below freezing if there is a wind-chill), so bring a warm jacket or sweater and a rain slicker in the event of heavy rain. Also bring a hat and sunscreen if you plan to go hiking, because the sunlight can be intense when there is no cloud cover.

The summit area features over 30 miles (50 km) of hiking trails and park wardens regularly give guided hikes. Check at the Park Headquarters Visitor Center (7,000 feet/2134 meters) or the Haleakala Visitor Center (9,740 feet/2969 meters) for that day's scheduled hikes. Free maps are also available. Trails range from the Hosmer Grove Trail, an easy half-mile loop through native alpine shrubland, to challenging all-day hikes. The Keonehe'ehe'e Trail (also called Sliding Sands Trail because of its steepness and soft cinder base) descends to the valley floor and is an extremely

A picnicking couple enjoys the view atop Haleakala.

strenuous trail; you can also take a half-day hike from the trailhead to the first cinder cone (Kalu'uoka Oo), which is five miles roundtrip.

When hiking the summit-area trails, be aware that the lower concentration of oxygen can cause a shortness of breath, as well as nausea, headaches and dizziness. Allow twice as long to climb back up a sloped trail as for hiking down. Hiking along a soft cinder trail is similar to walking across a sandy beach.

The Haleakala Visitor Center is located near the crest of Pu'u Ulaula (Red Hill), the highest elevation on Maui. In the immediate vicinity and just beyond the park boundary is a collection of telescope facilities run by the U.S. Air Force and the University of Hawai'i. The Haleakala High Altitude Observatory Site is above one-third of the earth's atmosphere and the 'seeing' conditions here can be as good as on the Big Island's Mauna Kea.

First protected as parkland in 1916, Haleakala crater (along with the Kipahulu Valley) became Haleakala National Park in 1961. Eight years later, the Kipahulu coastal area of Ohe'o was added to the park. The only access to Ohe'o Gulch is via the coastal highway extending past Hana. The lush and fertile Kipahulu Valley, a stark contrast to Haleakala's barren landscape, is a biological reserve that protects Hawai'i's largest intact rainforest ecosystem, and is not open to the public.

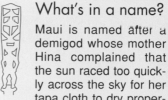

What's in a name?

Maui is named after a demigod whose mother Hina complained that the sun raced too quickly across the sky for her tapa cloth to dry properly. So Maui, known as the trickster, climbed to the top of Mount Haleakala – The Sacred House of the Sun – and waited in the pre-dawn darkness for the sun to appear. Leaping from his hiding place in the roots of an old wiliwili tree, Maui lassoed the emerging sun with a rope and beat it with an adze, breaking its strongest legs. The sun was left with only its weakest legs and henceforth had to crawl slowly across the sky, providing the people of Hawai'i with adequate daylight.

MAUI

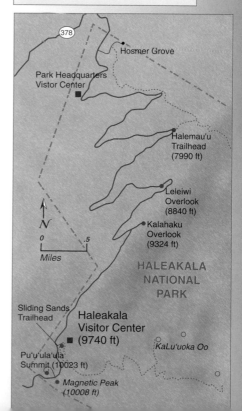

Hana Highway

This famous coastal highway runs along Maui's north coast from Kahului to Hana, a distance of about 50 miles (80 km). The first leg of the highway takes you to **Pa'ia**, an historic plantation town with vintage storefronts. It was founded in 1880 by Samuel T. Alexander and Henry P. Baldwin (of Alexander & Baldwin), who built a sugar mill here. By the mid-1960s, Pa'ia had become a ghost town. Today it offers visitors an interesting collection of boutiques and eateries, and is the last place to get gas before heading east along the winding road to Hana. A half mile east of Pa'ia is **Mama's Fish House**, a clifftop restaurant overlooking Ku'au Cove where some of Maui's best seafood is served.

The middle section of the Hana Highway is a serpentine road that snakes along the cliff-

Coastal overlooks and cascading falls punctuate a drive along the Hana Highway.

edged coastline, past stream-fed waterfalls and across green gorges. The road contains more than 600 curves and 54 one-lane bridges. There are no gas stations along the way and no restaurants, although there are a few roadside stands selling fruit and other items. The many hairpin turns of this narrow road demand slow and attentive driving, which is why some people let a tour operator do the driving so they can enjoy the scenery. If you're driving a rental car, there are numerous spots to pull over and enjoy the cliff-top views of hidden beaches and rocky headlands, many of which are seabird sanctuaries. The road is quieter in the morning.

The following are points of interest along the way.

Waipi'o Bay is where a major naval battle took place in 1791 when Kamehameha the Great's invading fleet of war canoes defeated the Maui fleet.

Kaumahina State Wayside is a rest stop with picnic tables and a sweeping view of the coastline.

Ke'anae Peninsula Lookout offers stunning views; its turnout, when eastbound, is just past the Keanae Arboretum.

Wailua Valley State Wayside provides coastal views of Wailua Village and surrounding taro fields, as well as inland views of the Keanae Valley and Ko'olau Gap in Haleakala's rim.

Pua'aka'a State Wayside is a five-acre park with restrooms and picnicking in a rainforest area of small waterfalls and pools.

A scenic pull-out and picnic stop above Wailua Bay.

Ulaino Road turns off the Hana Highway at the 31-mile (50-km) marker and leads to **Kahuna Garden**, set on a rugged lava coast overlooking the ocean. Part of the National Tropical Botanical Garden, this 500-acre (202-ha) tropical garden contains the world's largest collection of breadfruit trees and one of Hawai'i's last undisturbed native pandanus forests.

Kahuna Garden also provides access to **Pi'ilanihale Heiau** – a massive stone structure built by Pi'ilanihale, a 16th-century ruler of Maui. This five-storey-tall temple, the largest extant *heiau* in the state of Hawai'i, was completely hidden by jungle growth and remained undetected when the first archaeological surveys were done in the early 20th century. Only recently uncovered and opened to public viewing, this multi-tiered edifice remains shrouded in mystery. Pi'ilanihale Heiau can be viewed only when

(Top) Blue Pool. (Above and below) Wai'anapanapa State Park's rugged coastline.

Kahuna Garden is open, Monday through Friday, 10:00 a.m. to 2:00 p.m., by self-guided tour. Admission is $10 for adults, and no reservations are required. The visitor center is just inside the gate.

Ulaino Road also leads to Ka'eleku Caverns, where guided and self-guided tours of Maui's largest lava tube are available. At the end of Ulaino Road is a trail leading to a hidden waterfall and freshwater pool known as Blue Pool. This trail crosses private property and several streams, which become swollen during heavy rains. The growing number of tourists visiting what was once a local hideaway has caused resentment among some of the area's residents.

Wai'anapanapa State Park contains 122 acres of remote coastal wilderness. Its low-cliffed coastline features sea stacks, blow holes and a pocket beach of black sand. Wai'anapanapa means 'glistening waters' and a famous Hawaiian legend is attached to the Wai'anapanapa Caves, in which a princess once hid from her cruel husband. In his search he paused to refresh himself in the cave's cool water, and unexpectedly saw her reflection as he peered deep into the cavern. The park has picnic facilities and there is hiking along an ancient coastal trail (known as the King's Road) that leads south to Hana.

Hana

King Kamehameha's favorite wife Queen Ka'ahumanu was born in a cave at Ka'uiki Head overlooking Hana Bay in 1768. When she returned home with her warrior husband in 1790, they arrived with an enormous fleet of canoes that landed to the south of Hana and was said to blanket the beach for a distance of nearly five miles (eight kilometers). Hana's first sugarcane mill was built near Kauiki Hill in 1849 and the Hana Highway was completed in 1926 as a gravel road. In 1944 a retired entrepreneur from San Francisco named Paul Fagan established the Hana Ranch, bringing a herd of Hereford cattle from Moloka'i. When Hana's last sugar plantation closed in 1946, Fagan opened the Kauiki Inn (now the Hotel Hana-Maui) to attract tourists to the area. When Fagan died in 1970, a lava rock cross was erected in his memory on a hill overlooking the town. The hotel he founded has changed hands several times over the decades and is now owned by Passport Resorts. The 66-room Hotel Hana-Maui, serviced by about 200 employees, is Hana's largest employer. Other accommodations in Hana include a few bed & breakfasts and a condo hotel called the Hana Kai Maui Resort overlooking Hana Bay.

Local attractions are the Hana Cultural Center & Museum on the lower road leading to Hana

(Top to bottom) Hana Bay; Hotel Hana-Maui; Wananalua Church.

Bay, and the Hasegawa General Store, which two brothers from Japan established in 1910, and which the family's fourth generation continue to operate. When the store's brick building (built in 1958) was destroyed by fire in 1990, the family renovated the old Hana Theater and reopened a year later at new premises.

The road beyond Hana continues to snake its way along the coast to several scenic sites, including **Hamoa Beach** (see page 219), **Wailua Falls** and **Ohe'o Gulch**, which is where the Kipahulu Valley descends down to the sea and is part of Haleakala National Park (see page 253). This section of the park, located 10 miles (16 km) south of Hana, features waterfalls, streams and freshwater pools, including the tiered **Pools of Ohe'o** (also known as the Seven Sacred Pools). Park admission is $10 per vehicle (see page 252) and a free map is available at the Visitor Center. A half-mile loop trail leads past a grove of hala trees to an ocean viewpoint at Kuloa Point. People like to leave the trail here and scramble over the rocks to the lower pools of Ohe'o Gulch for a refreshing soak overlooking the ocean. A second cliffside trail traces the shoreline between Kuloa Point and the Kipahulu campground.

A third trail, Pipiwai Trail, is a four-mile (six-km) round-trip trail that traces the Pipiwai Stream and crosses footbridges past waterfalls, freshwater pools and a bamboo forest. A half mile up this trail is Makahiku Overlook, which looks down on a waterfall. The trail ends near the base of **Waimoku Falls**, which cascades 400 feet (122 m); be prepared for slippery mosses and mosquitoes. Pipiwai Stream (like all streams in East Maui) is prone to flash flooding, so check first at the visitor center for local stream conditions.

About a mile past Ohe'o Gulch is **Kipahulu**, which is

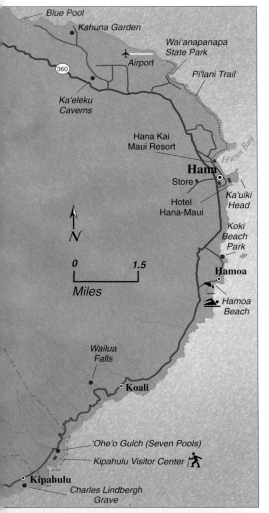

(Above) Hamoa Beach. (Right and below) Pools at Oheʻo Gulch.

where Charles Lindbergh's grave is located in a quiet cemetery next to Palapala Hoʻomau Church, built in 1857. The famous aviator spent his final years in the Hana area where he died in 1974 at the age of 72. The turn-off to the church is at Maui Stables. Nearby are the ruins of an old sugar mill.

The winding road past Kipahulu soon turns into a secondary road, which can be hazardous during heavy rains and is subject to landslides. It eventually diverges from the coast and leads inland to Maui's upcountry.

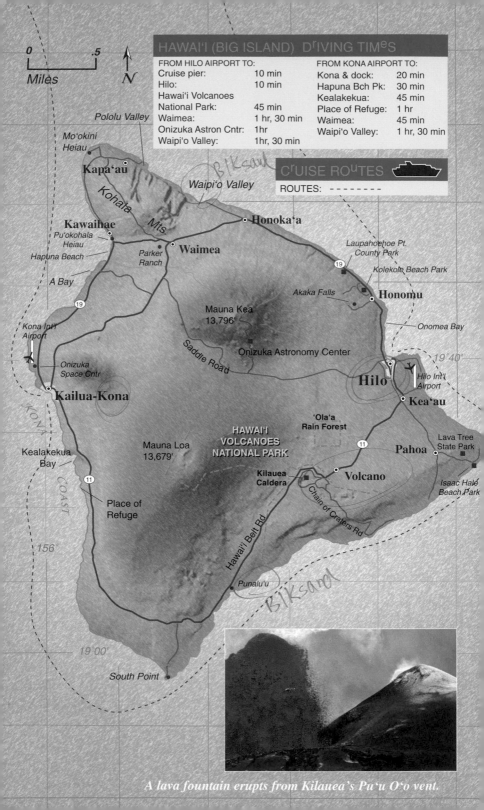

HAWAI'I (BIG ISLAND) DrIVING TIMes

FROM HILO AIRPORT TO:		FROM KONA AIRPORT TO:	
Cruise pier:	10 min	Kona & dock:	20 min
Hilo:	10 min	Hapuna Bch Pk:	30 min
Hawai'i Volcanoes		Kealakekua:	45 min
National Park:	45 min	Place of Refuge:	1 hr
Waimea:	1 hr, 30 min	Waimea:	45 min
Onizuka Astron Cntr:	1hr	Waipi'o Valley:	1 hr, 30 min
Waipi'o Valley:	1hr, 30 min		

0 .... **.5**

Miles

N

CrUISE ROUtES

ROUTES: - - - - - - - -

Pololu Valley

Mo'okini
Heiau

Kapa'au

BIKsaul

Waipi'o Valley

Kohala Mts.

Honoka'a

Kawaihae

Pu'okohala
Heiau

Laupahoehoe Pt.
County Park

Hapuna Beach

Parker
Ranch

Waimea

19

Kolekole Beach Park

A Bay

Akaka Falls

Honomu

19

Mauna Kea
13,796'

Kona Int'l
Airport

Saddle Road

Onizuka Astronomy Center

Onomea Bay

19'40'

Onizuka
Space Cntr

Hilo

Hilo Int'l
Airport

Kailua-Kona

KONA

Kea'au

'Ola'a
Rain Forest

Kealakekua
Bay

Mauna Loa
13,679'

**HAWAI'I
VOLCANOES
NATIONAL PARK**

Pahoa

Lava Tree
State Park

COAST

11

**Kilauea
Caldera**

Volcano

Isaac Hale
Beach Park

156'

Place of
Refuge

11

Hawai'i Belt Rd.

Chain of Craters Rd

Punalu'u

BIKsaul

19'00'

South Point

A lava fountain erupts from Kilauea's Pu'u O'o vent.

CHAPTER FOUR

HAWAI'I
THE BIG ISLAND

The island of Hawai'i is called the Big Island for good reason. Larger than all of the other islands combined, the Big Island encompasses 11 of the planet's 13 climatic zones due to its extreme range in elevation – from sea level to nearly 14,000 feet. When King Kamehameha ruled the Big Island but had yet to conquer the other Hawaiian islands, he and his chiefs enjoyed boasting that the magnitude, population and fertility of their island was equal, if not superior, to all the other islands combined.

Close in size to Connecticut, the Big Island is home to the world's highest island mountain, Mauna Kea, which rises to

Fertile farmland and lush valleys lie at the base of Mauna Kea.

13,796 feet (4,205 m) and supports the largest astronomical facility in the world. Snow falls on its upper slopes in winter, while cultivated crops flourish on its lower slopes.

Rolling ranch land at the northwest end of the island gives way to steep terrain along the northeast side, where waterfalls plunge off cliffs into verdant roadless valleys. Mauna Kea is a dormant volcano, but Kilauea Caldera to the south is among the world's

---

MUST SEE: 👁

Hawai'i Volcanoes National Park (page 271) for an up-close look at an active volcano
Waipi'o Valley (page 279) the legendary Valley of Kings
Kona Coast (page 290) historic bays and excellent snorkeling

Molten lava spills into the sea along Kilauea's East Rift Zone.

largest active craters. Streams of red-hot lava flow down its seaward slope into the ocean, adding to the coastline's blackened landscape of volcanic rock.

The island's South Point (Ka Lae) is the southernmost point of land in the United States. Swimmers who leap from the sea cliffs here are plunging into historic waters, for this could be the very spot where Polynesian voyagers first landed at the Hawaiian Islands. Their remote island kingdom remained undiscovered until the arrival of Captain Cook, whose two ships slowly sailed around the Big Island before landing at Kealakekua Bay on the west side. Today, when cruise ships sail around the Big Island, they linger off the island's southeast shoreline so passengers can enjoy a nighttime view of glowing red lava flowing down the darkened mountainside into the sea. Such a sight puts our human presence into perspective.

A Few Fast Facts

The Big Island's 150,000 residents comprise less than 15% of the state's total population. At 4,038 square miles (10458 sq. km), the Big Island is twice the size of all the other islands combined, and is still growing. The island's two active volcanoes are Kilauea and Mauna Loa ('long mountain'), which rises to 13,680 feet (4170 m) and is massive when measured from the ocean floor. Mauna Loa last erupted in 1984, while eruptions from Kilauea have been continuous since 1983. Gaseous emissions from Kilauea can create a haze referred to as 'vog' which is dispersed into the atmosphere by the trade winds.

Tropical flower farms thrive on the Big Island, where the east side's rainforest climate and light volcanic pumice soil create ideal conditions for cultivating anthuriums and orchids. Known as the Orchid Island, it is the largest producer for the state's tropical flower industry, generating about half of its total annual sales of about $100 million.

The Cruise Ports

There are two cruise ports on the Big Island, located on opposite sides of the island. Most cruise itineraries include a day stop at each port, but a few do not.

Hilo, a shipping center for the region's agricultural products, is located on the island's lush east coast and has docking facilities. Hilo's signature attraction is Hawai'i Volcanoes National Park, a 45-minute drive from the cruise port. Other highlights are the drive up to Mauna Kea's summit and the drive along the scenic Hamakua Coast to Waipi'o Valley.

Kailua-Kona, a tourist center on the island's sunny west side, is a small port providing access to nearby beaches and bays for swimming and snorkeling. Also

NCL's Pride of Aloha lies at anchor off Kailua-Kona.

in the region are major historic sites, Kona coffee farms and the Parker Ranch. At Kailua-Kona, cruise ships drop anchor and tender passengers ashore.

Shore Time Suggestions

It is impossible to see all of the Big Island in one day. With nearly 500 miles of paved road, the Big Island offers many scenic drives and far-flung attractions. Eco-adventure tours are popular with visitors because much of the island is rugged wilderness, dominated by barren lava fields and lush valleys accessible only by mule trails. A great deal of the coastline is laced with hardened lava and studded with black-sand beaches; however, in places you can find pockets of white sand tucked between the black-lava outcroppings as well as several splendid beaches along the island's west coast.

This chapter highlights the east half of the island in the

King Kamehameha

Hawai'i's great warrior king spent most of his life on the Big Island, which is where he was born and where he died. His royal connection with the island is evident in numerous places, including the *heiau* he built at Pu'ukohola to please his war god, and the replica *heiau* at Kailua-Kona where he spent his final years.

While his birth is shrouded in secrecy, as is the location of his remains, he himself was an extroverted man, warm and big hearted with his friends. He ruled his people with iron-fisted benevolence, and dealt shrewdly with foreigners while displaying his aloha spirit in a kingly manner. When he bid a final farewell to Captain Vancouver, who had spent several winters in the Hawaiian islands in the early 1790s, it was noted in the British sea captain's logbook that Kamehameha "in the most affectionate manner took his leave, not only of myself and all the officers, but of every person he saw on deck."

Hilo section and the west half of the island in the Kailua-Kona section. Shore excursions available through the cruise lines appear near the front of each section.

If you plan to rent a car on the Big Island, be sure to reserve one well in advance if you will be visiting during the Ironman Triathlon World Championship held at Kailua-Kona in October, or during the Merrie Monarch Festival in Hilo at Easter time.

Children perform the hula.

Hilo

Hilo is the Big Island's major center with a population of about 40,000. Settled by missionaries in 1822, Hilo is today a shipping hub for the region's crops of sugarcane, macadamia nuts, orchids and papayas. The downtown's historic parks and buildings reflect the city's plantation past, and its handful of hotels – which are modest compared to the beach resorts on the island's west side – are located mostly along Banyan Drive with views across Hilo Bay. Several historic mansions are now bed-and-breakfast establishments, such as the Shipman House on Ka'iulani Street where Queen Lili'uokalani came for tea and where former house guests have included Jack London.

Hilo was for years the location of one of Kamehameha's royal residences, where the arms and

Hilo's cruise port viewed from Reeds Bay Beach County Park.

ammunition he gradually acquired from merchant ships were stored in preparation for an invasion of Maui. He also liked Hilo for the surfing. King David Kalakaua (dubbed the Merrie Monarch for his love of entertaining) enjoyed vacationing in Hilo. A patron of the arts, King Kalakaua revived the hula when he ascended the throne in 1874 and Hawaii's most prestigious hula celebration, held annually in Hilo, is dedicated to his memory. Fans from around the world converge on Hilo to attend the week-long Merrie Monarch Festival, which begins on Easter Sunday with a music festival on Coconut Island and continues all week with free noon-day entertainment at hotels along Banyan Drive. The festival's three-day hula competition is always a sold-out event.

HAWAII

Hilo is not immune from natural hazards. Seven times since 1852, lava flows from Mauna Loa have threatened the community, including the most recent 1984 eruption, which sent lava flowing to within five miles (8 km) of Hilo. More devastating were the two tsunamis that swept ashore in the last century. The first struck on April 1, 1946, when an earthquake originating in the Aleutian Trench and measuring 7.4 on the Richter scale, sent a tsunami racing across the North Pacific to Hawai'i. All of the islands were damaged and 159 people lost their lives, more than 90 of them in Hilo, where a massive wave crashed over Coconut Island as it charged toward shore and sent white water crashing through the older downtown and residential areas. The second tsunami struck in May of 1960. It was generated by an 8.3 earthquake in southern Chile and it too sent a massive wave into Hilo Bay, where 60

A massive tsunami wave washes over Coconut Island in 1946.

people drowned.

In the wake of these devastating tsunamis, several measures have been taken to avert future disasters. A broad swath of the Hilo waterfront – where a railroad and commercial buildings once stood – is now grassy parkland upon which no development is permitted. In addition, the Pacific Tsunami Warning System, based in Honolulu, issues evacuation alerts if a suspected tsunami is heading toward Hawai'i.

Hilo's Cruise Port

The ships dock at a large cargo and container facility located two miles (3 km) from Hilo's historic downtown core and three miles (5 km) from the Hilo Airport terminal. Pay phones are available outside the cruise ship terminal. A volunteer greeting program called Destination Hilo offers assistance to cruise passengers coming ashore, and provides a $1 (each way) shuttle between the cruise terminal and downtown Hilo.

HAWAII

SHIP-TO-SHORE EXCURSIONS

Hilo's ship-organized excursions are predominantly land tours, including hiking and horseback riding. They include a visit to active Kilauea volcano (located in Hawai'i Volcanoes National Park) and to Mauna Kea (site of an international astronomical observatory complex), as well as the scenic valleys and waterfalls along the Hamakua Coast.

The following is a sampling of ship-organized shore excursions available from Hilo. Times are approximate. For general information on shore excursions, please refer to the Cruise Options section in Part I. **More detail on attractions listed below can be found within this chapter**:

- Hawai'i Volcanoes National Park (4.5 – 7 hrs, some with extensive walking to view molten lava)
- Biking in Volcano Park (5 hrs)
- Mauna Kea Summit (6 hrs) or Stargazing Adventure (7 hrs plus o/night stay in Waikoloa)
- Akaka Falls & Nani Mau Botanical Garden (4.5 hrs)
- Akaka Falls & Tsunami Museum (3.5 hrs)
- Lava Tree State Park & MacKenzie State Park (4.5 hrs)
- Hawaii Tropical Botanical Garden at Onomea Bay (2.5 hrs)
- Hamakua Coast (6 – 7 hrs)
- Waipi'o Valley (5 hrs) by 4X4, ATV, horseback or mule-drawn wagon
- Helicopter Tour (2.5 hrs)
- Volcano Golf (6 hrs)
- Hilo Bay Kayak (2.5 hrs)

Note: This is a general list of ship-organized shore excursions and these will vary with each cruise line. For more detail, consult your shore excursions booklet (supplied by the cruise line) or log onto your cruise line's website.

Getting Around Independently

At Hilo, your best option for independent touring is to rent a car. All of the major car-rental firms have agencies at the Hilo Airport and they run shuttle vans between the cruise port and the airport. From Hilo you can drive to Hawai'i Volcanoes National Park and explore the park at your leisure. Time permitting you can also visit the south end before returning to Hilo. Alternatively, you can drive to the summit of Mauna Kea or up the lush east coast to scenic Waipi'o Valley. The car return is at the east end of Airport Road.

Beaches

The beaches near Hilo are mostly small and rocky, and are not ideal for swimming or watersports. Reeds Bay Beach Park in Hilo is a pretty spot for a picnic but the water is cool for swimming due to a freshwater spring. Hilo's surfing beach is Honoli'i but the seas here are suitable only for experienced surfers, whom you can watch from a cliff-top vantage off Highway 19 north of Hilo.

Two black-sand beaches of note are Punalu'u Beach (see page 275) and Waipi'o Beach (page 279), but neither are recommended swimming beaches.

HAWAII

Hiking

Excellent hiking venues include Hawai'i Volcanoes National Park, which has 150 miles (240 km) of trails, and Waipi'o Valley, with trails along its eastern rim and valley floor. The Onomea Trail System (its trailhead on Onomea Scenic Drive) provides coastal views and shore access.

Golf Courses

If you've ever wanted to golf on a volcano, the Volcano Golf & Country Club provides your opportunity. Built in 1922, this 18-hole, par-72 course lies along the northern rim of Kilauea Volcano at an elevation of 4,000 feet (1200 m), where the air is cool and fog is often a factor.

Shopping

Local crafts and flower arrangements are sold inside the cruise terminal. In downtown Hilo, the shops are concentrated along Kamehameha Avenue, where refurbished historic buildings house shops and restaurants.

A free shopping shuttle is provided to Hilo Hattie and Prince Kuhio Plaza. An open-air farmers market is held on Wednesday and Saturday mornings at the corner of Kamehameha Avenue and Mamo Street. Some stores are closed on Sunday.

Hilo Attractions

Banyan Drive is lined with banyan trees that various VIP visitors to Hilo planted between 1933 and 1972. Each tree has a dated sign indicating who planted it. Hollywood director Cecil B. DeMille planted the first tree when he was in town filming *Four Frightened People*. Babe Ruth, Franklin D. Roosevelt and Amelia Earhart each planted a tree here in the 1930s.

A tranquil retreat off Banyan Drive is the **Lili'uokalani Gardens**, named for the last Hawaiian queen. This Japanese

HAWAI'I

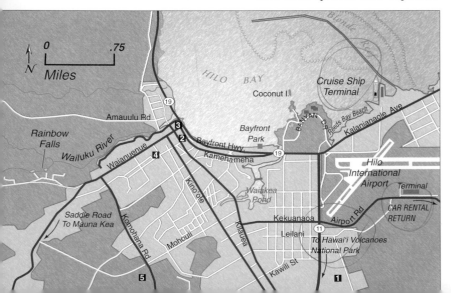

formal garden honors Hawai'i's early Japanese immigrants, and features ponds, waterways, half-moon bridges and pagodas. A footbridge connects the gardens with **Coconut Island**.

Pacific Tsunami Museum is **3** housed in the former First Hawaiian Bank building (1931), which survived both the tsunamis that brought death and destruction to Hilo in the last century. The museum's mission is to educate the public on the dangers of tsunamis, and past tsunami survivors are on hand to share their poignant stories.

The preserved Mission House standing beside the **Lyman** **4** **House Museum** on Haili Street is the oldest wood structure on the Big Island, which was built by a New England missionary family in 1839. David and Sarah Lyman raised seven children in this house, where they regularly hosted Hawaiian royalty and ship captains. Guests were served meals on a luxurious koa wood dining table set with fine china (www.LymanMuseum.org).

(Top) Lili'uokalani Gardens.
(Above) Bayfront County Park.
(Below) Pacific Tsunami Museum.

Imiloa Astronomy Center of **5** **Hawai'i**, located on the upper portion of Hilo's University of Hawai'i campus, is a new facility that opened in 2006. Housed beneath three titanium-covered cones (representing the volcanoes Mauna Kea, Mauna Loa and Hulalai), the center features a planetarium and showcases the world-class astronomical viewing taking place on Mauna Kea, as well as the mountain's cultural importance. It's open Tuesday to

HAWAII

(Above) Rainbow Falls. (Left) Locals swim in Boiling Pots when the water is calm.

Sunday, plus holiday Mondays (www.imiloahawaii.org).

The Wailuku River, which runs through a residential area of Hilo, consists of dramatic gorges formed over thousands of years from lava flows and water erosion. **Rainbow Falls**, named for rainbows that appear in their mist, plunge off a ledge of lava that formed some 10,000 years ago. Upstream are the **Boiling Pots**, a series of small pools eroded into the lava that partially filled the gorge. Their name is in reference to the swift-flowing water that makes swimming in these pools dangerous when a strong current is running.

Macadamia nuts, introduced to Hawai'i from Australia in 1921, are a major crop on the Big Island, and visitors to the Mauna Loa macadamia nut farm and processing plant on the southeastern outskirts of Hilo can learn all about growing and harvesting this tasty nut.

South of Hilo is the Puna District, where the lava flowing seaward from Kilauea has claimed anything in its path, including a town and beach. At **Lava Tree State Monument** you can view the lava molds of tree trunks created when a lava flow swept through this forested area. There are warm springs at nearby Ahalanui Beach Park and at Isaac Hale Beach Park on Pohoiki Bay.

Hawai'i Volcanoes National Park

Hawai'i Volcanoes National Park (HVNP) attracts a high number of visitors who want to witness first-hand the world's most active volcano. The summit of Mauna Loa, the world's most massive mountain, is within park boundaries; however, the big attraction at HVNP is Kilauea Volcano, which has been in continuous eruption since January 3, 1983. Lava flowing from Kilauea Caldera's Eastern Rift Zone has created more than 500 acres of new land along the Big Island's southeast coast.

Up to 2,000 visitors each day flock to HVNP to see this volcano in action. The flow of lava is, however, unpredictable. One week it could be oozing to the surface like cherry syrup squeezed from a bottle, the next it could be flowing seaward in a steady stream until plunging off a 20-foot cliff into the ocean where it hardens into new coastline. This lava is so hot (2,100 degrees Fahrenheit) it explodes into steam when it enters the ocean, blasting particles of rock skyward. For current information on volcanic activity, call 808-985-6000 or visit www.nps.gov/havo.

(Top to bottom) Steam Vents; lava fountain erupting from Pu'u O'o vent; overlook of Kilauea Caldera and its Halema'uma'u Crater.

HAWAII

(Above) Offerings to Pele at Halema'uma'u Crater. (Left, top to bottom) Lava blocks the Chain of Craters Road; hikers trudge across a lava field; inside the Thurston Lava Tube.

There is much to see at Hawai'i Volcanoes National Park even when the lava isn't flowing profusely. Crater Rim Drive (11 miles/ 17 km) encircles Kilauea's summit caldera and provides easy access to scenic overlooks and short hikes. Points of interest include **Steam Vents**, the **Jaggar Museum**, the walk-through **Thurston Lava Tube** and **Halema'uma'u Crater** where Pele, goddess of fire, is said to reside. To this day food offerings are brought to appease this temptestuous goddess.

Devastation Trail is a half-mile hike to the edge of Kilauea Iki Crater, while the longer four-mile Kilauea Iki trail descends 400 feet (120 m) into the crater. A map is available at the Visitor Center near the park entrance.

Entrance to Thurston Lava Tube

(Above) Holei Sea Arch.

Chain of Craters Road (24 miles/ 39 km) leads from Crater Rim Drive down to the park's coastal areas where points of interest include the **Kealakomo Overlook** and **Holei Sea Arch**.

The road dead-ends where a hardened lava flow crosses it. Visitors can park near this dead-end and walk across a lava field to view the flow of molten lava if the volcano is active that day. The terrain is very rough, the heat is intense and visitors are warned to be careful not to step on patches of thin lava crust which could possibly collapse into molten lava flowing just beneath the surface.

The cruise lines offer a variety of tours to HVNP (some of which include a walk across a lava field to view molten lava), or you can visit the park independently by rental car. Admission is $10 per car. Take a warm jacket for the cooler highland temperatures but also be prepared for extremely hot, dry conditions if you plan to hike across the lava fields to view hot molten lava. It is also impor-

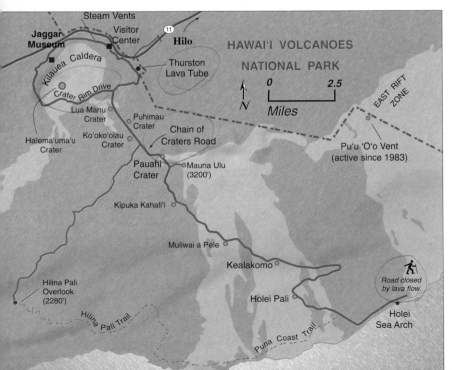

Those Tempting Lava Rocks

With acres of black lava rock lying around the Big Island, some visitors are tempted to take a small piece as a souvenir, while others get the urge to stack the rocks into neat little piles. Both practices are frowned upon. One is said to bring bad luck and the other could result in a stiff fine, even jail time.

Park rangers at Hawai'i Volcanoes National Park, where collecting lava rocks is prohibited, warn visitors not to rearrange the lava rocks into stacks alongside trails and overlooks because this makes scientific research more difficult. Many of these sites are also sacred to native Hawaiians, who compare this practise to sacrilege. Souvenir hunters who take a piece of rock belonging to the vengeful volcano goddess Pele risk being plagued with back luck. Such a fate has apparently stricken many, for nearly a ton of lava rocks has been returned since August 2002 when the Waikoloa Beach Marriott began a program for lava rock collectors wanting to reverse their bad fortune. A spot has been set aside on the resort grounds for collection of the returned rocks, which arrive from the U.S., Canada and Europe. On the first Wednesday of the month, cultural elders gather at a large outcrop of hardened lava to perform a ceremony requesting permission to return the rocks. Hotel staff then send a note to each rock's sender reassuring them that their rock has been returned to its proper place and they are now free of Pele's curse.

tant to bring along sturdy walking shoes, a wide-brimmed hat, sunscreen and bottled water. **Volcano Village**, located one mile outside the park entrance, has general stores, cafes and a gas station. (For more information on Hawai'i's volcanoes, see Natural Phenomena in Part I.)

Lava flows are best observed after dark (see top photo page 271), which is why most cruise ships arrange to pass Kilauea's seaward slope in the evening when – if the volcano is highly active – the sight of glowing red lava spilling from cliffs into the water is one of nature's most impressive spectacles.

The **Hawai'i Belt Road** leads south from Hawaii Volcanoes National Park to South Point. Along the way is **Punalu'u (Black Sand) Beach Park**, which is one of the few safe spots to swim and snorkel on the south coast, but the water is cool, the

Punalu'u (Black Sand) Beach

HAWAII

waves can be unpredictable, and there is often a bad riptide. However, this black-sand beach is a good place to view the green sea turtles that frequent this bay.

Turning off the main highway onto **South Point Road** (11 miles/18 km) of narrow, bumpy road), you will pass by the three-bladed generators of the Kamaoa Wind Farm on your way to the southernmost point of the United States. A rope ladder, used by fishermen, leads down to the water at the base of a cliff, from which locals like to leap (not a good idea if a current is running). Archeologists have discovered ancient canoe moorings at South Point, which is where they think the first Polynesians may have arrived at Hawai'i.

Mauna Kea ('white mountain') is, at 13,796 feet (4205 m), the world's tallest island mountain. A dormant volcano, it rises 32,000 feet (9,750 m) when mea-

(Above, left) Swimmers at South Point. (Left) The trail leading to Mauna Kea's summit. (Below) Observatories on Mauna Kea.

sured from the ocean floor and its summit provides an excellent viewpoint due to its high elevation above the clouds and the absence of city lights. The Mauna Kea Observatory is the largest astronomical facility in the world and is operated by the Institute for Astronomy of the University of Hawai'i. Several nations have massive telescopes at this observatory, their segmented mirrors adjusted by computer many times per second to produce digital images for study. Scientists from several nations work at Mauna Kea (and reside in Waimea).

You needn't be a professional astronomer to appreciate the desolate beauty of Mauna Kea, but you do need to drive a very steep and winding road to reach the summit. Guided tours to Mauna Kea are available through the cruise lines; these include a visit to the **Onizuka Center for International Astronomy** located at the 9,000-foot (2743-m) level. One tour (offered by NCL) features sunset viewing at the summit, followed by a hotel stay and reconnection with the ship the next morning at Kailua-Kona Please note: Reduced oxygen at the summit of Mauna Kea can present altitude dangers. Those who have gone scuba diving the previous day or plan to go diving the next day, as well as young children, pregnant women or people in poor health should not ascend Mauna Kea.

(Right) Scenic trails at Onomea Bay lead down to the water.

Hamakua Coast

This is a spectacularly scenic coast of plunging waterfalls and steep gorges once transited on foot or horseback, then crossed by cane-hauling trains. Waipi'o Valley lies at the north end of this highway (an hour-and-a-half drive from Hilo) and there are many scenic outlooks and parks along the way.

Onomea Scenic Drive is a four-mile (6-km) detour off the main highway. This narrow road hugs the coastline above Onomea Bay and winds past the **Hawaii Tropical Botanical Gardens** where indigenous and exotic flowers grow among the giant palm and mango trees. You can sometimes see sea turtles swimming in Onomea Bay.

Akaka Falls State Park features a half-mile loop trail through a lush tropical rainforest with plants as big as trees, which leads to scenic viewpoints of the cascading Kahuna Falls and the free-falling Akaka Falls, the latter plunging 442 feet (135 m) into a stream-filled gorge. Akaka Falls feeds the stream that flows through **Kolekole Beach Park**, which is a popular spot for locals (especially on weekends) who enjoy the picnic pavilions and freshwater pool – a popular swimming hole. (Swimming is unsafe off the park's black-sand beach.) The 1946 tsunami filled this valley with water over 30 feet (9 m) deep.

Railroad buffs will want to stop at Laupahoehoe to visit the Train Museum, housed in a restored station master's house. A road leads off the main highway down to **Laupahoehoe**

(Top to bottom) Onomea Scenic Drive; Akaka Falls; tsunami memorial and rocky shoreline at Laupahoehoe Point.

Point County Park where a foaming surf pounds lava rock outcroppings. A schoolhouse once occupied the park site, and standing on a grassy point overlooking the sea is a stone memorial to the 24 schoolchildren and teachers who were swept away by the 1946 tsunami.

The drive up the Hamakua Coast is worth the effort just for the cliff-top view at the highway's end of **Waipi'o Valley**. This magnificent valley (its name meaning 'curving water') is known as the Valley of the Kings, for this is a legendary place where ancient kingdoms were ruled by immortal gods and divine chiefs. A royal retreat and final resting place of alii over the ages, this pastoral valley is where the newborn Kamehameha was safeguarded until the threat to his young life had passed.

Several sacred sites once stood at the mouth of this valley, including a place of refuge, Paka'alana. The great *heiau* at Paka'alana was the most sacred

Waipi'o Valley from the air (above) and the lookout (below).

in Hawai'i until it was destroyed in 1791 by the chiefs of Maui, Oahu and Kaua'i in their war with Kamehameha. Upon receiving news of this attempted invasion, Kamehameha and his warriors suspended work on the *heiau* at Pu'ukohola and set sail in their war canoes for Waipi'o Bay, where Kamehameha's fleet counterattacked and routed the

Waterfalls plunge down sheer cliff faces in Waipi'o Valley.

invaders. This was Hawai'i's first modern naval battle.

Waipi'o Beach is over a mile in length and lies between 2,000-foot-high cliffs that guard both sides of the six-mile-long valley. When 19th-century white settlers visited Waipi'o Valley on horseback, they wrote glowingly of the scene spread below as they gazed upon this verdant valley of winding streams and gardenlike plantations of taro and other crops. Thatched huts dotted the valley

floor and shimmering fishponds fed by streams and springs lay close to the black-sand beach where they were separated from the ocean by a sand dune.

The residents of Waipi'o Valley established small taro factories here in the late 1800s. Taro was hand-pounded with stone pounders on wooden boards, then cooked in large, iron-bottomed boxes. Fresh water was supplied by a flume from Hi'ilawe Stream and water wheels provided power (later replaced with engines). The valley was abandoned for several decades after it was inundated by the tsunami of 1946, and again flooded in 1979.

A highlight of Waipi'o Valley is the spectacular double waterfall at Hi'ilawe Falls – the tallest in the state with a vertical drop of more than 1,000 feet (300 m). One of the mountain streams feeding these falls had been diverted in the early 1900s for sugar cane irrigation, thus reducing the flow of water to Hi'ilawe Falls, but in 2004 the stream was restored to its natural state.

Several thousand Hawaiians once lived in Waipi'o Valley. Today the valley's residents number less than 100. In 1992, the Bishop Museum, which is a major landowner in the Waipi'o Valley, conducted an environmental study to assess the impact of increasing numbers of visitors to this quiet and secluded setting. Subsequent measures included closing the valley on Sundays to commercial tours and allowing only foot traffic onto the far side

The Legend of Lono

It was in the Waipi'o Valley that the fertility god Lono descended the arch of a rainbow to find his bride, the beautiful Kaikilani living in a breadfruit grove beside the Hi'ilawe Falls. He made her a goddess and was devoted to her. However, one day he indulged in a jealous rage that caused a tearful Kaikilani to flee. A repentant Lono searched frantically for his wounded wife but could find no trace of her. When she did not return, Lono told his people he was setting off on a quest to search the entire island world and would not return until she was found. For centuries, Lono's people waited, unfoundering in their belief that their great god would one day return. When Captain Cook's ships appeared on the horizon, the Hawaiians thought they were witnessing the return of Lono. Some held this conviction until their dying days, but most did not, for Cook would not have died had he been a god.

of Waipi'o Beach.

If you want to explore Waipio Valley independently, you can hike down the steep road into the valley. Only 4X4 vehicles are allowed on this road. It's a one-mile descent to the bottom but it's the one-mile climb back up that is very challenging due to the steep grade. Once you reach the valley floor, you can turn right and head to the beach (swimming is not recommended due to dangerous rip tides). Or you can head up the valley along a rough trail that crosses back and forth through the stream bed (there are no footbridges). There are no visitor facilities in the valley (open to visitors between sunrise and sundown) and the only restroom is at the lookout at the entrance to the valley. A number of tour operators based in Kukuihaele offer guided tours of Waipi'o Valley and its rim, using various modes of transportation: 4X4 van, horses and mule-drawn wagon. Several of these guided tours can be booked through the cruise lines.

(Below) Kukuihaele's local eatery is a base for trail rides into Waipi'o Valley.
(Bottom) Shops line the main street of Honoka'a, on the way to Waipi'o Valley.

HAWAII

Kailua-Kona

The seaside village of Kailua-Kona is located in the famous Kona district, known for its clear waters and sunny climate. It is also steeped in history, and several important sites are within strolling distance of the tender dock. Coffee farms flourish on the slopes of Hualalai above Kailua-Kona, where the famous Kona coffee beans are grown. And each October, Kailua-Kona hosts the Ironman Triathlon World Championships.

Kailua-Kona is a picturesque resort and if you're looking to spend a few hours relaxing on a beach, you need venture no further than the crescent of white sand overlooking a turquoise lagoon opposite the tender pier. This is where Kamehameha, the great warrior king who united the Hawaiian islands, spent the last years of his life, from 1812 until his death in 1819. A thatch-roofed replica of his *heiau* , where he consulted with his chiefs and schooled his son Liholiho, stands on a point of land at the mouth of the lagoon.

Getting Around Independently

At Kailua-Kona, renting a car is problematic: the Kona Airport is eight miles away and you can spend a considerable amount of time waiting for your rental car agency's shuttle van, which often moves slowly in heavy traffic along Queen Ka'ahumanu Highway. This can be especially nerve-wracking if time is tight getting back to the ship.

You can reach the beaches south of Kailua-Kona without renting a car. Simply take the Ali'i Shuttle, which is a public

Ahu'ena Heiau overlooks the clear waters of Kamakahonu Lagoon in Kailua-Kona.

bus that runs along Ali'i Drive, between the King Kamehameha Hotel in Kailua-Kona and the Keauhou Beach Hotel at Kahalu'u Bay. The bus stops anywhere you want (just flag it down) and buses run every hour and a half, every day except Sunday. The first southbound bus departs from the King Kamehameha Hotel at 9:25 a.m. The fare is $2 each way.

If you want to go snorkeling at Kahalu'u Beach Park, the Kahaluu Beach Snorkel Rental Depot (808-937-7460) provides pickup at the tender pier ($15 per person for snorkel equipment and transportation).

Shore Time Suggestions

Kailua-Kona is an ideal walking port, with several historic sites overlooking the harbor and a lovely pocket beach right beside the tender dock (see photo on facing page). A Visitor Information Booth is located at the north end of the tender pier (under the 'Aloha' awning) where volunteer staff provide brochures and answer questions. Telephones and restrooms are also located here. Boating excursions depart from Kailua pier, many of which can be booked in advance through the cruise lines.

Should you rent a car, the north end of the island features rolling grasslands (the famous Parker Ranch is located here) and sites associated with Kamehameha the Great, who was born in this area. If you're looking for a good beach, numerous beach parks and luxury hotel resorts line the coast north of the Kona Airport. South of Kailua-Kona, places worth driving to include Pu'uhonua o Honaunau (Place of Refuge) and the Kona coffee-growing area.

Kailua-Kona's seawall leads from the tender dock to nearby shops and historic sites.

HAWAII

SHIP-TO-SHORE EXCURSIONS

Excursions from Kailua-Kona include a variety of water-oriented activities, as well as driving tours to various historic sites and the ranchlands north of the port. The following is a sampling of shore excursions available through the cruise lines. Times are approximate. For general information on shore excursions, please refer to the Cruise Options section in Part I. More detail on attractions listed below can be found within this chapter.

- Snorkel, snuba and scuba adventures (1.5 to 4.5 hrs)
- Honaunau Bay snorkeling & Place of Refuge tour (4 hrs)
- Party cruise aboard a 150-foot sailing canoe (2 hrs)
- Dolphin eco cruise (2.5 hrs)
- Atlantis Submarine (1 hr)
- Glass Bottom Boat (1 hr)
- Deepsea fishing (4.5 hrs)
- Kailua walking tour (1 hr)
- Historic tour of Kamakahonu Lagoon and Kohala (5.5 hrs)
- Kohala Coast & Parker Ranch (4.5 hrs)
- Kahua Ranch by ATV, horseback, wagon or hiking (5 hrs)
- Pololu Valley waterfall hike (6 hrs)
- Kona Coast cultural and historic sites (3.5 hrs)
- Kona Coffee Tour (4.5 hrs)
- Rainforest Hike (4 hrs)
- Helicopter tour (4.5 hrs)
- Championship Golf (6 hrs)

Note: This is a general list of ship-organized shore excursions and will vary with each cruise line. For more detail, consult your shore excursions booklet (supplied by the cruise line) or log onto your cruise line's website.

Shopping

A short stroll from the tender dock is the Kona Inn Shopping Village and other shops clustered along Ali'i Drive. A free shuttle will take you to Hilo Hattie and the Kona Coast Shopping Center, both located on Palani Road. (See map, page 290.)

The Kona Inn Shopping Village.

Beaches

Beaches of soft white sand aren't as plentiful on the Big Island as they are on the other Hawaiian islands, but there are several excellent ones on the west coast.

One of Kona's most sheltered beaches is right in the town of Kailua-Kona on Kamakahonu Lagoon (see photo, page 282). The beach hut there, run by Kona Beach Boys, rents beach umbrellas, lounge chairs and snorkel gear. Historic outrigger canoe rides and surfing lessons are also available.

South of Kailua-Kona, along Ali'i Drive, lie several good swimming and snorkeling beaches that can be reached by taking the Ali'i Shuttle (see Getting

Around Independently). **White Sands Beach Park** (a.k.a. Magic Sands or Disappearing Sands) is a lovely swimming beach with restrooms and showers. While heavy seas often wash away the sand here (usually in winter), it always returns. Locals like to body surf and body board off this beach, and board surfers frequent a shore break called 'Banyans' just north of the beach.

Kahalu'u Beach Park is good for swimming and snorkeling, except during a high surf when dangerous rip currents develop. Facilities include lifeguards, showers, restrooms, picnic pavilions and a lunch wagon. Surfing lessons are available.

Some of the Big Island's best swimming beaches lie north of Kailua-Kona in the Kohala District, and can be reached by rental car. At **Aneaho'omalu Beach Park** (called **A-Bay** by the locals) two, palm-fringed fishponds provide a scenic backdrop to a crescent of white sand. Public

(Above) The beach hut owner at Kamakahonu Lagoon shares some Hawaiian culture. (Below) Hapuna Beach in South Kohala.

HAWAII

access is at the south end of the beach; a concession at the north end rents snorkel gear, body boards, kayaks and windsurfers. Windsurfing lessons are available until mid-afterrnon, when the prevailing onshore wind becomes too strong for beginners. A blowing southwest Kona wind creates a crosswind at A-Bay, which allows windsurfers to go straight out to sea and back. A pleasant walk south of the beach leads past numerous petroglyphs.

Widely considered the best beach on the island is the one at **Hapuna Beach State Recreation Area**. This expansive stretch of soft white sand offers good swimming and body boarding on gentle summertime swells. In winter, during periods of high surf, there are dangerous rip currents and pounding shore breaks, and only experts should enter the water when waves are over three feet high. The beach park facilities

Snorkelers in Kealakekua Bay.

include a large parking lot, picnic tables, restrooms and showers. A Prince hotel overlooks the north end of the beach.

Directly north of Hapuna Beach is another of the Big Island's top-rated beaches – **Kauna'oa Beach** – which is overlooked by the **Mauna Kea Resort**, a famous hotel built by Laurance Rockefeller in 1965, its low profile designed to blend with the setting.

A good beach for small children with generally calm water is **Samuel M. Spencer Beach State Park,** just north of Kauna'oa.

Snorkeling & Scuba Diving

The Kona coast's clear waters are renowned for their snorkel and dive sites, which feature huge pinnacles, lava tubes and caves. Several snorkel and dive shops are located in Kailua-Kona, including Big Island Water Sports and Snorkel Bob's. The beach hut at Kamahakonu Lagoon (beside the tender pier) rents snorkel

gear, and tropical fish can be viewed in the lagoon's waters.

About six miles (10 km) south of Kailua on Ali'i Drive is popular **Kahalu'u Beach Park** where the sheltered waters teem with marine life, including green sea turtles, which come right into the 'lava wading pool' area of the shoreline to feed on seaweed and sun themselves on the warm rocks. This small cove is protected by the remains of a partially submerged rock wall, constructed in pre-historic times to confine fish. Entry is along sandy patches lying in between the shoreline's lava rock flats. You can rent snorkeling equipment onsite.

Kealakekua Bay (site of the Captain Cook Monument) is a marine preserve with excellent snorkeling. Spinner dolphins often come here during the day to rest. Boat excursions to Kealakekua Bay operate from Kailua-Kona and can be booked through the cruise lines.

Honaunau Bay, overlooked by Pu'uhonua O Honaunau National Historic Park, is fronted by smooth lava rock flats which provide easy entry for inner shoreline snorkeling amidst an abundance of tropical fish. Skin divers enjoy the deeper water in the center of the bay, which is also a popular scuba diving spot.

Pawai Bay (located between Kailua Bay and Honokohau Harbor) is another protected marine reserve and popular snorkel site. Body Glove Cruises runs snorkel excursions to Pawai Bay, departing from the Kailua Pier. The snorkeling is also good off Kauna'oa Beach on the Kohala coast.

Boat Excursions

You can enjoy underwater views of Kona's coral reefs and marine life in a glass-bottom boat or submarine tour, both of which depart from Kailua Pier. The *Marian*, a glass-bottom boat operated by Kailua Bay Charter Co., offers

Spinner dolphins escort a boat heading into Kealakekua Bay.

50-minute reef tours, which depart regularly throughout the day (except Sunday) and take passengers to within inches of shallow-water reefs and to the edge of a drop-off where depths plunge to more than 100 feet (30 m). Atlantis Adventures offers submarine tours into deep water.

Captain Dan McSweeney's Whalewatching Adventures runs boat tours year-round out of **Honokohau Harbor** (a few miles north of Kailua-Kona) which is also where numerous deep sea fishing charters are available.

Golfing

Mauna Kea Golf Course on the Kohala coast is a famous course designed in 1965 by Robert Trent Jones, Sr. The island's first resort course, Mauna Kea features breathtaking views of rocky coastline and of snow-capped Mauna Kea. Other top-rated courses on the Kohala Coast are those at the Mauna Lani Hotel and at the Hapuna Beach Prince

Hotel, the latter designed by Arnold Palmer. Close to Kailua-Kona is the Kona Country Club with its two 18-hole courses.

Kailua-Kona Historic Sites

Kailua-Kona is where the first group of New England missionaries landed in April 1820. They had left Boston on the brig *Thaddeus* five months earlier with four Hawaiians on board who had ended up in Connecticut on various trading and whaling ships. These Hawaiian men had learned the English language, converted to Christianity and adopted the New England mode of attire, which included a high-collared shirt, vest and jacket.

When the missionaries first arrived off the coast of Hawai'i and laid eyes on the locals, they were shocked by the sight of scantily clothed men, women and

Golfing on the famous Mauna Kea course, designed in 1965 by Robert Trent Jones, Sr.

(Top to bottom)
Ahu'ena Heiau;
Hulihe'e Palace;
Moku'aikaua
Church.

children frolicking in the water, floating on surfboards or lounging on shore. They knew their work was cut out for them as they headed ashore in a ship's boat to present themselves to King Liholiho (Kamehameha II) and ask his permission to remain in the islands and teach his people the gospel. The king carefully considered their request, consulting with his advisors for four days before granting the missionaries their request – allowing them to stay for one year on a trial basis.

The early months were challenging for the missionaries and their wives as they toiled under the hot Hawaiian sun in their heavy clothing. Their daily household activities of cooking and washing attracted as much attention from the natives as did their outdoor sermons. There was, of course, a language barrier and their initial attempts at conversion began falteringly with the king who was not an ideal role model for he refused to give up four of his five wives or abstain from rum drinking. The king, however, had abolished the ancient *kapu* system just months before the

HAWAII

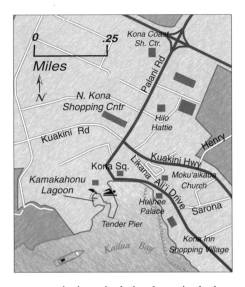

missionaries' timely arrival, thus creating an opportunity for Christianity to replace pagan worship in the islands. The king was hospitable and generous to the missionaries, and gave them prime land for constructing a church, which they did using grass thatch. Today, this site on Ali'i Drive is occupied by **Moku'aikaua Congregational Church**, the third church built here (in 1837) after the first two burned down, and its spire is today a town landmark.

Across the street from the church is **Hulihe'e Palace**, with manicured grounds that overlook Kailua Bay, where people paddle outrigger canoes in a scene reminiscent of the one that greeted the missionaries who first came ashore here. Construction of this royal palace was completed in 1838 and it became a favorite retreat of various royal families. Its walls are three feet thick and the interior is furnished with per-

sonal possessions of former royal residents. The Daughters of Hawaii, a non-profit corporation, maintains this historic property, which is open daily and has a gift shop (www.hulihee-palace.org).

Ahu'ena Heiau, at the entrance to Kamakahonu (Eye of the Turtle) Lagoon, is a reconstruction of the royal grounds occupied by Kamehameha the Great in his final years. A footpath leads past informative plaques. Hawaiian artifacts (including a royal feather cape) are displayed in the lobby of King Kamehameha's Kona Beach Hotel overlooking the beach at Kamakahonu Lagoon.

Attractions South of Kailua-Kona

The Ali'i Express can be taken to **Kahalu'u Bay** (location of Kahalu'u Beach Park) where you can view numerous historical sites in the vicinity, including several *heiaus*, a royal fishpond and King Kalakaua's Beach House, the latter two sites located on the grounds of the Keauhou Beach Resort. One of the smallest churches in Hawai'i – **St. Peter's Catholic Church** (nicknamed Little Blue Church) – was built in 1889 upon one of the platforms of Kuemanu Heiau – a temple dedicated to the sport of surfing that overlooks Kahalu'u Bay.

At **Keauhou Bay** there stands a monument marking the birthplace of Kamehameha III, a son of Kamehameha the Great. Nearby, across the road from the club house of the Kona Country Club golf course, is the upper portion of a stone ramp once used for the ancient sport of lava sledding (called *holua*). The south end of Ali'i Drive is the site of the Kuamo'o Battle, which took place in 1820 when newly converted Christian supporters, led by King Kamehameha II, defeated the supporters of the ancient *kapu* system. The remains of slain warriors are said to be interred within the battlefield's rock cairns.

The Big Island's famous Kona coffee beans are cultivated on the slopes of Hualalai, within a 20-mile-long, two-mile-wide corridor containing 600 small, independent farms. Here the rich volcanic soil and prevailing weather patterns are ideal for growing coffee trees, which bear bright red berries called 'cherries.' Each cherry contains two beans, and 4,000 beans (the yield of one coffee tree) are needed to produce one pound of roasted coffee. Everything at these farms, from planting to picking, is still done by hand. An American missionary was the first to plant coffee in Kona in 1829, and two decades later a coffee export pioneer named Henry Greenwell arrived from England to begin Kona's coffee industry in earnest. **Kona Historical Society and Museum** now occupies the Greenwell ancestral home. Tours are available at Greenwell Farms and at Kona Coffee Living History Farm in Captain Cook.

Kailua-Kona

White Sands Beach

Kahalu'u Beach Park

Keauhou Bay

Ali'i Drive

KONA

COAST

0   2.5
Miles
N

11

Kona Historical Society Museum

Captain Cook

Captain Cook Monument

Kealakekua Bay

Napo'opo'o

Painted Church

HAWAII

Pu'uhonua O Honaunau National Historical Park (Place of Refuge)

The snorkeling is excellent off the Captain Cook Monument at Kealakekua Bay.

HAWAII

Kealakekua Bay

No other bay in Hawai'i is more steeped in maritime history than Kealakekua Bay. It was here that the Hawaiians greeted Captain Cook as a god, then later killed him for being an impostor. It was also here, in this sheltered bay, that Kamehameha the Great conducted much of his business with foreign ships visiting his island domain.

At the south end of Kealakekua Bay, overlooking Napo'opo'o Beach, is the Hikiau Heiau, which is where priests once worshipped Captain Cook as their god Lono and which is now part of **Kealakekua Bay State Historical Park**, accessible by road off Highway 11. A mile across the bay from this park is the **Captain Cook Monument**, a white marble obelisk erected on a patch of ground deeded to Great Britain to commemorate their famous explorer. A nearby plaque marks the exact spot where Captain Cook was slain. Visitors

to Kealakekua Bay are discouraged from entering the roped area of the monument. The monument is hard to access by land, for the rough trail leading down from the highway takes several hours to hike back up. Kayakers launch their craft at Kealakekua Bay State Historical Park and paddle over to the monument. One of the easiest ways to visit Kealakekua Bay is by taking a snorkeling excursion from Kailua-Kona. The entire bay is a protected marine sanctuary and you can snorkel right in front of the monument. Spinner dolphins are often seen in this bay.

St. Benedict's Church, known as the Painted Church, is located up the road from Kealakekua Bay. Its splendid interior is decorated with biblical-themed frescoes that a Belgian priest painted at the turn of the last century.

Pu'uhonua O Honaunau National Historical Park ('Place of Refuge at Honaunau') is the most complete restoration of an ancient religious sanctuary in

Prisoners in Paradise

When an angry chief of the Kohala district sought revenge against a cruel sea captain named Simon Metcalfe, he seized the *Fair American*, a small schooner under the command of Metcalfe's son. All of the crew were murdered with the exception of Isaac Davis, who attempted to escape by swimming through water thick with canoes, only to be captured, beaten nearly to death and eventually taken into protective custody by another chief who took pity on him.

The elder Metcalfe's ship, the *Eleanora*, was anchored in Kealakekua Bay at the time. When news of the massacre reached Kamehameha, he detained John Young (the *Eleanora*'s boatswain, who was ashore at the time) to prevent word of the blood bath from reaching the elder Metcalfe. Kamehameha took Davis and Young under his protection, and the distraught English sailors eventually accepted their fate. Granted the status of chiefs and given large tracts of land, they became important members of Kamehameha's royal court, serving as interpreters whenever a British or American trading ship arrived in local waters.

John Young married a niece of the king, who made him governor of the island, and he became an important figure in Hawaiian history. His son was Minister of the Interior and one of his daughters was the mother of Queen Emma. Isaac Davis also prospered in Hawai'i and he refused an offer of passage back to England from Captain Vancouver who, upon his return, placed an advertisement in a London newspaper notifying friends and relatives that these two men were alive and well. Davis's sister wrote him a letter (now in the State Archives of Hawai'i) begging him to come home, but Davis stayed in Hawai'i.

Hawai'i. Situated on a point of land at Honaunau Bay and surrounded on three sides by water, it adjoins a royal compound where Hawaiian high chiefs once held court. Royal palms flourish throughout the palace grounds and a royal fishpond overlooks the beach-lined cove that was used for royal canoe landings. No commoners were allowed to enter the royal compound, and violators were punished by death – unless they were lucky enough to reach the *pu'uhonua* next door

Pu'uhonua o Honaunau
National Historical Park.

before the king's warriors caught them. A stone wall up to 10 feet (3 m) high and 17 feet (5 m) thick stood between the royal grounds and the place of refuge, so most violators would try to swim to safety. Upon reaching the lava rock shoreline of the *pu'uhonua*,

Hale o Keawe Heiau stands at the end of the Great Wall.

the *kahuna* (priest) would perform a ceremony of absolution and the offender could then return home safely.

The bones of Keawe, who was a great chief of Kona and a great-grandfather of Kamehameha, were entombed in Hale o Keawe Heiau at the end of the Great Wall, and his *mana* (spiritual power) infused this temple with great cleansing powers. The National Park Service has reconstructed a temple on this site and replica *ki'i* (wooden images) stand guard outside it. The Great Wall, which was built around 1550 without mortar but by carefully fitting the stones together, has been stablized and repaired. The park's self-guided half-mile tour provides a fascinating stroll through one of the most significant historic sites in Hawai'i. (www.nps.gov/puho)

Kohala

Kohala's seaside is often referred to as the 'Gold Coast' although the first color that comes to mind when driving north along Queen Ka'ahumanu Highway is black, for lying on either side of the road are vast fields of hardened black lava. Its only when you turn off the main highway and head towards the ocean that the emerald green golf courses and white sand beaches reveal themselves.

Just north of the hotel resorts, standing atop **Pu'ukohol**a ('Whale Hill'), is one of the last major sacred structures built in Hawai'i before outside influences permanently altered traditional life. Kamehameha the Great built this stone temple in 1790-91 after a prophet told him its construction would please the war god Ku and thus guarantee Kamehameha success at conquering and uniting all of the Hawaiian islands.

Thousands of men, including Kamehameha himself, hauled water-worn lava rocks to the site.

Upon the *heiau*'s completion, its platform measured 224 by 100 feet (68x30 m), and was enclosed on three sides with 20-foot-high (6-m) walls. Three terraces ran the length of the platform's fourth side, which was open to the sea and held ceremonial structures – thatched huts, an altar and a row of wooden figures representing the Hawaiian gods.

Kamehameha invited his cousin and chief rival Keoua to attend the *heiau's* dedication ceremonies. When Keoua and his entourage arrived by canoe, they were slain during a scuffle on the beach. His body was carried up to the *heiau* and offered as the principal sacrifice to Ku. With Keoua out of the way, Kamehameha was the undisputed ruler of the Big Island and went on to unite all of the Hawaiian islands through conquest or treaty.

Pu'ukohola Heiau was abandoned following the death of Kamehameha in 1819, when his son and successor abolished the *kapu* system and destroyed the idols. A National Historic Site since 1962, Pu'ukohola was officially opened in 1974. Admission is free and the visitor center is open daily from 7:30 a.m. to 4:00 p.m.; self-guided walking tours of the park include the ruins of a second temple built by Kamehameha's ancestors that was converted into a fort during Kamehameha's rule with the aid of John Young, who was a stranded British sailor and trusted advisor to the king (see page 293). The site of Young's homestead is

(Top) Entrance to Pu'ukohola Heiau historic site.
(Above) Kawaihae Harbor.

also on the park grounds. One of the best places to view Pu'ukohola Heiau is from **Kawaihae Harbor**, along the road leading out to the breakwater. You can also access the *heiau* on foot from Spencer Beach Park.

Five miles north of Pu'ukohola Heiau, on the lower slopes of the Kohala Mountains, is a 45-acre (18-ha) arboretum and botanical gardens called **Pua Mau Place**. The name means 'ever blooming' in reference to the continuously flowering tropical flowers, shrubs

HAWAII

HAWAII

(Top to bottom) Kapa'au's main street; Parker Ranch wagon ride; Kohala Mountain Road winds past pastures of grazing cattle.

and trees. Open daily, the visitor center's wraparound deck provides panoramic views in all directions and is a good vantage for sighting humpback whales (from December to March) in the waters below (www.puamau.com).

At the northern tip of the island is **Mo'okini Heiau**, built in 480 AD and enlarged over time. One of the most bloody temples in the islands, it was dedicated to the war god Ku, whose rituals demanded human sacrifice. About a thousand yards from the *heiau* is the birthsite of Kamehameha the Great, who received his birth rituals at Mo'okini and later worshipped here before rebuilding Pu'ukohola Heiau. The lands surrounding Mo'okini and the Kamehameha birthsite (which is marked by a stone wall enclosure and birthing stones) are owned by Kamehameha Schools.

While many visitors to Hawai'i are familiar with the King Kamehameha statue in downtown Honolulu, fewer are aware that the original is displayed in the village of **Kapa'au** in North Kohala (see photo, page 264). This statue, sculpted in the late 1800s by an American artist living in Florence, was lost at sea en route to Hawai'i, so a replica (displayed in Honolulu) was made. The original statue was eventually recovered (see page 171) and mounted in Kapa'au's Kamehameha Park where it is draped with 22-foot-long floral lei each June 11 for the local Kamehameha Day Celebration.

Dominating the Kohala District is the historic **Parker Ranch**. When Massachusetts-born John Palmer Parker jumped ship in Hawai'i in 1809 at the age of 19, he befriended King Kamehameha who hired Palmer to round up the cattle running amok on the island. Palmer eventually married one of the king's granddaughters whose royal status entitled her to 640 acres (259 ha) of land in 1847 when the Great Mahele (land division) took place throughout the Hawaiian kingdom. Over time, the Parker Ranch grew in size to 500,000 acres under the Parker-family dynasty. Private ownership of the ranch ended with the death of Richard Palmer Smart in 1992, who had established the Parker Ranch Foundation Trust to benefit the Waimea community. Sections of the ranch had already been sold to

fund ranching operations, such as the low-yield pasture lands along the Kohala coast where luxury resorts now stand. The Parker Ranch Visitor Center and Museum are located in Waimea; wagon rides and other tours are offered. (www.parkerranch.com)

Guided hikes are available into **Pololu Valley**, which is private land and is explored via the Kohala Ditch Trail. Built in the early 1800s, this three-mile (5-km) trail clings to cliffs rising 1,000 feet (300 m) above the valley floor. The highlight is the section of trail that leads behind the Kapoloa Falls, where it cascades from its crest 300 feet (91 m) above and plunges another 200 feet (61 m) into a deep chasm below. Hawaii Forest & Trail is the exclusive tour operator to Kapoloa Falls (331-8505; www.hawaii–forest.com); this excursion is available through some of the cruise lines.

Hawaiian Cowboys

In 1793, off the Kona coast, Captain Vancouver unloaded a hungry bull and cow into a chief's canoe for delivery to King Kamehameha. Initially, the king was wary of these strange creatures, and his people fled at the sight of them. However, Vancouver delivered additional cattle the next year and when one of these cows gave birth to a calf, the Hawaiians were so excited they bundled the young animal in cloth and carried it on their backs across the island from Kealakekua Bay to Hilo to show King Kamehameha. Soon there were so many cattle roaming freely about the island, cowboys from the Spanish missions in California were brought over to teach the Hawaiians how to ride horses, throw lassos and round up cattle. These Hawaiian cowboys became known as *paniolo*.

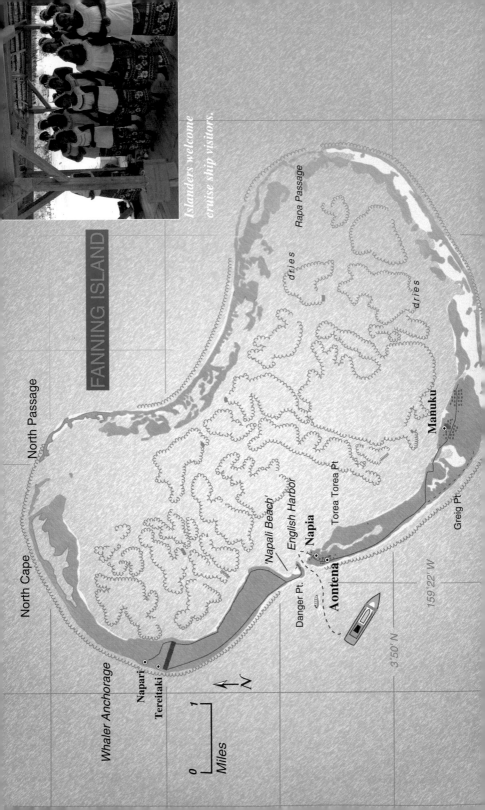

FANNING ISLAND

North Passage

North Cape

Whaler Anchorage

Napari
Tereitaki

Napali Beach

English Harbor

Danger Pt.

Napia

Aontena

Torea Torea Pt.

dries

dries

Rapa Passage

Manuku

Greig Pt.

3 50' N

159 22' W

N

0   1
Miles

*Islanders welcome
cruise ship visitors.*

CHAPTER FIVE

FANNING ISLAND

Fanning Island is not exactly a household name, but anyone who has seen an episode of Gilligan's Island will have caught a glimpse of this palm-treed atoll lying in the middle of the Pacific Ocean, for it was the South Seas island featured in the television show's closing credits. Gilligan and his skipper were taking their boat passengers on a three-hour tour, but Norwegian Cruise Line takes its passengers on a two-day crossing of the open Pacific before landing at Fanning Island, which lies nearly 1,000 miles (1,600 km) south of Hawai'i .

This coral atoll – like the other Line Islands – was uninhabited except for seabirds when discovered by the American explorer Edmund Fanning in 1798. Then, in 1855, Captain Henry English

brought 150 laborers from Manihiki to Fanning Island to harvest coconuts for their oil. Twenty years later the island's guano deposits were mined and shipped to Honolulu.

Great Britain annexed Fanning Island in 1889, and it became officially known as Tabuaeran when it gained independence in 1979 as part of the Republic of Kiribati. A member of the Commonwealth of Nations, the Republic of Kiribati consists of 33 islands scattered across 2,400 miles (3,860 km) of ocean on both sides of the equator.

Fanning Island lies 185 miles (300 km) north of the equator. Its maximum elevation is about 10

Norwegian Wind at Fanning Island, with English Harbor and Napili Beach in foreground.

*Tenders bring ship passengers
ashore to English Harbor dock.*

feet (3 m) above sea level and the total land area is about 13 square miles (33 sq. km). Primitive by western standards, the island has no electricity, no telephones and no running water. The 2,000 or so people who live here are Micronesian, and they speak Gilbertese/Kiribati, although the official language is English. They live in thatched huts and, until recently, used only bicycles or bare feet for getting around the island, which has a single dirt road. They grow most of their own food, including taro and breadfruit, and they fish local waters.

For decades, the only visitors to Fanning Island were an occasional sailboat and the scheduled cargo ship that delivers supplies every few months. This all changed when Norwegian Cruise Line decided to expand its presence in Hawai'i with roundtrip cruises out of Honolulu. Due to a longstanding American shipping act that restricts foreign-flagged ships from traveling exclusively between American ports, NCL sought a foreign port of call for its Hawai'i cruises. The company chose Fanning Island and, after signing an agreement in 1998 with the Kiribati government, *Norwegian Dynasty* became the first cruise ship to make scheduled visits to Fanning Island. Since then, NCL has launched three U.S.-flagged ships, offering seven-day Hawai'i-dedicated cruises, but the company continues to position one of its foreign-flagged ships on 10- and 11-day Hawai'i itineraries that include a

call at Fanning Island.

The regular arrival of North American cruise passengers has had a major impact on the islanders' subsistence economy, one that was traditionally based on barter. Some cruise ship visitors come ashore bearing gifts for the children, but most have American dollar bills in their pockets. The locals have responded by setting up a straw market beside the tender dock, where handcrafted items range in price from $2 to $20. They also perform traditional songs and dances for their visitors.

The island has three primary schools, one junior secondary school and one high school. The schoolchildren do their homework on hand-held chalkboards and they start learning English in Grade 5. The NCL Primary School was renamed this on November 24, 1998, in recognition of the company's commitment to Fanning Island and the benefits this brings. The Republic of Kiribati receives visa fees and Fanning Island collects a passenger head tax. Both corporate

(Top) Kiribatians perform traditional songs. (Above) Locals hired by NCL unload payment in the form of food staples.

funding and personal donations from NCL crewmembers and passengers have helped the community. In addition, ship doctors have come ashore to provide medical services, and NCL has delivered bags of rice from Honolulu, as well as medicine, canned goods, clothing, books and other supplies.

The sheltered lagoon inside the atoll is a classic South Pacific vision with crystal clear, aquamarine water and palm-fringed beaches. But a visit to Fanning

FANNING

(Top to bottom) The beach at English Harbor; NCL pavilions; bike hut; truck tours.

Island is not just a beach stop, it is an opportunity to experience an isolated culture that has only just begun to adjust to outside influences.

A Few Fast Facts

The Republic of Kiribati is one of the poorest countries in the world. Its leading export is copra (a coconut product). Other sources of income include licenses issued to foreign fishing fleets, remittances from Kiribati citizens working as sailors on foreign merchant ships, and development assistance from nations such as the United States, Japan, the United Kingdom, Australia and New Zealand. The official currency is the Australian dollar. The Kiribati flag is based on the country's coat of arms. The waves of white and blue represent the Pacific ocean, and the tropical sun symbolizes Kiribati's location astride the equator. The frigate bird represents power and freedom.

The Fanning Island Experience

Cruise ship passengers arriving at Fanning Island are tendered ashore while the ship stands off in deep water outside the atoll. Large boats are used and the tendering is usually completed by mid-morning, unless a bad swell is running, in which case the process is slowed down as extra caution is required to safely load passengers into the tenders. Passengers have the option of taking a tender to the main beach at English Harbor or booking a shore excursion to quieter Napali Beach.

At the English Harbor tender dock, the beaches serviced by NCL lie to the right as you disembark, and a straw market is on the left. The beach closest to the tender dock is usually the most crowded, so proceed to the farthest beach if you're looking for a quieter spot to suntan, swim or snorkel. NCL brings bottled water, lunch fare and refreshments ashore for its passengers, and maintains restroom facilities adjacent to the beach.

Passengers heading to Napali Beach disembark at a dock that is located about 10 minutes on foot along a path to the beach where beach chairs are provided along with a limited supply of hammocks and floating mattresses. An All Day Sports Package (about $15) can be purchased at the beach hut, which provides access to Hobie Cats, paddleboats, sea kayaks and bicycles. There are no food or restroom facilities at Napali Beach, but a tendering service to the main beach in English Harbor is provided.

Passengers can rent bicycles for touring the island; registration as at the bike hut (a short walk to the right as you exit the tender) and you will need your key card.

An island tour by flat-bed truck is available, or you can simply walk part of the atoll, which is about 11 miles (18 km) long. Aontena village, one of seven traditional villages on the island, is less than a mile from English Harbor and is about a 45-minute roundtrip walk. The vegetation on Fanning Island is dominated by coconut plantations, with small areas of forest and woodland.

Other tours offered include a snorkel excursion to Barracuda Reef, and a photography tour that is conducted by one of the ship's photographers.

Be Prepared

The sun is extremely hot at Fanning Island, so be prepared with a sun hat, sunscreen and bottled water. Also take some insect repellent, and your NCL key card. Gifts are welcomed by the local people, but refrain from bringing candy for the children, who do not receive regular dental care. Educational materials, musical instruments and sports equipment are good choices. The local soccer team often plays NCL's crew on ship day, and running shoes are always needed.

HELLO - ko na mauri
THANK YOU - ko raba
GOOD-BYE - tia bo

Napili Beach.

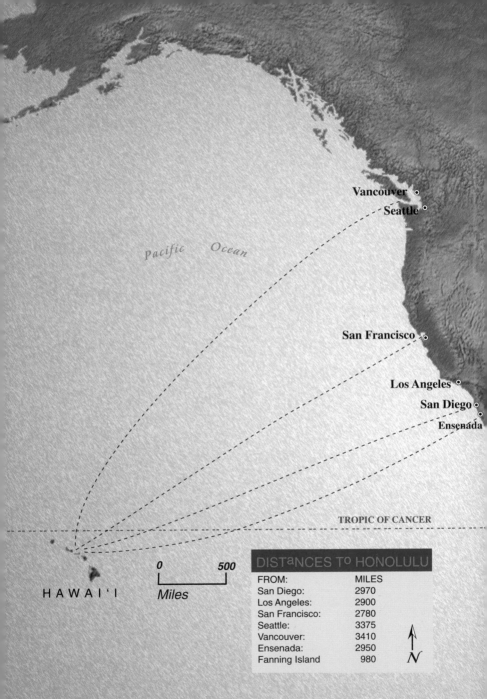

Vancouver

Seattle

Pacific Ocean

San Francisco

Los Angeles

San Diego

Ensenada

TROPIC OF CANCER

0	500

Miles

HAWAI'I

DISTANCES TO HONOLULU

FROM:	MILES
San Diego:	2970
Los Angeles:	2900
San Francisco:	2780
Seattle:	3375
Vancouver:	3410
Ensenada:	2950
Fanning Island	980

N

Fanning Island

CHAPTER SIX

MAINLAND PORTS

Several cruise lines offer round-trip Hawai'i cruises from various mainland ports, or one-way cruises between Honolulu and one of these west coast ports. San Francisco was the major California port during the early days of steamship travel to Hawai'i, but Los Angeles and San Diego are now the two busiest ports for round-trip Hawai'i cruises.

San Francisco

The cruise ships dock at historic Pier 35, within walking distance of several waterfront attractions, the cable car stations and the vintage street cars that run along The Embarcadero – the city's revitalized waterfront area of stylish shops and restaurants. The cable cars can be caught at the turnaround stations or at various stops along the way. Union Square, North Beach, Nob Hill, Chinatown and SoMa can all be reached by cable car, while other areas of interest, such as Haight Ashbury, Golden Gate Park and Presidio can be reached by city buses, street cars or taxi. Alcatraz Island can be accessed by passenger ferry from Pier 41. The retail area around Union Square and Market Street is the city's best-known shopping enclave, containing premier department stores such as Saks Fifth Avenue and Macy's.

A taxi from the airport to downtown San Francisco costs about $35, and the minibus shuttle is $11.

Pride of America departs from San Francisco.

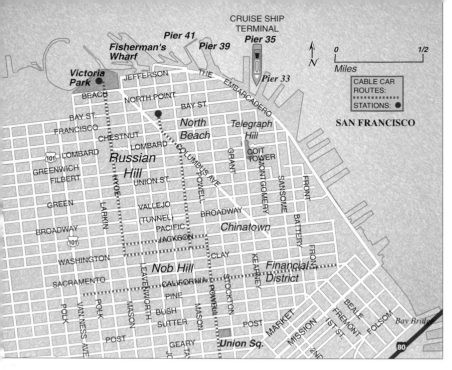

CABLE CAR
ROUTES: ▪▪▪▪▪▪▪▪▪▪▪▪
STATIONS: ●

SAN FRANCISCO

Los Angeles

The cruise lines that use Los Angeles as a base port for round-trip Hawai'i cruises include Princess Cruises, which sails year-round to the Hawaiian islands. Celebrity Cruises also offers a selection of roundtrip sailings to Hawai'i from Los Angeles, as does Royal Caribbean International.

Los Angeles Harbor, situated in San Pedro Bay, is one of the world's greatest manmade harbors, built with breakwaters, channels, piers and wharves. Downtown Los Angeles is 21 miles due north of Los Angeles Harbor, and Hollywood is seven miles northwest of downtown.

Los Angeles Harbor.

Long Beach Harbor.

The Los Angeles International Airport is about 20 miles from Los Angeles Harbor.

Long Beach Harbor is about five miles east of Los Angeles Harbor, and this is where the *Queen Mary* has been permanently docked since 1967. Daily tours of this 1930s Cunard liner are available to the public, its onboard facilities including several restaurants and shops as well as a hotel. The geodesic dome beside the *Queen Mary*'s dock used to house Howard Hughes's *Spruce Goose* before being converted into a cruise facility by Carnival Corporation, which also constructed an adjacent docking pier for its cruise ships.

San Diego

The cruise lines currently providing roundtrip Hawai'i cruises from San Diego include Holland America Line, which offers these cruises from October through to March. Celebrity Cruises also offer several Hawai'i sailings from San Diego, as does Royal Caribbean International.

The San Diego International Airport (also known as Lindbergh

Field) is a 10-minute drive from downtown and the adjacent cruise ship terminal on San Diego Bay, where miles of waterfront parks, hotels, restaurants and marinas line the shores. South of the terminal is the city's spectacular Convention Center with its glass-enclosed lobby and landscaped

Port of San Diego.

outdoor plazas and terraces.

Seaport Village, next to the Convention Center, is a large waterfront complex of shopping, dining and entertainment (and is also a good place to observe the U.S. Navy's Pacific fleet of cruisers, carriers, destroyers and other large vessels docked across the bay at Coronado Island). The architecturally acclaimed Horton Plaza, with its six open-air levels of upscale shops and restaurants, was built in the 1980s and began the downtown's revitalization. Adjacent to the Plaza is the historic Gaslamp Quarter, where shops, galleries and restaurants are housed in restored 19th-century buildings.

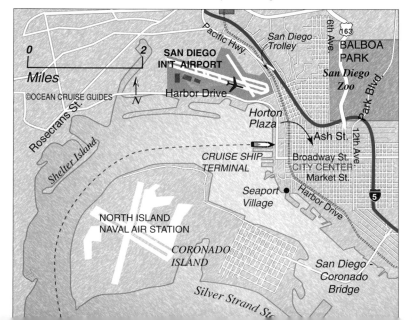

MAINLAND

Ensenada

The Mexican port of Ensenada is located just 70 miles south of the U.S. border in Baja California. Ships returning to San Diego or Los Angeles from Hawai'i will make a short service call at Ensenada (to comply with U.S. shipping regulations), while a few embark or disembark passengers here who are taking a one-way cruise between Ensenada and Honolulu.

Ensenada's new cruise terminal has two berths to accommodate arriving cruise ships, each with its own market village selling Mexican handicrafts and liquor. The town is within walking distance or a 5-minute drive; shuttle vans charge $2 each way, and drop you off in the center of town near several shopping streets and an outdoor crafts market selling excellent Mexican handicrafts.

Vancouver

The Vancouver International Airport is a 30-minute drive to the two downtown cruise ports. **Canada Place Cruise Ship Terminal** is located at the north end of Howe Street in the very heart of downtown Vancouver. It's a city landmark and instantly recognized for its majestic white sails, which crown a complex containing the Pan Pacific Hotel and Five Sails Restaurant, a Food Fair, promenade shops and an IMAX 3D Theatre. Long-term parking is provided here, and taxis, lim-

ousines, public transportation and car rentals are all easily available.

Vancouver's secondary cruise facility – **Ballantyne Pier** – is located about one mile east of Canada Place at the foot of Heatley Avenue.

The downtown core is easy to explore on foot, starting at the Tourist Info Centre (200 Burrard Street, Waterfront Centre), where maps, bus and ferry schedules and other information are all available.

Canada Place Cruise Terminal.

Carnival Spirit, 2000 – 88,000 tons, 2,125 passengers

Carnival Cruise Lines

This family-oriented cruise line of 'Fun Ships' offers spring and fall sailings to Hawai'i aboard *Carnival Spirit*. These 12-day one-way cruises run between Ensenada and Honolulu, and between Honolulu and Vancouver. Ports of call are Nawiliwili (Kaua'i); Kahului and Lahaina (Maui); Kona and Hilo (the Big Island), with an overnight stay at Honolulu. Well-known for its excellent children's facilities, Carnival has introduced fine dining fleet-wide with gourmet dishes created by French master Chef Georges Blanc. Officers are Italian and service staff are international. (www.carnival.com)

Celebrity Cruises

This upscale cruise line offers 14-night Hawaii Circle Cruises from Los Angeles and San Diego, each

spring and fall (October through December), aboard two Millennium-class ships, *Infinity* and *Summit*. Ports of call are Hilo, Kona, Lahaina and Honolulu. Celebrity also offers 12-night one-way cruises between Honolulu and Ensenada in November and March aboard *Mercury* (77,713 tons; 1,850 passengers). Celebrity is popular among cruise aficionados, with ships featuring gourmet cuisine, sophisticated service and modern decor. All ships have facilities for children and teens. Officers are Greek and service staff are international. (www.celebritycruises.com)

Holland America Line

This Seattle-based cruise line offers 15-day round-trip Hawai'i cruises out of San Diego from October to April, as well as a 17-day Hawai'i round-trip cruise from Vancouver and a 16-day Hawai'i cruise from Seattle to Vancouver. Ports of call are Hilo and Kona (Big Island), Lahaina (Maui), Honolulu (remaining overnight on some itineraries) and Nawiliwili, Kaua'i (on some itineraries). HAL's Hawai'i cruises are currently serviced by the *Zaandam*, a mid-sized ship carrying 1,260 passengers. HAL's spacious ships have distinctive blue hulls and are finely appointed with extensive artwork. HAL appeals to mature cruise travelers seeking refinement and attentive

Summit, 2001 – 91,000 tons, 1,950 passengers

Zaandam, 2000 – 63,000 tons, 1,440 passengers

service. Officers are Dutch and service staff are Indonesian and Filipino.
(www.hollandamerica.com)

Norwegian Cruise Line/ NCL America

NCL America is an offshoot of Miami-based Norwegian Cruise Line, with its head office located in Honolulu. NCL America is the only cruise line with U.S.-flagged ships offering Hawaiian inter-island cruises that remain in local waters. NCL America offers year-round roundtrip cruises out of Honolulu on *Pride of America*, *Pride of Aloha* and (until January 2008) *Pride of Hawai'i*.

Pride of Aloha and *Pride of Hawai'i* are Hawaiian-themed, with colorful floral leis painted on their hulls and interiors featuring Hawaiian decor. Many of the ships' all-American crew are Hawaiian, and passengers can drop by the cultural center and partake in activities such as lei-making.

A new feature on *Pride of Hawai'i* is its selection of court-yard and garden villas with access to a private courtyard area with pool, hot tub and sundeck. (Note: *Pride of Hawai'i* is leaving Hawai'i on January 28, 2008, for a 12-day cruise to Los Angeles, where the ship will be renamed *Norwegian Jade*, modified and redeployed to Europe.)

The decor on NCL's other

(Above) Pride of America, 2004 – 81,000 tons, 2,138 passengers (Below) Pride of Aloha, 1999 – 77,000 tons, 2,002 passengers

U.S.-flagged ship, *Pride of America*, reflects the many regions of the United States, including a Capitol Atrium, an Alaskan gold rush saloon and a Hawai'i Museum.

Facilities found onboard NCL America ships include a pro shop

that rents golf clubs, arranges tee times and provides information on the courses included in NCL's Golf Hawai'i Program.

Each NCL America ship has a teen club and a children's playroom, as well as an arcade, ball court, fitness center and health spa, but no casino. NCL also features Freestyle Dining, which offers passengers the flexicility of dining each night at their choice of restaurant at their chosen reservation time. The service on NCL America ships is very friendly and is more casual than ships with European staff.

NCL America itineraries include seven-day roundtrip cruises from Honolulu on *Pride of America* and *Pride of Aloha*. These itineraries feature two calls at the Big Island (a full day each in Hilo and in Kona) as well as overnight stops at Nawiliwili on Kaua'i and at Kahului on Maui. *Pride of Aloha* also offers 10- and 11-day Hawai'i-only cruises which include an overnight in Honolulu and in Nawiliwili, Kauai, as well as three days on

(Top) Pride of Hawai'i, 2006 – 92,000 tons, 2,466 passengers

Maui (two days in Kahului, one day in Lahaina). Also included is scenic cruising past the sea cliffs on Kauai and on Molokai, and a night-time sail past an active volcano on the Big Island.

Pride of Aloha also visits the foreign port of Fanning Island, in the Republic of Kiribati, on 11-day round-trip itineraries from Honolulu. This itinerary features four Hawaiian ports of call (Hilo, Lahaina, Nawiliwili and Kona), a day at Fanning Island, and four days at sea (traveling to and from Fanning Island). (www.ncl.com)

Princess Cruises

This popular line offers year-round 15-day circle cruises to Hawai'i out of Los Angeles. The itinerary features port calls at Hilo and Kona (Big Island), Nawiliwili (Kaua'i), Honolulu and Lahaina (Maui), and is currently serviced by *Island*

Princess, an elegant ship appointed with Italian marble and exotic woods. The ship carries 1,970 passengers in mostly outside cabins with private balconies. (This abundance of private balconies on all of the line's new ships has become a Princess trademark.) Princess ships successfully appeal to a broad market. The childrens' facilities are excellent, as is the nightly entertainment, and passengers can choose between traditional set times for dinner in one of the main dining rooms or the more flexible Personal Choice dining offered in the other main dining room. *Diamond Princess* (116,000 tons; 2,670 passengers) will take over the line's Hawai'i itinerary in September 2007. (www.princess.com)

Royal Caribbean International

This Miami-based cruise line offers a few cruises to Hawai'i, including 14-night circle cruises from Los Angeles and from San Diego aboard *Radiance of the Seas* and *Serenade of the Seas.*

Island Princess, 2003 – 92,000 tons, 1,970 passengers

These sisterships carry 2,500 passengers and feature an impressive central atrium with glass elevators. Children's facilities are excellent and include a water slide and wading pool. Other features are a miniature golf course and and rock-climbing wall, the latter now a trademark feature on every RCI ship. Officers are Scandinavian and service staff are international.
(www.royalcaribbean.com)

Serenade of the Seas, 2003 – 90,090 tons, 2,500 passengers

PHOTO CREDITS:

Photos, Michael DeFreitas
2,5,6, 16 (top), 17 (2nd), 23 (bottom), 24 (both),27 (bottom), 46 (top), 49 (bottom), 51 (middle), 63 (middle), 80, 87, 94 (bottom), 95 (bottom), 98 (bottom), 109, (all) 113, 114, 115 (bottom) 116, 133, 144 (middle)149, 151, 156, 202 (middle), 215, 222, 223, 226, 238 (bottom), 240 (middle), 241 (middle), 246 (middle), 252, 259 (bottom), 261, 272 (3rd), 276 (all), 280, 288,

Photos, Alan Nakano
9, 17 (top), 18 (bottom), 27 (top), 31 (bottom), 32 (top), 38 (bottom) 43 (bottom), 46 (bottom), 75 (bottom), 85, 90, 91, 96 (top), 101, 103 (bottom) 104 (bottom), 118, 119, 144 (top), 147, 228 (top), 230, 236, 263, 294,

Additional Photography
4, art by Kerne Erickson
10 Norwegian Cruise Line
14 Royal Caribbean Int'l
15, Phil Hersee
21 (both), Florida Int'l Univ.
22 (bottom), Turtle Bay Resort
35, Hawaii Tourism
36, Norwegian Cruise Line
50 (top) painting by Herb Kane
50 (bottom), USGS
51 (bottom), National Parks Service
52 Evert Gerretsen
53 (bottom), Hawaii Tourism
54 (both) Pacific Tsunami Museum, Hilo
55, Hawaii Tourism
57, Hawaii Tourism

60, Hawaii State Archives
61, Hawaii Tourism
62, Painting by Herb Kane, used by permission
63, Painting by Herb Kane, used by permission
63 (bottom) Hawaii Tourism
65 Painting by Herb Kane, used by permission
66 Painting by Herb Kane, used by permission
67, Sandwich document, R. H. Judd Archives
65 Painting by Herb Kane, used by permission
72, Painting by John Horton, used by permission
73, Vancouver Map, R.H. Judd Archives
74, Painting by Herb Kane, used by permission
75 (top) Hawaii Tourism
76, Painting by Herb Kane, used by permission
77, Hawaii State Archives
78, Hawaii State Archives
79, Hawaii Tourism
81 (top) Bishop Museum
82, Hawaii State Archives
83, Library of Congress
86, Hawaii Tourism
92, Hawaii Tourism
93, Bishop Museum
94, (top) Hawaii Tourism
95 (top, bottom) Phil Hersee
96 (bottom) Hawaii State Archives
98 (top) Hawaii Tourism
100, Jack Jeffrey, Photo Resoure Hawaii,
102 (all) Hawaii Tourism
103 (mid), Hawaii Tourism
105 (both) Hawaii Tourism
107 (top), Hawaii Tourism
107 (bottom), Phil Hersee
108, Dave Matilla, NMFS
115 (top) Peter Stevens
117, inset, Hawaii Tourism
122, Douglas Peebles / CORBIS
128, Mike Sedam, Corbis
134, Hawaii Tourism
145, Corbis
165, Phil Hersee
169, Norwegian Cruise Line
174, Bishop Museum
175, Bishop Museum
177 Phil Hersee
183, Hawaii Tourism
184, Mark Johnson/Corbis
186, Hawaii Tourism
187, Hawaii Tourism

189, (both), 190, 192, 193 Library of Congress
205, Turtle Bay Resort
207 (middle, bottom), 211, 214, 221 (middle) Hawaii Tourism
224 (top) Dave Glickman, NMFS
224 (bottom) R. Cartwright, NMFS
227, 228 (bottom), 235 Hawaii Tourism
238 art by Kerne Erickson
249, 250, 251 (top, middle), Hawaii Tourism
251 (bottom), Peter Stevens
256, 259 (middle), Hawaii Tourism
260 (inset) USGS
262, 264 (bottom) BIVB
266, Pacific Tsunami Museum, Hilo
271 (middle) USGS
272 (bottom), 275, 279, 286, 293, 297, BIVB
298 (inset) Wayne Messenger
299, Norwegian Cruise Line
300 (all), 301 (all), 302 (all), 303 (all) Wayne Messenger
305, Norwegian Cruise Line
308, Corbis
309, Port of Vancouver
312 (bottom) Wayne Messenger

All other photography by Anne Vipond.